PRINCE
& THE
POPPER

Jim Brydon

Prince And The Popper
Copyright © 2018 by James Brydon

No part of this publication may be reproduced, distributed, or transmitted in any form or by any means, including photocopying, recording, or other electronic or mechanical methods, without the prior written permission of the author, except in the case of brief quotations embodied in critical reviews and certain other non-commercial uses permitted by copyright law.

Tellwell Talent
www.tellwell.ca

ISBN
978-0-2288-0042-2 (Hardcover)
978-0-2288-0041-5 (Paperback)
978-0-2288-0043-9 (eBook)

Table of Contents

GET THEM SAYING YES IMMEDIATELY............................1
MAKE THE FAULT SEEM EASY TO CORRECT.................25
HAPPY TO DO WHAT YOU SUGGEST...........................35
BEGIN IN A FRIENDLY WAY..45
IN TERMS OF OTHER'S INTERESTS...............................55
LET THEM DO THE TALKING..63
APPEAL TO NOBLER MOTIVES....................................89
QUESTIONS OTHERS WILL SAY YES TO.......................105
THE OTHER PERSON'S IDEAS AND DESIRES.................125
TALK ABOUT YOUR OWN MISTAKES............................139
THE OTHER PERSON'S POINT OF VIEW........................151
DO IT SINCERELY..167
THE SWEETEST SOUND IN ANY LANGUAGE................181
DON'T CRITICIZE, CONDEMN, OR COMPLAIN.............193
BE GENUINELY INTERESTED IN OTHERS.....................203
SMILE...215
DRAMATIZE YOUR IDEAS..229
THE BEST OF ANY ARGUMENT: AVOIDING IT..............251
AROUSE AN EAGER WANT.......................................265
ADMIT YOU'RE WRONG..287
BE HEARTY IN YOUR APPROBATION.........................307
...AND LAVISH IN YOUR PRAISE................................333
CALL ATTENTION TO YOUR FAULTS FIRST..................349
...AND OTHER'S MISTAKES—INDIRECTLY...................363
AND, OF COURSE, LET OTHERS SAVE FACE.................373

GET THEM SAYING YES IMMEDIATELY

Torpor. It means listlessness. You can look it up, if you like. I'll wait.

Nothing much was happening. I'd been at Yamnuska Centre Legal Aid for going on two years. It's not how I had intended to spend my career but things don't always work out the way you expect them to. After three years of clawing my way along the partnership track, I had chosen an alternative vocational path. Less charitable souls would say I'd been canned. They'd be right, of course. But less charitable souls might have called my previous life "spelunking up the rectum of the legal profession in search of my great reward." I think I might just have found it there.

When you work for Legal Aid, one of two things is probably true. You are charged with a mission to help save the poor and woebegone from the travesties their lives have become through no fault of their own. Or, you are waiting for something better to come along.

I don't much care for the poor. Mostly, they drink far too much, far too often. They whine. They consider the supermarket tabloids Holy Writ. And they always seem to have that characteristic smell about them. You know, *Eau des Pauvres*: three parts despair to one part lemon gin. Retirement planning is done through the Western Canada Lottery Corporation. And they take a fiendish glee in rediscovering the telephone at difficult times: say, any Friday before a long weekend, preferably shortly before closing time, or 2:00 a.m., any weekday, especially when your bedmate is a light sleeper or some sort of social critic.

But lately, I hadn't much cared about anything better coming along. I was eating regularly. My house was paid for. Forays to the grocery store for Wonder-Chow or whatever was needed to tempt the pallet of Rollo—my ostensible roommate and faithless canine companion—didn't leave me scouring the ditches for a few extra bottles to cash in just to make the final total. Having disposed of my larcenous ex-wife—by divorce, I should add; I am an officer of the court and a gentlemen, for the first couple of hours, anyway—I was no longer slaving to satisfy the local maintenance-enforcement brigade.

I think you get to a point in your life where it is just easier to go along with whatever is happening and leave the ambition to the eager young things with stars in their eyes, hope in their hearts and holes in their heads. I'd been there and wasn't looking to do that again for a few years. I like to think of this as my resting period.

My liquor cabinet never seemed quite full. I hadn't managed a vacation this year because I didn't know where I might want to go. It wasn't a question of money, only interest. Gossip seemed all recycled and there are only so many times you can listen to the same story, no matter how it may have been amended and improved in the week since you last heard it. A small city just keeps turning up the same faces, day after day, week after week, month after month. If anyone had died, even someone I might like, it would have been a definite improvement.

Lately, even my sex life had reached a state of torpor. My usual resort of last resort, the cunning prosecutor, Ms Kathy Markle, was now spending her nights attempting to spawn with her farmer husband, Brian. She told me so the last time we were together—in the together sense, at least. Lately, when I saw her haunting the halls of the court house or bundling goodies into the back of her new SUV, she smiled at me, knowingly. I trusted that Brian was doing his part in this enterprise. It's probably just as well. I don't much like human *larvae*. They seem to spend their leaf-chewing years being almost as much of a household pest as young aphids. Society looks down on even the most careful application of DDT.

I have to admit, I was feeling pretty down. Fall can do that to you (autumn, not a negligent injury. I can't afford those). Aside from slaking my lusts, I had pretty much gotten over being in actual love the last time and hadn't worked my way up to doing anything equally stupid lately.

I suppose that it's only polite to introduce myself after all that.

My name is John Appleby Prince—Jack, to those who care, and goodness only knows what to those who don't. Appleby was my mother's maiden name. I guess it seemed the right thing to do at the time.

I will be thirty-four on my next birthday and, as you may have figured out already, I am a lawyer. Quite frankly, if you haven't figured it out yet, you haven't been reading too closely, which means you might be a lawyer, just not a very good one. I still have all my teeth, thanks in no small part to the generosity of the United Church of Canada, which employed my father, the late Rev. Hugh Richard Herbert Prince in various inconsequential parishes about Ontario, until he and the church secretary disappeared together. I believe that he was in the process of divorcing my mother at the time of what is now called "his passing" and hadn't yet suffered whatever humiliation there might be in being defrocked. (Given what he and Ms Enderby had likely been up to, I figure he was probably used to it.) This means that if I am ever left to chew buckskin as part of tanning a moose-hide, it will prove that I have at least one legitimate job skill.

Because I work for Legal Aid, I earn about twenty per cent of what I would have if I'd stayed in Toronto but with far fewer temptations to commit larceny. The last time I checked, our trust account consisted of three paper clips and assorted elastics tied around a pink telephone message. Stealing from my clients would amount to receiving stolen property.

At the time I begin this, our office was headed by Angus Black, legal director, boon companion and husband of the Black Madonna. She probably knows both more law and has a good deal more direction than Angus. That said, since his heart attack, he is always careful to take a walk around the block twice a day and usually makes it back without asking directions.

Of my two fellow toilers in the garden of earthly legal aid delights, preeminent was Lawrence (never Larry) Kennedy. Lawrence comes from a long line of deeply committed rich people. He drives a very nice, new car and lives in a less than modest "community" of socially-committed professionals who defend their hard-earned possessions like a mother bear her cubs. He subscribes to such progressive notions as freedom, equality and the maximization of his RRSP at tax time. His partner, never his wife, the indomitable Allison, forms his entire social conscience and works for all manner of good causes, in keeping with her master's degree in sociology.

The other was William James Wallace MacLean, or Scottie, to the pure of heart. Scottie is married to Mako, a Japanese woman of exacting standards, or so he claims. Frankly, from all the evidence, I doubt it extended to her choice of mates. They have two children, Euclid and Clytemnestra. In Scottie's mind, Greece is equidistant between Scotland and Japan.

For all this, we were short a body since our sole family lawyer and leavener of testosterone had left us. Given the choice between replacing her and taking on the extra work among ourselves, Angus had made the executive decision to do nothing. We still had the usual keening hordes of women—children looped, whorled and wedged about them—wanting to take the old man to court. Mrs. Stockard, the firm drover of our herd of secretarial staff, was tasked to tell them that we had no one who could help them and that they should contact Legal Aid Central. Few of them seem to have bothered. Either the old man came back and all was well or they could do quite well enough without him. Nothing seemed to have stopped the ever vigilant Allison from being quoted in the local press and elsewhere about the lack of legal services to women in our region. The only one who ever seemed to listen to Allison also had to sleep with her, and that seemed more than enough punishment for any human being.

* * *

Into our little world of peace and tranquility, to say nothing of torpor, strode the premier of this good province. I always thought of Premier Steven Beakman as a good and decent man, one to be emulated if you go in for that type of thing. He had his job to do and I had mine. So long as he kept the cheques flowing every couple of weeks, far be it from me to have had any but the kindest of regards for him. He probably even liked dogs—or would say he did if he thought he could have gotten Rollo onto the voters' list. For reasons that quite escape me, however, he seemed to have gotten it into his head that we should have an election. I believe that this is what is called "dropping the writ." Once the writ was dropped— an act of gross negligence, in my view—from his fumbling fingers, things were never quite the same.

I recall one of my political science professors saying that elections developed as a peaceful means to replace the ravages of revolutions, wars of succession and regicide. She was probably one of those who also believed that there could be peace on earth with just a modicum of social equality. I didn't hold it against her: she was sort of cute, actually.

But I don't think she ever lived in Yamnuska Centre. Here, elections are celebrated with all the low-intensity bloodletting and rapine savagery of any good medieval crusade and with even less tolerance than, say, the St. Bartholomew's Day Massacre or the Spanish Inquisition. Within days the land was laid waste by placards, signs and enough other detritus to choke an environmentalist. Every cranny, nook and waste site was scoured for any and all provender for the various political hordes, all intent on battle to the last drop of their campaign chests.

I am studiously apolitical, especially when I vote. If forced by circumstances or the need to impress someone, female and pleasing to the eye, I can recite chapter and verse of all party platforms. Like I said, my poli-sci prof was sort of cute and claimed that all political platforms can be fairly dealt with by trashing the opposition and noting that everyone likes the electorate and no one will raise their taxes or be rude to their children. In short: vote for me and I'll make you happy, not like those other guys. A brisk reading of any good front page will fill in the details. I used to think that elections were just hopeless wastes of money. Now, they just tart up the landscape and provide Rollo with additional targets during his nightly rambles.

It was not too terribly surprising, though, that the day after the premier's announcement that we were all his new best buddies for the period of the next thirty-five days of the campaign, Lawrence called Scottie and me into what he had taken to calling his chambers. (Lawrence gets that way when he spends too much time with his rich relatives—or when Allison is holding out on him.)

"I have an announcement that I'm sure will be tremendous news for all of us."

"Ye've nae got the wee lass up the stump, hae ye?" Scottie is nothing but profoundly direct. For him, if it doesn't deal with whisky or sex, it's too much like work.

"No, nothing like that, I believe. I mean, not that I know of." Lawrence seemed perplexed. It wasn't that much of a stretch, I guess, but he was trying to cover his bases as a man of the world.

"Aye, 't's a'ways the man's the last to know." Scottie nodded and smiled. "We'll leave . . . so ye can call the wee wifie, to be sure." He turned and was steering me out when Lawrence recovered.

"No, it's not that . . . not that at all."

"Bu' ye shuid call her, lad. Let her know ye care and that ye'll make a fine pa."

"But I don't care about that right now. This is important!"

"Ach, Prince, he's outta he's heid. Ah'll nae tell the fair Allison and it'd be a tru' kindness if ye'll nae mention it."

"It's about an election, Scottie!"

"Ah've heerd tha' bu' ne'er pronounced tha' way, Lawrence."

"Well, at least you can listen, Jack."

"Why not? I'm here and I can explain it to Scottie later."

Lawrence sat down and laced his hands behind his head. His smile was almost ethereal. He closed his eyes and shook his head. "I am our official agent."

"Do we really need one?"

"Absolutely. It's in the act!" He leaned forward and smacked his right fist onto a copy of a little booklet. I craned my head to discover that it read, "Elections Act."

"Our? Does every office need one or something?" Quite honestly, it had been a while since I last voted. Things change.

"No, Jack. Our party needs one in every riding. And I'm it in Yamnuska Centre and the Lakes."

"Well, I'm happy for you."

"You should be happy for yourselves. I mean, this is a great opportunity. We can make some real progress here, some changes to the system."

I didn't have the heart to point out to Lawrence that the last time he had tried to make "real progress," he had tried to get me fired. So, I nodded. I might even have smiled. Small talk is good at times like these, so I ventured, "How are our chances, then, Lawrence? Pretty good?"

"Good? They've never been so good. I'm mean, in the time this government's been in power, look at the changes we've made and look what's going to happen."

I half expected him to take on the likeness of a newly collectivized peasant in one of those socialist realist posters from the 1930s. You know, stiff jaw uplifted, collar open, revealing tight pectorals, sweating with the strain of the task ahead. Sinewy arms ending in tight fists grasping a hoe. A face turned heavenward in search of the New Jerusalem and a mouth already belting out a lusty, rustic version of the bloody "Red Flag" or "The Internationale." Of course, if Lawrence had burst into song, I would have had to hit him. Quite hard, too. Maybe, Scottie could hold him while I worked him over. But then, Lawrence seemed to know when to quit. Good political instincts, I'd say.

"So, you'd say it's pretty much a sure thing, then?"

"We've held this riding for the last fifteen years. It's in the bag."

"Great!" I was edging my way out. I had a sense that Scottie already had the doorknob turned.

"Of course, we can't be too confident. If the voters sensed that, it would be a different matter. And in any election, it's always one vote at a time."

"So, you're confident but not over-confident. Sort of a quiet confidence, then."

"But we still have to work, you understand. Like I said, it's always one vote at a time." This wasn't sounding too promising at all. It was beginning to seem as if Lawrence had a plan to dump all his files on the two of us while he became chief assistant to the deputy in charge of licking stamps . . . or boots. "No, we've come this far. It would be tragic if we were to be hauled back into the old days and the old ways."

"I must have missed those but I agree it would be . . . what is it? Tragic?"

"Jack, you have no idea . . ." Here, he seemed to launch into a grim reverie. I almost expected him to pull pictures out of his wallet of black-eyed waifs, grimy of hand and face, stern and resolute as they opposed evil landlords, who snickered as they threw kith and kin out of ramshackle hovels, probably killing kittens as they went. Mostly, it was about the joys of rural electrification and paved roads so that Farmer Brown could rush home from the fields to catch the last of the soap operas on his flat-screen TV. Or maybe, share reruns with the pigs on their portable in the barn . . . Lawrence ended with, "But we have to work and work smart. Not one corner of this riding is going to the polls without knowing the name, Myron Horschewicz."

"Who?"

"Myron Horschewicz. Our candidate!"

"That's actually a relief, Lawrence." He looked at me quizzically. "I hadn't heard of him and now I have. That means you've started your campaign with a big bang." I smiled. "I take it he's not the incumbent, though."

"Do you ever watch the news, Prince?"

"Only if they have something interesting on it."

Scottie felt impelled to interject. "No, the T and A news, Jack!"

"Well, that can be interesting, too. I mean Lawrence, here, is a man of the people now, Scottie, and he has to appeal to all tastes or lack of same."

"I'll pretend you didn't say that."

"You're sure learning this political stuff pretty fast, Lawrence. Wow!" I was almost out the door. I had even turned and tossed this last remark over my shoulder.

"But we have to work as I said."

"I know, Lawrence . . . it's one vote at a time. But, look, we've all got a lot of files—"

"I'm not talking files, Jack. I'm talking volunteering, making phone calls, stuffing envelopes, maybe even making the occasional speech. We have to make our candidate a man that everyone will want to vote for."

"You could dress him up in a red suit and have him pass out candies to children, but I sort of thought running him as a socialist was more or less the same thing."

"You scoff, Jack, but I know you don't mean it." I was about to tell him otherwise when he reminded me of our last Christmas party. He'd drawn my name and had given me the gift that just keeps on giving: a membership in the party. Well, it was anything ten bucks or under. "As a party member, Jack, you'll want to be in good standing . . . for when the plums are being passed out."

I didn't agree immediately, so he added a bit of incentive. Lawrence does have his capitalist heritage, after all. "But if you really aren't interested in the fortunes of the next government . . ."

He might have winked then. I hope not. I prefer to think he didn't.

* * *

As the old saying goes, discretion is the better part of valour. It is almost the whole of utter cowardice.

So, I found myself on the phones the next Saturday afternoon. I picked that time because I didn't want to face the wrath of people freshly wakened from a hard night's drinking with the party's carefully prepared message that went like this:

> "Hi there, I'm [*state name*] calling from the Myron Horschewicz campaign for the legislature. How are you today, sir/madam? [*Pause for answer.*] I don't know what you know about

> Myron but he grew up on a farm right around here in Yamnuska Centre. He left the farm at 18 to attend university and, since graduating with an honours degree in political science, Myron, along with Premier Steve Beakman, has been working with the government to make this province a better place for you and me. I'm sure you'll agree that we're all better off in the last eight years and I'm hoping that you can find your way to vote for Myron Horschewicz. Can Myron **count** on **your** vote? [*Wait for answer. Respond positively to any questions relying on the points listed in the printed materials.*] Thank you for your time and have a good day, sir/madam."

If Lawrence hadn't written this cloying patter, he must have an even more evil twin.

I was met by an elfin figure, long-bearded and kindly. He introduced me to a room of fellow party loyalists, all lined up along one wall working the telephones with glee. The elf gave me a list of names, telephone numbers and addresses, pointed me to a desk and telephone and set me to work calling each of them. After each call, I was required to indicate on the sheet whether my impression of the response was very positive (two + signs), positive (one + sign), neutral (a zero, appropriately enough), negative (one - sign) or downright hostile (two - signs). I think the idea was to identify the positive vote, although it wouldn't surprise me if it was a cheap way to do a survey. And there is no twin quite that evil. I reminded myself that, after all, it was one vote at a time.

The first few calls were no problem. I got a couple of hang-ups in the first ten seconds. I put them down as single negatives. I mean, they didn't swear or question my patriotism, parentage or sexuality; so it was good. The third call brought into question Myron's but that was his problem. I put down two negatives. Much more of this and he'd owe votes.

The next name was one I recognized from my client list. I tried to get the attention of Santa Claus between Christmases but he was busy trying to talk someone out of voting for the demon Conservative, Jeff Wooster. He looked as if a nice sit-down and a cup of tea might do him and his blood pressure a world of good. The rest of his elves all seemed tied up in serious party business. No one responded to my pleading look.

So, I dialed.

Mona Moonias answered. "Yeah." I don't think I have ever talked to Mona when she was fully sober. She usually needs a bit of heart-starting first thing in the morning and on cool days, she doesn't want the antifreeze to drop too low.

"Hi there, I'm Jack Prince, calling from the Myron Horschewicz campaign for the legislature."

"So, who the fuck're you?"

It seemed a fair question and there were those instructions, "Respond positively to any questions relying on the points listed in the printed materials."

"I'm Jack Prince."

"Whaddaya want, eh?"

An excellent lead-in to the next part of my spiel, I thought. "How are you today, madam?"

"I'm pissed to the gills and I wanna know where the fuck my ol' man is. Ya know him? Bert Manyfeathers? Ya know where the prick is?"

Obviously, one of the primary political skills is lying. I did, in fact know Bert. Since I had presided over his sentencing not two days before, I could make a pretty good guess that he was in the local correctional centre finishing off three months for drunk driving. "I'm afraid I don't, ma'am."

"Well, if ya see him, tell him he's got my bottle and I want it. Ya got that?"

"I certainly will. I am calling from the Myron Horschewicz campaign office..."

"Who the hell's this Horseshit guy?"

It seemed to fit, so I continued on script, "Now, I don't know what you know about Myron but he grew up on a farm right around here in Yamnuska Centre. He left the farm at 18 to attend university and, since graduating with an honours degree in political science, Myron, along with Premier Steve Beakman, has been working with the government to make this province a better place for you and me. I'm sure you'll agree that we're all better off in the last eight years and I'm hoping that you can find your way to vote for Myron Horschewicz. Can Myron **count** on *your* vote?"

"Wha's someone named Horseshit gonna do, paw the ground with his hoof? Hawr, hawr."

"Probably. Can he count on your vote?" All right, I was getting a bit nastier than I should. But I was wasting a good Saturday afternoon talking to drunks and I wasn't even getting paid for it.

"Why the fuck should I care?"

I looked around. Still, no one was paying much attention. The Jolly Old Elf had gone to the back, no doubt, to carry around some large reams of folded paper. My fellow telemarketers all had their heads down, furiously currying politically favourable cold calls. "'Cause he'll cut the price on all your favourite brands and even bring you a bottle personally."

"A 26 or a 40?" She had sobered up a bit.

"Whatever."

I put her down as a double positive.

I made my way down the list a bit farther until I came to a familiar name: Robert Morceau, judge. Spouse: Barbara Morceau, teacher. It had been a while, almost two years, since I had spoken to Mrs. Morceau and I was hoping she wouldn't recognize my voice. On the other hand, it had been just over twenty hours since His Honour and I had exchanged pleasantries. I looked around. There seemed to be no appealing for a substitute. Santa was consulting with the other socialist elves and everyone else seemed to be smiling and chatting away to happy voters everywhere. I was hoping for Mrs. or no answer.

Luck was not with me. On either score. I am sure that when I am consigned, quite justifiably, to an ever-burning hell, the first voice I hear will be that supercilious, superior, oily moan that only a lifelong adherent to sadomasochism and criminal procedure and an undying affection for the torture of perfectly pleasant legal aid lawyers could muster.

"Hello." It seemed that he had done me an irredeemable favour in even lifting the receiver, let along spouting two relatively inane syllables. I'd had enough of him. I'd had enough of trying to get Myron Horschewicz elected. And I'd certainly had enough of grubbing for votes, one at a time.

"Yeah, I'm calling from the Jolly Jeff Wooster campaign office. Jeff is looking for your vote. Has he got it?"

"I don't know. Who is Mr. Wooster running for?"

I was surprised that Morceau didn't have his name already chiselled into some portico in the courthouse. "The Conservative Party. Sir." I'm not sure why I said "sir," but maybe it was from force of habit. It usually made him turn sort of a cerulean blue when I said it in court instead of "Your Honour."

"And what does Mr. Wooster stand for?" Trust Morceau to be comparison shopping during an election. I mean you're either against one or you're against the other.

The temptation to say that he was for the slaughter of big-eyed kittens and forced self-mutilation seemed a bit over the top so I replied, "Mr. Wooster is a positive, progressive thinker who's in favour of the conservative values of the family, personal responsibility and, uh, yeah, that's right, tax cuts."

"Really?"

"No, sir, I phoned you up on a Saturday afternoon, just because I had nothing better to do than try to get you to vote for him because he's a sex-crazed, thrill killer whose pomposity can only be compared to the most megalomaniacal dictators and genocidal crazies of the last century. At least this way, we can get him out of town. So, if you don't mind, I'm going to go off and commit serial acts of Tantric sex with a group of people I keep in my garage just for occasions like this."

"Your Mr. Wooster sounds like a fine person. You, young man, seem mentally unbalanced. I'm going to be calling party headquarters to complain."

I hung up and marked him down as definitely neutral.

Then, I felt a hand on my shoulder. It was the elf. He looked deeply concerned. Somewhere, I'd heard that he was a local high school guidance counsellor who had set up wonderful programs for unwed mothers and young drug users in his school. He had that look of soft concern about him. He smiled as he seized my lists and virtually hauled me from the chair.

"Thank you so much for all you've done for us. You've been a great help." He steered me to the door. I looked back. No one else was leaving. In fact, some were blushing and chattering to themselves. The more sensitive simply looked away, seeking that special mote up next to the ceiling.

"But, I'm not done. We have to work and work smart. Not one corner of this riding is going to the polls without knowing the name, Myron Horschewicz!" I think I had more or less worked up to a fairly high pitch at that time. I was about to say, "But it's always one vote at a time," when the door slammed behind me. It had no knob on the outside.

I was home in fifteen minutes. Rollo, at least, was impressed.

* * *

I had the sense that, when I came to work the next Monday, Lawrence was trying to avoid me. I'm not sure why. Maybe, it was the little things. The turned back. The snort of derision whenever I said something. Little comments to Gail, my faithful confidante and assistant, "I hope Jack's happy with his little performance on Saturday." I got the impression that the local party was a bit like the Bolsheviks of old who blamed the sponsor when his nominee screwed up. Unlike the Bolshies, though, I didn't have the impression that there was any sort of local version of the Lublyanka Prison where Lawrence could look forward to a quiet walk in the hall with his special guard and a bill for two cents sent to his survivors—to cover the costs of the bullet. The price of ammunition might have gone up. Inflation and all that.

Lawrence called an office caucus late one Thursday afternoon and even allowed me to attend.

"The party is deeply concerned about the way things are going." He was doing his best to be serious. So was I, but I'm not as good as Lawrence.

"I thought we've held this riding for the last fifteen years and it's in the bag."

"I also said that we have to work. Some of us have and some of us have merely played around at being serious about this business." He looked at me. I'd checked already—there was no one behind me.

"Surely, you're not saying..."

"You know very well what I'm talking about, Jack. You couldn't have done any more harm if you'd picketed with a Jeff Wooster sign in front of this office. According to our polling, we're running behind and we have to do a lot of work to catch up."

"We could always work and work smart—you know, make sure not one corner of this riding is going to the polls without knowing the name, Myron Horschewicz."

"Maybe I'm not being clear, Jack." I looked at Scottie and mouthed "one vote at a time" but he was counting ceiling tiles. "Your *help*, so far, has involved, what? Attempting to bribe a First Nations person with an incipient alcohol problem with a bottle of rum?"

"That's a flagrant exaggeration, Lawrence, and you know it!"

"And precisely which part of it is a misstatement, Jack?" He was actually snarling and showing his teeth. Rollo might have quivered.

"The part about the rum." Lawrence looked at me. "Well, we never really settled on what it was supposed to be." He rolled his eyes at this, so I continued. "And who says that Mona's an incipient alcoholic?" I said, leaving aside the fact that she'd probably passed that stage sometime in her late teens. "Well, I was just trying to help."

"Who?"

I didn't think to improve his grammar so I said nothing. He pursed his lips and started barking commands to Scottie and Angus, who both nodded gravely. "And Jack, don't do anything more for the party."

I shrugged. It's in the best of political traditions in this country, I'm told, so I shrugged.

* * *

I spent the remainder of the campaign safely ensconced in my little house with Rollo, watching American cable TV. At least they weren't having an election that year, for a change. Besides, their commercials are far more entertaining if you're one for 'roided rasslers and stock cars.

It was a few nights before the vote. It must have been a Thursday. I was home. It can't have been that late. I hadn't taken Rollo out yet to do what damage he still could to the forest of election signs dotting the roadway. He'd taken a liking to those of the Liberal Party lady. She had made it clear that she didn't care much for politics; she was just putting her face out there to take up time at the local all-candidate debates: roadkill on the political highway, as it were. If I hadn't already been committed to The Party, I might have considered her in preference to Mighty Myron Horschowicz or Jolly Jeff Wooster.

There was a knock at the door. I was surprised because I had installed a doorbell. The ever vigilant Rollo yawned, licked himself suggestively and went back to sleep. I was still in my law suit, tie and all, when I answered.

She was not that tall, maybe five-two or three but she had a smile that gleamed. "Hi. I'm Janice and I'm from the Jeff Wooster campaign. I was wondering if I could interest you in some of Jeff's ideas." She clicked up the smile another two or three hundred watts.

One must be fair in any election campaign. These are contests of ideas and one look told me that she might just have something of interest for me. "Sure. Come on in."

She fairly bounced. Given everything, the verb was quite appropriate. She smiled some more and handed me some literature. I flicked it over. It had the grinning face of a man who had become some sort of devotee of Dale Carnegie or suffered from some form of dementia. Maybe it was drugs. He was surrounded by an equally addled family: two blond daughters, a tow-haired lad who looked adoringly at his father, and a wife who seemed eager to get her husband launched successfully so she could cut ribbons or bake cookies or whatever it is that political wives do. Mostly, I suppose, she wanted out of town and into the big city during sittings where she could shop. There was no dog. I checked. Well, Rollo wasn't on the voters' list, after all.

I smiled.

"I was wondering just what I can do to convince you to vote for Jeff." She had a whispery voice and one of those round faces that works so well on bouncy, young things. I believe they are often referred to as pixyish.

I have never thought of myself as a particularly cunning person. I try it often enough. But, I felt no great need to let her know that I was already committed to the opposition, at least on paper. I shrugged. I told you it had a fine political tradition. "I don't know. Why don't you sit down and have a drink and we'll see what comes up?"

She unleashed yet another of her one-thousand-watt grins and found her way to the couch. I grabbed the Johnny Walker Red, changed my mind, and took the Jack Daniels, clinking the bottle as I did. "You . . . uh . . . old enough?"

"Sure!"

You might think that I was asking whether she was old enough to drink. I mean there is an age limit in this province. I should know. I spend half my time defending what they call "minor consumes," where some fifteen-year-old gets caught with the better part of a case of beer. The judge gives him a lecture about the evils of drink and hits him with ten hours of community service. I figure the really big punishment is that he loses the better half of a dozen Molsons or Labatts. But if you think that was my big concern, let's just say that they don't put you in jail for supplying liquor to minors, if she was one. It's harder and harder to tell at my age.

I snuggled down beside her and put her drink on the coffee table. She whipped open the brochure and started her spiel. "Jeff's a family man, Mr., uh . . ."

"Jack." I smiled and nudged her.

"Are you a family man, Jack?"

I hung my head at this. "Unfortunately not. I've . . . never been that lucky, I guess."

"But you'd like to be, I'll bet."

Her enthusiasm was contagious. "You have no idea how hard I've tried but . . . I guess sometimes things just don't work out." I tried a pained expression.

"I'm sorry to hear that, Jack." Her spiel seemed to taper off at this point and it looked like she might just pack things up and put me down as a 0.

"Not half as sorry as I am—what is it? Janice? I like to think of the family as the foundation of everything that's good in our society. I just am so confused about ... these things."

"So, you haven't been able to—"

"No." It was fairly breathless. Then, I looked up at her with eyes as sad as I can make them. "I'm *so* confused about a lot of things, you know. There just never seems to be the right person, someone who can understand me and ..." I think I added a sniff just then.

I must have because she put her hand on my arm and rubbed me. "You're not ... *gay* or something like that, are you, Jack?"

"How can I be sure? I mean, I've been in those bars and I've been propositioned by those ... you know, those people ..."

"Oh, I'm sure you're not." She stroked my hair and brushed my face ever so lightly.

"Thank you." All right, it was a bit of a croak but things were looking up.

"Would it be all right if I hugged you?" This was far more positive attention than I'd ever gotten from my own party. I mean, no recriminations, no lectures, no appeals to purity and sobriety.

"That would be wonderful. I just don't know how voting for Jeff will make me feel better about these things."

"It will, I'm sure." She seemed to be quite clear about this as her arm stroked my back up and down.

"Would it be all right if I ... kissed you? I mean, you seem like such a ... I don't know ... a nice person."

"If you'd like." I did. It was considerably more than a friendly peck on the cheek and I have to admit that my political passions were becoming aroused.

"I had considered voting for that other guy, you know, Myron Whateverhisnameis ..."

She pushed me back. "You wouldn't ..."

"I'm so confused. I mean, he seemed so . . . understanding. Someone who would be more accepting . . . and all that." I took advantage of this confusion to move my hand where no gentleman should. I suppose we had gotten to the point of the heavy lifting of actual political persuasion and at least one of us was putty in the hands of the other. My hand was up her shirt and any thought of political friction had been replaced by a far more basic variety.

"We try to be understanding of people like you, Jack." And sympathetic, it definitely seemed.

"Like me? What do you mean by people like me, Janice? You don't—"

"Oh, no, no, no. I don't mean that there's anything wrong with you, Jack. I mean . . . you haven't done anything like those people . . ."

"I've been so tempted over the years. You've no idea. I'm just so confused that I don't know what I should and shouldn't do."

Janice might well have considered a career as a lawyer, once she got politics out of her system. In fact, she was the one who definitely steered me to the right—my bedroom was in that direction, after all—leaving her Jack Daniels largely undrunk. She was gentle. It didn't hurt a bit. In fact, she was accommodating enough for me to make several points, none of them of a particularly political variety. Before she left, she extracted a promise that I would definitely vote for Jeff Wooster. It wasn't quite a sacred vow, but I felt bound by it.

When I got up the next day, I felt invigorated. I noticed that her glass was now empty.

* * *

The day after the election was a sad one in our office. Lawrence had obviously spent the entire night watching the results. He'd done a fine job, too. Myron Horschewicz came within fewer than fifty odd votes of defeating Jeff Wooster. There would be a recount but it was clear that

Mr. Horschewicz had been swept aside in a quite unexpected landslide for Jeffrey R. Wooster and his band of Jolly Conservatives.

"This is a disaster!" Lawrence kept repeating this. I half expected to see lifeboats launched over the side of our office and having to pack Mrs. Stockard into a lifejacket. Finally, the refrain changed to, "How could this ever happen?"

I felt that this question deserved some sort of answer. "Well, maybe Wooster's campaign was somehow more appealing to the average voter."

"But we offered everyone everything."

"Everything?"

"As far as we could. No free liquor or anything."

"Hmm. Sometimes that just isn't enough, I guess, Lawrence."

"Who could vote for that . . . that . . ."

"I read he was a real estate agent in Strawbrook, Lawrence."

"Exactly. A small-town, money-grubbing land shill gets elected over a fine guy like Myron. It shouldn't happen. Ever. Can you explain that to me, Jack? I mean who would vote for a guy like that?"

"According to what I heard, a lot of people who don't like to pay a lot of taxes. You know, that and 'all it takes is one vote at a time.'"

"Yeah, taxes that go to paying for healthcare and good schools and legal aid."

"Steady, there, Lawrence. I don't think the average voter cares for us that much."

"But they should, Jack. They really should. I can't imagine any of us or any of our clients with any brains wanting to vote conservative."

"But I expect a lot of them did or didn't bother to vote."

"Why would they?"

"Not bother to vote? My guess is—"

"No. Vote for those . . . barbarians."

"Like the old saying goes, 'Politics makes strange bedfellows.'"

He kept on with this until I left for court. His Honour Judge Morceau was practically ecstatic, cackling as he cracked the judicial whip over the backs of the usual suspects with rather more vigour than even Simon Legree might have thought appropriate. But I wasn't feeling that well and excused myself early. It wasn't the election results or even the weird ecstasy of His Honour that was bothering me. The downstairs plumbing wasn't working that well and, quite frankly, it had begun to itch.

MAKE THE FAULT SEEM EASY TO CORRECT

I don't know if you ever bought condoms as a teenager. Unless you could wait until everyone in the washroom had done his business and left you with an intemperate vending machine, you were left with the expedient of buying them on the open market. When I was young, that involved marching in and asking the store clerk for some. In my small town at the time that meant dealing with a grey-haired hag who played bridge with my parents and made Ms Stockard look hot. We resorted to minor thefts. Actually, I was more a receiver of stolen goods. Nowadays, you can just trot down to the local welfare office and dip into the goldfish bowl full of them, left out for the picking up. (Lately, I've had a lot of chances to see welfare families. They must take them home and let the kids use them for balloons. You can almost hear the kids begging mom to go back for more.)

The STD clinic at the hospital is a bit like that. You don't really want anyone to watch you go in. Which is really rather silly, when you think about it. How many adults do you know who aren't having sex with somebody? And if you're old enough to do the deed, why should you be worried about the usual by-products? If you had made a public vow of chastity, maybe. But in a day and age when we are pretty much relieved to discover that the local bishop has limited himself to consenting, adult women, what's the big deal?

But I was pretty uncomfortable about the whole thing. I just told my Gail that I had a doctor's appointment and I'd be back "whenever—you know how doctors are."

The hospital in Yamnuska Centre has agglomerated over the years. Sometime in the '20s, they had put up a nice little sandstone building, modern for its time. I suppose people brought their chickens and turnips up the broad stone steps, along with little Martha who'd come down with "the fever." God willing and with the best of care and intentions, little Martha would either bound down those stairs all the better and thank you doctor, or not.

Not being wasteful, sometime in the '40s or early '50s, a government, looking to shore up its support here, had thrown up a clapboard extension. Now, little Tommy could have his tonsils out in the cleanest and most modern of facilities, all shot through with penicillin and the wonder drugs of the age. The sandstone relic was consigned to old folks who might just appreciate its retro feel. Besides, they had the morgue there and a loading dock out back for added convenience.

Later, in the '70s or '80s, when the world was a more caring place, they decided to slap up the latest in modern buildings and jam it full of the latest in things that whir and beep and tell them your innermost secrets—literally. This bastion of steel, chrome and tinted windows was just chunked down to the left of the clapboard extension, like a horizontal medical stratum. If they kept this up, in another hundred years or so they would have a pretty good museum.

I'm a modern guy. I chose door number three.

A sensitive hospital would have had a discreet sign between varicose vein repair and X-ray—"Venereal Diseases: This Way"—and maybe a circumspect little doorway, half-covered by a curtain. Blue would be tasteful . . . Not in an age of universal illiteracy, I guess. Instead, they had installed a scrawny gnome, bedecked in a blue uniform and burdened by a sense of self-importance. He sat bolt upright in an open kiosk that replaced the soothing fountain that should have stood in the echoing atrium. He calmly shuffled papers and kept his eye on a bank of television screens. Currents of the vaguely ill sauntered about, dragging IV poles and looking for places to smoke. Concurrent streams of puzzled visitors, concerned, guilty or mildly curious, intersected with them, occasionally doing the dance of avoidance with the others. There was a thrum of muted conversation punctuated by the slap of footwear on the all-weather carpeting mixed with the rustle of nylon, corduroy and denim. It was not quite church-like, more modern library.

The gnome gave one of his TV screens a whack as I made it to the counter. His telephone rang. In the best modern tradition, he looked right at me, then answered it. Better a disembodied electronic voice than having to deal with a living being—you can always hang up. His caller seemed someone near and dear to him; he was, therefore, forgiven. He whined into the receiver, ending with an extended sigh.

"You want something?" It was without a smile, all bruised officiousness. Ah, the tender ministration of concern and humanity we've come to know and expect from the health care system! I was thinking that the call had to be from his wife.

I leaned in. I wasn't in the mood for sharing. "Yes, I was wondering—"

"Speak up, young man. I'm not a lip reader."

I cleared my throat and checked, left and right. "Yes, I was saying that I—"

"Don't lean on the counter, sonny. It's not made for leanin'."

"Sorry." I bellied up to it but tried not to lean. Still, I wanted him to hear. "Look, I'm looking for the STD clinic."

"You'll have to speak up. I can't hear what you want."

So, I leaned in, anyway, and said it as loudly as I dared. "The STD clinic! Where is it?"

The lobby stilled. We were everyone's concern at that instant. He looked at me as if I had sprouted horns and a tail. It was all pious condemnation and disgust. "To your left. All the way down the hall." He flicked his head showing me the way. "And, you don't have to shout, young man. Nothin' wrong with my ears!"

I felt my face flush. There was only the sound of throats being cleared. So, I turned to the blue-coated gnome and in my loudest voice added, "Your ears may be good, old man, but once the tests come back, some of the smaller bits might just fall off." I turned and left before he could die of the shock. Or have me arrested.

It might have been more appropriate for the STD clinic to be in the clapboard building, but irony is often lost on provincials. I walked all the way to the old sandstone. When I arrived in the lobby, I found myself surrounded by old people all tilted over and sitting in a circle, humming mindlessly. And tunelessly. Or it might have been a more modern composition. Much as this put me in mind of the Court of Appeal, I had things to do. So, I bowed courteously and went in search of a sign—the printed kind, not a religious epiphany. Although, by now, that wouldn't have half-surprised me.

"It's downstairs."

I looked up. The nurse was older but not unkind— just the sort to leave mama with as she slides off into senility and, from there, the graveyard. I guess I looked surprised. "Pardon?"

"You want the VD clinic, right?"

"Yes, but—"

"I think I know all the family members." She looked about at her charges. "You aren't one of them. Even if I didn't, you didn't walk up to one of my guests and ask them how they were. That's the first thing they always do.

Probably figure there's a little extra in the will for each time they ask. Besides, you look confused enough for the clinic." She smiled and pointed the way.

* * *

It was a warren of tiny rooms, each with an examining table covered with a sheet of paper in case we dripped, I suppose. A desk commanded the waiting room "personned" by a woman who looked like she knew the business end of a syringe and could use it. She looked up.

"Name?" I almost expected a bit of engine oil to seep from the corner of her eye.

"Uh, Prince. John."

She handed me a clipboard and pen and steered me to one of the rooms. "Okay, Prince, John"—I think I heard the comma—"fill out the form completely and honestly. Doesn't help if you lie or leave stuff out. Then strip down. Order's not that important. When you're done, put the clipboard through the slot so we know you're ready." She grabbed a gown from the inside corner and tossed it to me. The door closed behind her and she left the world to darkness and to me, in the words of the poet. Not really but I was shut up in a space a bit bigger than a coffin that smelled like a vat of Windex.

After I was more or less naked, I launched myself onto the examining table and set to work on the questionnaire. I was doing pretty well—I'd been around thirty-odd years and I mostly remembered my birthday and address—until I got to the question about "sexual contact." It is probably considered less than genteel to have anonymous sex but all I could put down was "Janice." I mean, we hadn't been formally introduced before we got to know each other—Biblically, at least.

The next question had to do with the "date of sexual contact." I put down, "Thursday before election day." It's not the sort of thing you scrawl on your kitchen calendar along with the dental appointments. Besides, it wasn't something I wanted to remember that badly.

The balance of the questions had to do with the type of activity, its location and details that I had never considered. We live in liberal times, I guess. There were suggestions there that I'd never even heard of.

I tried to be honest. Not because I really wanted to. Mostly, it was all the notices of what would happen to me if I didn't. The last part of the questionnaire was a pamphlet advising me of the dire consequences of untreated sexually transmitted diseases. When I finished, I just wanted to grab my groin and run. But I put the clipboard in the slot and awaited my fate. All the while, I thought about the list of potential damage I had done to myself. I didn't care that much about sterility but blindness, death and insanity aren't that high on my life's list. About that point, my eyes started bothering me and I had the sense of a clawing ache in my groin. It was moving north.

My reverie was interrupted by the nurse who had cranked open the door, armed to the teeth with medical implements and my clipboard. She sat on a stool that she had produced from beside the examining table, going right to the nasty part: who, what, when, where and, of course, why and how. She shook her head and flipped my gown up over my waist. I had the impression that she'd seen and done it all before as she hauled out a Q-tip and ground it into the head of my penis.

Apparently satisfied, she flipped the gown down and shook her head. "Was it good for you, Prince, John?"

"No, but I guess only one of us has to be satisfied."

"Well, you're not going to be too happy about any of this. We'll have to wait for the lab tests but I'm pretty sure that you've got *Neisseria gonhorrhoeae*."

"What's that?"

"Clap."

"Do you really think applause is appropriate?"

She smiled. "I've heard them all but that's pretty good." She got more serious. "You don't have a last name for this Janice woman, do you?"

"No, things didn't work out."

"I'd guess they did for you."

"You might say so, but I'm sitting here in a gown with no back, practically stark naked, with my best parts sticking out and talking to a woman who has no great interest in me—sexually, I mean."

"Oh, don't say that, Mr. Prince. I have nothing but interest in you sexually. Just not the way you'd like. But, like you said, I guess only one of us has to be satisfied."

I nodded. "Well, now you put it that way."

"So, let me guess. Maybe five-two or three but a great smile? I'd say, what, uh, nineteen, maybe twenty years old? Brown hair, short and bobbed? Let's see, brown eyes?"

"That's amazing, although I'm not sure about the eyes. How can you tell?"

"Oh, let me finish. She worked for the Jeff Wooster campaign. Right?"

I didn't say anything.

"You're not the first, Mr. Prince. We've had thirty-seven men in here in the last three weeks, all with the same symptoms as you. All of them promised to change their vote for her. She's quite effective."

"I'd probably say defective."

She checked the clipboard again. "You work for the government, I see."

"Legal Aid, actually."

"Oh, I don't think that matters much. I expect you'll be down-sized, too. You may just have done the unbelievable, Mr. Prince."

"Oh? What's that?"

"Literally screwed yourself."

That was comforting, but I asked what was going to happen.

"Oh, you'll be fine. Medically, I mean. You've come in early. No venereal blindness or trips to the funny farm for you. Just four weeks of antibiotics, no drinking and total abstinence from sex. You can handle that, can't you, Mr. Prince?"

"Well, I think I can take the pills. I wasn't getting any of the other anyway. Why no booze?"

"You might just get drunk and lucky at the same time." She hauled a bottle of pills from her pocket. "Not allergic to antibiotics, are you?"

"What's the alternative?"

"Oh, they used to use mercury. The clap didn't kill you but the cure sure did."

"I suppose that's progress."

"Put on your clothes and I'll give you some more pamphlets before you leave." I noticed her name tag: "Heather Horschewicz." She saw me notice.

"Wife?"

"Sister. Myron isn't . . . married."

***

I don't think you're supposed to meet any of the other guests at the STD clinic, privacy and all that. But I couldn't miss him since we emerged from our caskets at more or less the same time, like vampires at dusk. Normally, it wouldn't have mattered that much and I wouldn't have noticed. By now, I didn't much care. I'd been ignored by a gnome, drooled on by the elderly and manhandled by the medical staff. Besides, my sex life, drinking career and peace of mind were all on a four-week vacation.

But he tried to duck back in. Which meant I saw him.

Of all the people I expected to meet at an STD clinic, the last was the very fey and gay Bobby Cherry, Crown Prosecutor and common sufferer with me in the courts of this good province.

I guess he decided that he was busted so he came back out and shook his confidence into place. He looked at me as if to say, "You have at least as much as I have to be ashamed of."

"Two questions, Bobby."

"I can imagine what heterosexist remarks you seem to think are funny, Prince."

"Are you batting for the other team now?"

He shook his head, almost in disgust at the idea. "What else?"

"So, how did they get you to change your vote, then?"

HAPPY TO DO WHAT YOU SUGGEST

Prostitution has one advantage over marriage. On a price per transaction basis, it's considerably cheaper. Besides, hookers have a way of leaving and letting you go to sleep. They don't seem to feel any great need to hang around and cuddle. Or talk about deworming the cat.

But we don't get a lot of prostitution charges in Yamnuska Centre. We don't have a "stroll" with young bits of alluring flesh bluing in the winter winds. Nor are there those daring, midnight raids on suburban bungalows with half-dressed citizens spilling out windows amidst the clamour of sirens and the glare of flashing cruiser lights. Maybe, it's all the amateur competition.

My thirty days of sobriety and chastity were up and I was given the task of defending Monica Ponace for being a "common streetwalker," actually communicating for the purposes of prostitution. I had never been on this side of a prostitution defence before. When I articled, I had been to court with a client whose greatest wish was to go to "John School" so his wife, loved ones and business associates would remain blissfully convinced of his virtue. As I recall, my preparation time in the washroom — nervously peeing and throwing up --- accounted for about ninety per cent of the final bill. But I am made of sterner stuff now. And I earn about two thirds of that final bill.

But, back to Monica. She was hardly the picture of a homecoming queen. I don't think she'd made it much past grade four before her excesses had consumed her. Even if Yamnuska Centre had a stroll, she'd have starved on her earnings. I doubt anyone could get quite *that* drunk.

But, back in January, she had been stopped by Constable Wayne Venale for drinking and driving. As they stood on the dark shoulder of the highway, he asked her to provide a sample of her breath, blood or other bodily substance suitable for testing to determine the concentration, if any, of alcohol or any other drug that might be coursing through her bloodstream. She apparently offered to have him provide her with some of his own bodily fluids in lieu.

"When I read the demand to her, Ms Ponace then made, uh . . . an improper suggestion to me." The good officer sucked on his closed lips at this, as if holding in bodily secretions of a more digestive variety. I took it from this that he was usually on the bottom during acts of love, lest he suffer from motion sickness.

"And what was that, Constable Venale?" A new kid was subbing in for the Crown. His ears coloured. There we had it: green for the witness and red for the Crown—Christmas colours!

"The demand?" It was a strangled croak.

Morceau, ever eager to get to the squalor in people's lives, chimed in, "I believe we already have that, Constable. What else did she say?" As in, "get to the dirt."

Venale looked at his feet—all size twelve of them—then sucked half the ambient oxygen from the room. He grunted and gave it back to us, along with bits of carbon dioxide in the process. "She, uh, made the suggestion that I might want to, uh . . ." Here, he trailed off in mumbles.

It was my turn at the thumbscrew. "I'm sorry, Your Honour, I didn't catch that." I didn't bother getting up, just sat back and pointed it out over my notes.

Normally, Morceau would have commented on this but he was far more entranced by the prospect of seaminess to come. "Speak up, Constable!"

Venale sucked in another deep breath and looked about him. He pursed his lips. "She said . . ."

Scottie's lessons of a year hadn't failed and I stood up. "I object, Your Honour. This is a statement to a person in authority." Constable Venale breathed again. Much more of this and one of us would have to resort to mouth-to-mouth resuscitation.

"Mr. Greene?" He looked to my "learned friend," who apparently wasn't.

"Uh, yes, sir . . . uh, I mean, Your Honour?" He had that look one associates with bunnies and fawns in the worst of Walt Disney. And it was a near miracle that his voice wasn't reverting to a prepubescent quality.

"Mr. Prince"—the words were well salted with appropriate venom—"has made an objection. Do you have an answer for him?"

"Uh, yes, uh . . ." An entire course in the law of evidence flashed before his eyes, I'm sure. You could almost hear the pages flicking by.

"What. Is. It?"

"I . . . I'm not quite . . ."

"Well, you could say that the officer wasn't a person in authority. Or you could ask for a *voir dire* to prove that the statement was voluntary. Or you could say that it was a spontaneous utterance. Hmmm?"

"Yeah, the last one."

"Good guess, Mr. Greene. You might also have said that the statement was the *actus* of the offence." He smiled his feral smile and turned to me, content that he, at least, could do his job. "Overruled, Mr. Prince."

"No fair. Two against one." It was almost whispered and I hoped the trusty court tape machine hadn't picked it up.

"I have acute hearing, Mr. Prince."

"And a cute appreciation of evidence, too, if I may say so." It wasn't my day to be cited for contempt. Morceau had other fish to fry—or a barrel of them he could shoot, first.

He turned on the witness. "Well, Constable Venale, just what did Ms Ponace have to say to you?"

The police officer glanced from one side to the other. "She . . . uh . . . said that . . . if I didn't make her blow . . . she would offer me some . . . uh . . . sexual services." He paused, breathed out, and then hurriedly added, "Into the breathalyzer, I mean." He took on a shade of red I have seldom seen among mammals.

"Satisfied, Mr. Greene?" That was a question someone should have asked of the officer. All of this suggested to me that Constable Venale was either freshly hatched under a cabbage leaf somewhere or both he and my client had been holding out on us — informationally speaking. I checked her for smirks but she was busy mouthing curses in a language somewhere between Cree and English. I guess he hadn't quite measured up to her exacting standards.

My opponent tried to read between the lines of the juristic face. There is often much hidden between the scowl furrows and the crow's feet. "I . . . guess so. . ."

"Well, I'm not." Shock of shocks! "Exactly what did Ms Ponace say, Constable? And I don't want a lot of mumbling about 'sexual services' either. What did she say? Exactly!"

"She said that if I didn't make her give a breath sample, she would . . . uh . . . blow me until . . . my eyes . . . mmm . . . popped out."

"That's a lot better, don't you think?" Before Venale said anything more, my client removed all doubt with a sudden chortle and smirk. Both caught me by surprise.

"Control your client, Mr. Prince. If you can, that is." He was doing his best to remain magisterial but there were just too many impulses brimming over. "Or want to."

"Your Honour, that was quite uncalled for."

He bared the fangs that I'm sure he sharpened every fortnight. "As you noted, Mr. Prince, I have an acute appreciation of the evidence... all the evidence!"

"You may have misquoted me." I stood to cross-examine but my heart wasn't in it.

* * *

"In the end, it comes down to this, in my view, gentlemen. Did Monica Ponace offer illicit sexual services to Constable Venale, seeking a benefit for them?"

I was sort of hoping he would get into a diatribe about "prurient activities" and the like but he was eager to return to his chambers to practise foaming at the mouth.

"It seems pretty obvious to me and any other right-thinking person that Ms Ponace was offering sexual services. I am quite familiar with the vernacular meaning of the term, 'blow,' in the sense of a 'blow job,' as is any other ordinary person of business in our society today." I smiled. Perhaps, Morceau didn't spend his entire private life dismembering small animals. Or maybe, he had an extensive library of pornography. Or a really good dictionary.

"I can and I do take judicial notice that it refers to a perverse sexual activity sometimes found within the legal rubric of sodomy." The dictionary was definitely winning out here and my respect for Barbara Morceau, his long-suffering wife, rising. She had once told me that she knew when and how to keep her mouth shut. And I thought she only meant keeping mum at inopportune times.

"I say this because, although he has not admitted it, I am sure that Mr. Prince is more than familiar with this terminology. And I have no doubt that Ms Ponace knows and uses it, herself."

I turned to Monica and mouthed, "You haven't, have you?" The look on her face told me she might not have much taste but she did have her limits.

"She did use it that night and I am sure that she intended that she would engage in oral sexual gratification of the officer in return for a personal benefit to her that the officer might—indeed, could—bestow." No doubt, "oral sexual gratification" and "personal benefit" were terms Monica used regularly. But, I suspect her personal life had never risen to so literary a height.

"Was it prostitution? Or merely a sordid attempt to escape her legal obligations by resorting to her feminine wiles? I don't see that it much matters in this case. Ms Ponace offered a disgusting sexual favour in return for having the officer not do his full duty. That was the contract for sexual services that she offered, that she communicated publically. He was right and exhibited a fine example of being bound by his duty in resisting that offer and also by charging her as he did. I suppose we expect no less from our police officers than that but I am proud that this young man has resisted the temptations offered to him and has brought her to court today.

"Monica Ponace, I find you guilty as charged."

* * *

After he had subjected poor old Monica to thirty days of mopping the floor at the Women's Correctional Centre, it was almost time to go home. I decided a quiet breaking of my alcoholic fast was in order. Thirty days is a long time. So, I stopped off at the Beaver Hill House Hotel beverage room, suitably referred to as "The Lodge," for a post-litigation infusion of common sense.

I ordered my usual "Jack and Jack"—Jack Daniels straight up—and sat back at a table to let it make its way into my bloodstream, and, from there, to rot what remained of my brain cells.

It wasn't as if she were a presence. She sat at the bar under the full glare of the overhead track lighting. Still, she was good-looking enough to consider her a good time, if not a long time. And recall, I had remained celibate for a full thirty days with only my dirty mind to sustain me. I considered her as she sat at the bar nursing one of those drinks that comes in several colours and contains enough fruit to keep the dreaded scurvy away. She was dressed in a light grey pantsuit, which suggested that she had spent time in a city somewhere that gum boots aren't considered the equivalent of loafers. In these post-smoking days, she appeared hard-pressed for something to do with her hands, so she waved the left one about like a demonic orchestra conductor, occasionally brushing strands of long, brown hair from her forehead, when she came to the *con brio* parts.

I continued to watch her, considering the correct approach. She was clearly not a hick, so references to country music and cattle roundups were probably not going to work.

She turned, as if surveying the room. She had a pleasant enough face, not improved by a somewhat recessed chin and a large, narrow nose. I had the impression of nothing so much as a bird, bony-framed with a beak for drawing insects from those hard-to-reach corners and furrows. Still, she seemed pleasant and of an age where such suggestions as seemed to upset Judge Morceau would not be summarily dismissed.

I settled for the quiet, perhaps not too sophisticated "Can I buy you a drink?" and let her know that I was, in fact, a lawyer. That might impress her—if she didn't ask too much. I made my way to the stool beside her at the bar.

"Hi there. I was wondering if I could buy you a drink."

"Were you?" It wasn't quite cold but the ice I was trying to break seemed just a bit thicker.

"Yes. May I?"

"You don't seem to be too observant."

"Pardon?"

"I said, 'You don't seem to be too observant.' I have a drink." At this, she pushed the flora dangerously close to that nose and sucked on the straw. She turned away from me. I took it as a rejection but "faint heart ne'er won fair maid" or any other version of the female of the species.

"You waiting for someone?" I tried to keep it as breezy as possible. You know, the friendly West and all that.

"No. I just thought I'd have a pleasant drink."

"And a fruit salad, it seems."

"What?" It wasn't a question so much as a challenge.

"A fruit salad." I pointed to her drink, the assorted cherries and grapes now floating about halfway down the glass.

"Look, I don't know who you are or what you think I'm going to do but I just came here for a quiet drink."

"It was pleasant before."

"Yes, it was, until you showed up."

"I mean your drink."

"Yes, it was."

"Now, it's quiet. I don't think you can have it both ways."

"Well, I'm having it my way. Alone. Got it? I thought this was a nice place but I guess I was wrong." She had raised her voice enough that I took this as total rejection and retreated to a nearby table. But she wasn't done. She rounded on me and proceeded to remind me of my place in the order of things. In her mind, it was somewhere between tree slugs and slime mold. I turned my back and pretended that the pictures of softball teams sponsored by The Lodge held incredible fascination for me.

"This guy bothering you, lady?" It was Constable Wayne Venale, now in civilian clothes. He had the lacquered look—every part of him gleamed as if he'd been squeezed out of a tube of hair gel.

"No, not really. I was just making myself clear."

"Actually," I added—I figured it was my turn by now. "She was establishing my place in the biological hierarchy and I was just pondering my Latin name. I think she's passed on *rejectus familiaris*."

"This guy just doesn't take rejection well."

"Rejection? You're past that, well into humiliation and working on annihilation, actually. But, I am going to ignore all this and sit here and finish my drink."

"Well, you just leave the lady alone. All right, sir?"

"All things considered, Constable, that's a great idea." I turned back to my softball team pictures and tried to work out just which of them were probably my clients. I couldn't help but hear the two of them behind me.

"Are you really a cop? I mean, a police officer?" She gushed and giggled.

"Yeah, sure, cop's fine. Don't worry about it." He chuckled.

"So, you'll protect me against the big bad guys out there?" She tittered.

He leaned in. "So, whaddaya do?"

"I work the other side of the street. I'm a lawyer." Another giggle and another drink.

"Really?" He chuckled again

"Yeah, you got a problem with that?"

"Nope. Just don't sue me, 'kay?" This was apparently fiercely funny and she fairly whooped.

And so it went. She nickered at his every comment, which were many and ones that even I wouldn't have stooped to. I'm not sure why I stayed but I figured, once humiliated, I might as well stay and see how this would all turn out. He had her on her fourth drink but she held out for another before they got up to go.

She stumbled as she got up and he caught her. "I'm pretty woozy. You're gonna have to put up with a mouthful of booze."

"That's okay. We can use it as disinfectant."

"And we're gonna need it, too, aren't we? I mean your little guy's gonna get awf'ly dirty."

She cackled at this. "What're you gonna do for me, Waynee?"

"I don't know. You do this for me, maybe I'll give you or your clients a pass sometime." He fairly leered.

She leaned back and smiled. "You think?"

"Sure." He laughed again.

She walked over to me and cuffed me on the head. "That's how a gen'leman does it, bub. He knows how to make a woman do it right."

I'd only had three so I was past sober but only philosophical. "According to his sworn testimony in court, he doesn't even know what you're talking about."

Wayne Venale didn't seem too happy about this, so I added, "That was an offer to engage in oral sexual gratification in return for a personal benefit that you, as an officer of the law might—indeed, could—bestow. It was a contract for sexual services that she offered, that she communicated publically. You were right and exhibited a fine example of being bound by your duty in resisting that offer. Good night, Constable. I hope she doesn't charge you. Or bite you—for that matter."

BEGIN IN A FRIENDLY WAY

People always turn up where you least expect or want them. And so it was with the lawyer from the bar.

There she was in the "seven items or less" line, hawk-nosed and chicken-legged, dumping items ten through thirteen before reaching for the sugarless gum. Cinnamon, I believe.

And my trip to the bakery seemed incomplete without her braying about the cinnamon buns from whatever place she'd recently left. Or been thrown out of.

Finally, there was the encounter in the leash-free park where Rollo was ever wont to gambol and play. Or sniff crotches of whatever species. There she was in full plumage, a jogging suit so gaudy it would surely have gotten her arrested in even the gayest parts of Toronto. She shuffled along, plodding to whatever she had crammed into her iPod, in a world all her own, if that doesn't summon up images too frightening for small children. She tossed her ridiculous mane about, slewed her $150 shoes side to side and raised her nose into the wind in spite of the obvious resistance.

Rollo had taken the opportunity to recycle whatever I'd been feeding him and had left it, plus some scratchings of turf and cinders, in the midst of the walkway. Before I could pull out my baggie and reverse it over my hand, I heard that unmistakable sound of foot on fodder—pre-chewed and digested. I turned to see her look down and emit a most unladylike interjection. Mind you, it was appropriate to the situation. It had squirted rather farther up than I might have expected, suggesting that I needed to readjust Rollo's roughage.

The growl that came from her might have been enough to call Rollo to battle if he hadn't turned tail and run for the tall grass. She tore out her earbuds and rounded on me, literally spitting venom. Or something that colour, anyway.

"You need to control that dog of yours!"

I smiled and held up the bag. I was hoping the bar had been dark enough that she wouldn't recognize me. Or that her encounter with Constable Venale had erased her memory entirely.

"And what's that supposed to do, eh? A little late to do me any good! These shoes are ruined and my pants . . ." Here, she peeled back several layers of pink, purple and puce plastic clothing to reveal suitably soiled white gym socks. Or they had been. Rollo's digestive juices gave them a new and less than subtle shading.

"You and that . . . *animal*!" she said, as if either Rollo or I would be insulted by such a reference. "I've got half a mind to have one of you destroyed and the other one sued." I was tempted to ask her to take her time, since she was admittedly handicapped, and to choose the right one carefully. "Don't they have a dog bylaw in this, this . . . pathetic excuse for a town?"

"Um . . . Yamnuska Centre is actually a city." It was the most innocuous thing I could think of at the time.

"You!" Her nostrils flared and I almost expected bolts of fire to snort out. And I guessed that my anonymity was lost.

"Yes, it's funny how we should meet like this, isn't it?"

"You think this is *funny*, do you? *Funny*! Do you have any idea what a Marc Poulot jogging outfit costs? To say nothing of the Hermès joggers." I took these to be the shoes

"Well, to be perfectly hon—"

"No, how could you? Marc Poulot wouldn't sell his scraps to this manure pile in the sun!" She was swiping away at her ankle with a hand and fingernails that had been sprayed with paint to match her Marc Poulot duds.

"I don't think you want to do that." I was trying to be helpful but she continued with several more sweeps until she stopped, turned her hand to her face and let out a cry fierce enough to match her sordid plumage.

"You bastard! You . . . you fucking pig! You disgusting pervert!" She was bound to get it right sooner or later. I reached down to help her. "Get your stupid hands off me or I'll call the cops."

I had done my best to scrape Rollo's flattened leavings into my baggie, then stood. "I suppose you should. After all, you've got an in with them, don't you? Or is it the other way 'round?"

I whistled for Rollo and left her to uphold the honour of Marc Poulot and all who worship him. Hermès, as I recall, hasn't been worshipped since the days of the Greeks.

* * *

Rollo isn't used to being barked at by anything on two feet. Four he can handle; two make him neurotic. I had to spend quality time with him for several hours that day and he insisted on coming to work with me the next. I couldn't blame him. He has a delicate psyche.

But, we were late, what with all the stenches, odours and just plain interesting smells that had been deposited in the preceding day.

I hauled open the front door of the office, surprised to see that none of the secretarial staff was there. A throaty growl from Rollo could have warned me but he just nosed his way into my office and curled up in the corner. I went to my desk and shuffled files between piles, like a Mississippi gambler reduced to doing tricks at children's parties. I had more or less shuffled and reshuffled them into their original stacks when Gail poked her nose into my office.

"Mr. Prince! You're late." I could tell by the fact that she called me Mr. Prince that something was wrong.

From behind her came a voice, "I'll handle this," followed by the beak and right wing of Rollo's nemesis. "I understand your name is Prince. Well, Mr. Prince, office hours are 8:30 to 12:00 and 1:00 to 5:00 p.m. Not whenever you drag yourself in. You are late."

"Well, one of us should be, don't you think?"

She had traded her Marc Poulot in for something beige and formidable and her running shoes for something capable of doing a bit more damage in a serious scrap. They were nicely polished, though, and I speculated that they wouldn't show stains quite so readily. She ignored this and barked that the rest of the office was in the middle of a meeting and "Wouldn't I like to join them?"

Rather than being strictly honest, I did so, in the room where we keep what books we have or have liberated from the courthouse. We call it the library.

The masses were arrayed as if in a particularly rigid form of Protestantism, ladies on the left and men—the lawyers—on the right. Subbing in for our regular divine, was the Bird of Prey. Appropriate in this setting, don't you think? She began.

"For the benefit of Mr. Prince, my name is Carrie Anne Bloodworth." She looked directly at me. "I have been sent by the new Conservative government to make some changes around here."

Scottie shuffled over to me. "Di' the wee berd say't her name was Bloodbath?" This caught a hawk-like stare and the beak twitched ever so slightly.

"I've got quite perceptive hearing Mr., uh . . . MacLean, is it?"

"I've nae doubt yer misperceptive abou' manny things, ma'am. Just confused aboot the name s'all."

"It is... Bloodworth, Mr. MacLean. Please learn it." This last was schoolmarmish. If I hadn't known Scottie, I would have expected him to be put off.

"So it's Bloodwerth, then, is it? As in wha' y'd say at the blood bank? 'Wha's yer blood werth?'"

Some of the staff snickered at this. I checked Lawrence but he seemed to be pondering a well-thumbed copy of *Das Kapital* or *An Intelligent Woman's Guide to Socialism and Capitalism*, the Quiller-Couch edition. Angus sat rigid, staring into a crack in the wall behind Ms Bloodworth. He was the colour of parchment.

Not taking the bait, our overseer continued. "I will be speaking with each of you individually as to some strategic reassignments we are making in this office and throughout Legal Aid generally. These changes are long overdue in this office and they are long overdue in the entire system."

If anything, Angus's pallor found an even cheaper grade of paper. Lawrence, God bless him, was finally stirred to action.

"I, for one, am quite curious as to just how the system is to be changed and what strategic reassignments are intended."

Ms Bloodworth squared the sheets she had in front of her. "As I was saying, I will be meeting with each of the lawyers individually. I am not prepared to say anything beyond that. Other than this. Mr. Black is being seconded to Legal Aid Central, pending new assignment. I am sure we all wish him well in his new posting. As of 8:30 this morning, I am the new Legal Systems Coordinator for the Yamnuska Centre Service Unit. We will continue to be known as Legal Aid for the time being. A new designation is in the works. I'm afraid that I am not able to say much more than that at this point in time."

We all looked to Angus, just the way we always had before. He stood like a grieving father, rubbing the soil from the grave of his child, shaking his head. He started to speak, then shook his head and just crept from the room, so old.

* * *

The leash-free park was usually dog-free, as well, come noon time. This is not to say it was deserted. Far from it. All manner of spandexed, sneakered and otherwise repulsive forms of human life took the opportunity to tempt cardiac arrest by flitting past each other, constantly monitoring respiration, heart rate, blood pressure and, no doubt, stock prices on a variety of watches strapped to flailing arms. So intense was this exercise that they regularly fought tiny turf battles over lane space by flinging muttered curses as they trotted past each other like the ill-bred thoroughbreds they so vainly imitated. Or, at least, I imagined they were cursing each other. Certainly, mouths moved and reactions were had to what passed between them. And, given the looks of fury displayed and the sudden bursts of energy expended with each passing, I had the impression that what might have been said were not words of encouragement.

It all seemed rather pointless—a bit like practising law, actually—to run around endlessly in a circle in order to get fit. And the overall reduction in blood pressure occasioned by the exercise was counteracted by the increase in blood pressure from swapping dark threats and imprecations. This much exercise made me want to close my eyes and think of better things. One was the possibility of improving this sport with the addition of handheld weaponry, the better to clear the track for the fittest of the fit. After any given noon hour, the police could be summoned and the winner carted off to jail for all the carnage he—or possibly she—had caused. Think of the added competition for innovation in sneaker design! Besides, Ms Bloodworth was a public jogger. My plan might solve many problems at once. (Black Angus always had the good sense to avoid strenuous feats once he had finished jumping to conclusions, running off at the mouth and lifting our flagging spirits.)

Of course, I couldn't close my eyes as I had to keep watch for Rollo and his habit of providing additional hazards to the sport of jogging. All things considered, these could be seen as gifts for the super-healthy, something to add that soupcon of challenge for the overconfident. Exercise is frequently accompanied with a pungent air of health, light breeze and sweaty socks, all wholly incompatible with *eau de la merde chieneuse*.

Rollo had exchanged one form of public indecency for another, having located and started a spawning dance with a frisky young hound of dubious breeding and no apparent pedigree. The bench beside me creaked and leaned to my right. It was Kathy Markle.

"Come on, Prince. You've done some family law. Whaddaya think it'll cost if he knocks her up?"

"That's Rollo's problem. He'll have to get a second job, I guess."

"What's his first?"

"Funny you should ask. He's a SALTEA dog."

"He doesn't look too nautical to me."

"No, he's a service dog pursuant to the provisions of the *Service Animals Licensing, Training and Exemption Act*. It's a real statute. You can look it up."

She looked dubious. "When did acquire this exalted status?"

"Oh, about twenty minutes ago when I looked it up."

"Do tell." Rollo, oblivious to his newly elevated status, had now begun the part where the two of them chase each other a bit. There wasn't much growling and nipping yet.

"I don't know if you've met our new and inglorious leader, yet. The ever so well named Carrie Anne Bloodworth, dominatrix."

"I saw the memo. We've got our own new Queen of Mean."

"Not Bobby Cherry! Say it ain't so."

"It ain't so. No, this one comes with all the equipment—horns, tails and membership in the right political party. I don't think Bob quite fits in with her crowd."

"You worried?"

"Nah. Brian gave them a big lump of cash. I think he may even've signed me up as a party member. I don't know."

"Not for Christmas, I hope."

"No. I got a mink."

"The same way a mink gets a mink?"

She snorted. "Maybe. I'm a married woman after all."

"I'd noticed lately." She smiled.

"So what's with Carrie Anne Whatshername?"

"She's made a big splash. Big changes at Yamnuska Centre Legal Aid. Oh, yessiree! Big changes!"

"Don't tell me they fired you?"

"You think I'd be here with my SALTEA dog if I'd gotten fired? I'd be in the bar and he'd be out of a job. Just another canine bum in the alleys of Yamnuska Centre, sniffing cans and stealing trash."

"A charming thought. What's he up to now?" Having finished with the courting dance and the usual sniffing, snarling and snapping that is the wont of doggie dating, he had raised himself and settled in for the *coup de grace*.

"Starting a family like you. I should try it."

"I don't care. It's not *my* dog!" She reeled back and slapped her leg. It was enough to break the moment of bliss for the randy rapscallions. The female yelped and ran off in the general direction of downtown. Rollo just looked disgusted. He shook himself all over, looked about and trotted over to us, tail wagging. He nuzzled Kathy—quite inappropriately, I thought. She laughed some more and petted his head.

"So, what's been going on?" she asked.

"Bloodworth's bloodletting. Angus is being sent off to Legal Aid Central to act as some sort of legal mole. He figures they can't afford to fire him but, if they make it miserable enough, he'll quit."

"And Lawrence? I expect he's on the chopping block."

"I wasn't in the room but I get the impression that he'll be returning to the family fortune, whether with Allison or alone. Lo, the prodigal hath returned."

"What did he say?"

"I didn't understand all of it but the words, "reactionary," "stunted" and "profligate" were all used in conjunction with Ms Bloodworth."

"It makes you wish he swore, you know, normal words."

"I figure Lawrence'll die young and when they open him up to see what killed him, all those words will just come spewing out in a big, black ball. The pathologist will go deaf and the nurses, running for their lives."

"Quite a picture, Prince. You have a talent."

"One of my two."

"I can imagine what you think the other is."

"Well?"

"I'm a married woman, Jack. I'm trying to have a baby with my husband."

"So, what's holding you up?"

She sighed. "Sometimes, it's what isn't holding him up."

We sat there patting Rollo and looking at other things. The wind, the sounds of traffic, the chittering of the birds weren't quite enough.

"What about Scottie?"

"He's packing up his office."

"She didn't . . ."

"No. Scottie was given a choice. He could collect Unemployment Insurance . . ."

"It's called Employment Insurance now, you know. You should keep up with the times."

"That sure made me feel better when I was getting it."

"Employment Insurance?"

"What else?"

"Oh, nothing. I was just, you know, checking." She smiled her crafty smile.

I got her drift. "Well, that too. Always."

"So what was the choice?"

"Not getting it."

"No, I mean for Scottie."

"Oh, that. He could take the EI or he could move to some place called Sunareka, wherever that is."

"Oh, you don't want to know."

"No, eh?"

"Kind of nowhere much. You have to see it to believe it."

"You can't tell me then?"

"Oh, I could but it would spoil all the fun. Think Siberia."

"With or without the Gulags?"

"Both." We sat there some more and looked at the trees. The last of the athletic enthusiasts had run off to shower and appall their fellow citizens with their bright glows of health. "What's happening with you?"

"I don't know. I had to wait until after lunch."

"And the SALTEA dog?"

"He's staying, too. Can't do without him. He's my wingman."

IN TERMS OF OTHER'S INTERESTS

Even if I'm pretty sure what is going to happen, I still feel like a kid called to see the principal when I get The Great Summons to the boss' office. My palms get sweaty, my heart rate climbs and there's this gnawing sense of acid eating away at the walls of my stomach. But I figured with Lawrence, Angus and Scottie all gone, I was the institutional memory of Yamnuska Legal Aid, if you ignore Ms Stockard—and I, for one, always do—and I thought they needed someone from before to take care of little matters like telling people where the bathrooms are, let alone the courthouse. Angus represented the time before (probably the time before they started keeping time), Lawrence worked with the opposition and Scottie . . . well, Scottie was Scottie. Besides, they hadn't fired him; he was on his way to sunny Sunareka.

You can tell a lot about a person by the way he or she keeps an office. Scottie, ever the anarchist, keeps various paraphernalia of his minor triumphs over the forces of righteousness and good—a photo here, a blood-stained rock there—stashed amidst his files and briefs. He describes these arrangements as "organic," likely due to the bits of single-celled life clinging to them.

Lawrence is more of a modern-day kitsch man. Everything is molded plastic, stainless steel and shining lights, all arrayed in a spectrum that varies from faun to puce. He even has a mauve-coloured laptop. Lawrence is secure in his masculinity and needs to demonstrate solidarity with those of alternate lifestyles and challenged tastes. I suspect the edifying influences of the lovely Allison in all this. But it made for fewer sharp edges.

Black Angus is an Early Western rumpus-room kind of guy. Pictures of various, long-forgotten local likelies shaking hands with Angus or his good lady wife, the Black Madonna, bowling trophies, and posters of places in Europe that hadn't looked like that for forty years festooned the premises, all set about with dark, faux oak paneling. The floor was draped with a rug that was supposed to pass for Persian, according to the tag from Wal-Mart. And Angus kept the lighting low, so even the most adept lawyer couldn't read what he had on his desk. (It is a rudimentary skill, to say nothing of a habit, practised by all good lawyers to read what's upside down. It saves time and embarrassment later.) Of course, his monitor was always perched so you couldn't sit in the tatty black "client chair" and actually look at Angus; it dissuaded repeat visits.

When I got to what had been Angus's lair, I found the door closed. Having been summoned, I felt entitled to enter. This startled Carrie Anne and a middle-aged character, resplendent in pastel shirt and red suspenders, crouched over the corner of what appeared to be a new modular desk. She looked up. "You might have knocked, Mr. Prince."

"I might have seeped in under the door, too." This was for Red Suspenders who likely had. He was stringy enough. "I believe that you called for my presence at 1:30 p.m. and, by my watch, it is." I brushed aside a newly ensconced plant. Dieffenbachia, I'm told. I didn't know that before. You grow. Whether it would, is another question. But, given the number of its mates, now strewn about the place, Ms Bloodworth was doing her part to reduce global warming by creating a carbon sink, however isolated. The rest of the office had been gutted, new carpets laid and a "gee whiz" computer system installed. It whirred and clicked, either digesting data or chewing up nanobots, whatever they are. The drapes that had kept this space darkened had been supplanted by the latest in Venetian blinds of a shade that only decorators could have named. Angus's feature wall of fame was now superseded by Carrie Anne's certificate corner.

I was amazed and more than a little impressed at how quickly the new age cometh and the old passeth away.

"I'd like you to wait outside."

Rather than invite her to compare our respective likes, I smiled, said, "Oh," and retreated to the space just outside the door. I don't think I shared too much in common with Red Suspenders and our discussions of likes and dislikes wouldn't have found much common ground. I looked about for someplace to sit and discovered that the chair that Angus had thoughtfully placed there was gone. But I was here, as required, and I didn't have much else to do. I found a place on the floor and occupied it by right of adverse possession: not by force of arms, not in secret and not to anyone's danger, as I recall.

From my roost, I considered many aspects of our office, its layout and better use. I considered how much paper it might take to wall up the door and wondered whether I would leave fingerprints, if it happened to fall on Carrie Anne and injure her fatally. Time flies when you're fantasizing impending doom. Whoever's.

After twenty minutes of this and other more personal considerations, the door opened. She peered out, missing me initially. I stood. Stretched. Yawned. Smiled. She did not.

"I am a busy person, Mr. Prince. I don't appreciate interruptions and I don't like slackers."

"Where do you stand on sarcasm?"

She grunted in disapproval and pointed for me to enter. I did. Red Suspenders tipped his glasses back but didn't stand to shake hands or introduce himself. I smiled and said, "Jack Prince. Thrilled to meet you." It wasn't mutual. Carrie Anne slipped in behind me and sat at her desk. I looked for a place to sit but found none. Red Suspenders occupied the two-toned, creamy seat matching that commanded by my new boss. I debated sitting on the floor but moved to the windowsill, pushed up the blind and just leaned. I think I even crossed my legs. This forced Carrie Anne to reposition herself and made it impossible for Red Suspenders to look at me. He frog-walked his chair across the room and tried to work with his file in his left hand. I was glad. I'm sure it offended some long-held, personal philosophy never to deal with anything on the left.

"This is Gavin Turcotte. He's from the minister's office." I took it that she was referring to Red Suspenders, which gave me the advantage of an actual name.

He cleared his throat. "I suppose you want to know why the minister has sent me."

"Not really." It could be that there were just too many people there and someone had to come to Yamnuska Centre, just to ease the crowding.

"No? Well, I'll make this as simple as I can."

"I'll try to keep up." I smiled. He didn't.

"We think that this office and the whole of the legal aid system needs a serious upgrading and repositioning in the realm of delivery systems for the government. I think it's safe to say that the mission of this organization has become obscure and caught up in bureaucratic decay. Are you following me?"

"Perfectly."

He launched into a similarly flavoured rendition of business-speak that had passed its "best before" date ten years ago. Still, he carried it off with a straight face for a good five minutes, ending with, "So, are you on board, Jack? Are you with us?"

I forewent a hearty "Argh!" a warm "Aye, aye, Cap'n, sir!" and even "To the ends of the Earth" and responded with a smile and "But, of course, Gavin. One hundred per cent."

This seemed to be somewhat of a surprise. He looked over to Carrie Anne. "Really?"

I hadn't understood a thing he'd said but, I suspected, neither did he. Carrie Anne was an open question. She scowled and shuffled some papers in a file. She sorted through it, at last finding the Holy Grail that looked oddly like a copy of my party membership.

"Is there a problem?" I try to be helpful. Sometimes, I even tell the truth—if it isn't too painful. And sex isn't involved.

"No." He didn't seem convinced so he checked his file. "It's just that we had expected, uh . . . perhaps, some resistance."

"Resistance?" I smiled. "I try to be as . . . flexible as possible to all new experiences. From what I've learned from my brief acquaintanceship with Ms Bloodworth, I know she has the same flexibility. I only hope I can emulate this myself." (With this I glanced up at my immediate superior and looked past her to the Certificate Wall and what appeared to be a degree in sociology and religious science "With Great Distinction" from an American university of dubious provenance and lesser reputation. I think it was founded by a televangelist who'd sinned, sought public redemption and lost ground ever since. He'd called the school "his gem" and its graduates, "truthful seekers after justice." It figured.) The recollection of our first meeting was on Carrie Anne's face.

"Well . . ." With this, Gavin stood. "I guess I'll get back to the capital. It was good to meet you, Mr., uh, Prince." He stuck out a sweaty palm that I grasped and squeezed ever so slightly more than was called for.

"Good to meet you, sir. I trust this will be just the first of many profitable meetings." So, it was lying for a good cause. Me.

He left and I was almost to the door when she called me back. "Just a minute, Mr. Prince. We're not done." I walked back, twirled Gavin's chair until it was suitably positioned, and sat. It was a comfortable improvement. "I don't know what you think just happened—"

"I think that I just met some guy from the minister's office, who probably outranks you. I think you had it in your mind to can me and set this whole circus up with a new roster of clowns, and you, the ringmaster. And I think you were going to do all this because you think I belong to the wrong political party, which would result in an ugly lawsuit, just when you are getting used to the soft chairs and the fuchsia blinds. Am I warm?"

She sat silent. In another part of my life, I would have thought she was pouting. But pouting is beneath a director in our legal aid system so I'm sure she wouldn't. Finally, she smiled. "You have a . . . *reputation*, Mr. Prince. And don't think we don't know it, either. But I'm going to keep you around for a while. And not just because you think you might sue me. No, I've got a new job for you." She twisted a smile as she picked up her pen and torqued its cap sadistically back and forth. I believe Freud had something to say about this. I could just imagine how it might actually feel in her hands.

"Really. I can hardly wait." My smile was at least as fake as hers.

"Yes. I think we need someone of your . . . experience and . . . *qualities* to undertake a *special* role in this office."

"Oh?"

"Yes, in addition to your other responsibilities, I think you'd service our clients best if you also took on the many conflicts and other difficult files that occasionally crop up in various offices about the province."

I had the sense that "servicing" had the same meaning as it did among bulls and cows. Despite the apparent possibility of pleasure, they'd all wind up in the slaughterhouse. "Or you could leave your resignation with me by the close of business."

I'm afraid I'm addicted to such minor luxuries as eating regularly and having a roof over my head. "Sure. Why not?"

"Oh, Mr. Prince. One other thing."

"I can hardly wait."

My discomfort seemed to please her. "I was wondering about that dog, the one in your office."

"Shh! We never use that word in Rollo's presence. He's offended by it. You never can tell just how he'll react."

She rolled her eyes at this and sighed. "Be that as it may, Mr. Prince, he is a dog."

"I believe you may be mistaken."

"Mr. Prince, I've had just about as much of your silliness and fakery as I can take. That dog is . . . a dog! He is a dog, a whole dog and nothing but a dog!"

"So help you dog." For the dyslexic, you understand.

"What?"

"I am afraid, Ms Bloodworth, you are quite mistaken. Rollo is so much more than a dog to me."

"I'm sure you'd like to think so, Mr. Prince, but that animal is nothing but a dog and we can't have a dog just lolling about this office. I mean, consider the liability issues alone. If he up and bites some client, we could be sued for millions."

"Rollo would never bite a client."

"It's happened before."

"Never. He has much more elevated tastes." I tried not to think of his recent choice of romantic partners. "He doesn't like their flavour."

"Mr. Prince, I'm not going to fence with you about this. Either that dog goes or you both do. Do I make myself clear?"

"But you can't do that!"

"And why not?"

"Rollo is a service animal as defined in paragraph 2 (1) (t) of the *Service Animals Licensing, Training and Exemptions Act*. As such, he is entitled to remain with me, as needed, in any public building where I might be. I trust that makes an end of your quite improper suggestions. And if that is all, I'll bid you a good day."

I got up and left, thinking only of how I could justify Rollo's presence to Judge Morceau, when next I went to court.

LET THEM DO THE TALKING

"Jack, I'd like you to go to Moskolsippi." Carrie Anne Bloodworth seemed to be developing a bad habit of suddenly and silently turning up like the ghost in a Shakespeare play or a bad smell at a wedding. Besides, there was no telling what semi-intimate acts you might be up to.

"Do I pack my mukluks or sun hat?"

"Pardon?"

"It sounds like you're sending me to Russia or the Magnolia State. I should tell you, I'm not licensed to practise in either place."

"I hadn't thought of that." Ms Bloodworth looked puzzled. She seemed quite good at it, actually. I think she'd been practising most of her life. Then, she smiled. "Oh, yes. I get it now." I was glad. It seemed like progress.

"So . . . ?"

"What?"

"Which is it? The snows of the Kremlin or mint juleps and southern belles?"

She smiled, but it didn't go too deep. Nothing much did. Except maybe Constable Venale. Then, again. . . . "Neither one, actually. Moskolsippi is a town three hours north of here. You can drive to it." That was a relief. I had visions of mushing with Rollo in harness. He really would be a service dog then.

"When and why?"

"Thursday. I'd like you to see a man there named Harry Popowicz."

"The blind monkey sings at midnight." She looked puzzled. "Isn't that the countersign?" I was trying to be helpful.

A shake of the regal head betrayed no sign of operating parts within: no grinding gears, sproinging springs or even a helpful ticking. I wasn't surprised. "Jack, are you always this bizarre?"

"People *have* been saying that since . . . you know . . . the accident." I struggled to keep a sob out of my voice.

This time she looked at me, actually peered, and bobbed her head twice in my direction, like a robin pecking at a worm. When she came up wormless, I half expected her to ask about "The Accident" but, like most people, she just looked away. To be perfectly honest, the only accident in my life was when the Rev. Hugh Prince's condom broke. That's my mother's story, at least.

Gathering herself, she grunted, tsked once and continued. "Harry Popowicz is a client."

I nodded as if taking things in as quickly as I could. "A client."

"He's a bit of a problem."

"A *bit* of a problem."

"Yes."

"For whom?"

"Whom?"

"Yes. The objective form of who, if you recall your grammar."

"Uh . . . for everyone, I guess."

"Oh." I continued sitting, contemplating my artistically arranged desktop. She was leaning, provocatively, I thought, against the doorframe. Had I not known about Constable Venale, I might have thought the fleet was in town.

She became more forthcoming . . . verbally I mean. "Harry Popowicz is charged with causing a disturbance at the police station. He's been having some sort of problem with the town for some time now. Something about a bus contract. Ms Stockard has the file."

I looked down at my desk. "Why?"

"You don't seem to read any of the memos I send out, Jack. Why is that?"

"Of course I do, Carrie Anne. My nightly reading. I must have misplaced it. Please do tell."

"I have appointed Ms Stockard as disclosure coordinator in this office. She is appropriately trained and I have tasked her with the compilation and distribution of all materials for files emanating from the Crown's office. It was necessary because of the utter mess . . . and I don't mean to be disrespectful of Angus. I know he was doing his best. But there were mounds of material scattered throughout this office. I just don't know how any decent office could cope with such a pig's breakfast of paper."

"I'm told they eat slops."

"Who do?"

"Pigs. For breakfast, I mean." I laid my pen carefully on my desk so that it cascaded down the mound of files I had erected before she came in.

"What do pigs eating have to do with files?"

"Precisely my point. You *are* quick!"

She squinted at me, her head cocked to one side, then shook her head. "All I was saying is that Ms Stockard has the file materials and will give them to you. You can pick up your car on Wednesday from the Central Vehicle Authority. And Jack—" This was a parting shot if ever I heard one. "Be back by Friday night. We're on strict budget constraints."

I have to admit, this last confused me but I let it pass. "Is there something special about this place that I should know?"

"No, I just don't want any . . . malingering." She turned to go, then looked back. "What's that statute again? The one for your dog?"

"The *Service Animals Licensing, Training and Exemptions Act*. SALTEA, like the crackers."

"And where do I find it?"

"Wherever fine statutes are kept for sale."

She closed my door behind her, for which I thought to thank her, but couldn't. Then, I heard her ask someone, "What happened to Jack Prince?"

Gail answered, as usual, without much thought. "He was fired once." After a bit of a pause, she added, "And he drinks sometimes."

I looked at Rollo but he just yawned, put his head on his paws and went right back to sleep.

* * *

I'd checked the map. This meant nothing. Maps never tell you what you really need to know. Oh, they'll tell you how far things are. And how many of that company's gas stations you can drive by. Sometimes, they even get the names of things right. They're like those guide books that tell you where to go to see this painting or that statue. But if all you're looking for is arts and crafts, you might as well stay at home and watch PBS. You see it all there sooner or later.

No, I think that any decent tourist brochure should let you in on the best bars to pick up women. Where to buy good dope. Hotels that won't question you when you come home drunk with a likely partner on your arm. Or wherever. And, of course, the places not to go to get rolled. Or not get rolled. Whatever. Maybe, when I get disbarred, I can go into guidebooks. They'd be colour-coded and talk about the things that people really go to Europe for: sex, dope and a generally good time. Face it, going to Europe for the art is like going to a singles bar for the music: it's loud, trashy and highly unlikely.

Moskolsippi was bundled up within a national park I'd never heard of and tucked in behind a lake that promised boring driving around. It looked like the sort of place you wind up in when even Legal Aid lets you down.

I rounded up a car easily enough. Actually, things turned out fairly well. The young lady who signed it out to me was worried about my clutch sticking. It didn't. Neither did she the next morning. Something about a job. And here, I was going to let her take care of Rollo. She probably hated dogs, too.

So, I showed up at the office to pick up my file from Ms Stockard, only to find Carrie Anne personning the battlements of Fortress Yamnuska Centre Legal Aid. Constable Venale must have pulled the night shift. Or not. I left the engine running to keep it warm and the window cracked so Rollo could stick his head out. I brushed off the rain as I came in, careful to spray as much as I could in her direction.

"Mr. Prince, you're not taking that animal with you, are you?"

"No, I left her at the Central Vehicle Authority." This puzzled her. Most things seemed to.

"That dog . . ." She made a strong sighing sound that went on far too long.

"That's an unkind thing to say about a fellow government employee."

"That animal does not work for the government." To disabuse any and all doubt, she actually pointed at my boon companion and wingman.

"Who? Rollo?"

"That would seem to be his name."

"Of course. He is my companion animal pursuant to the—"

"I talked to Jeff."

"Jeff?"

"Yes, Jeff Wooster. He's our MLA, you know."

"Oh, yes, Jeff."

"That seems to cause you some discomfort, Jack."

"No, no. The antibiotics cleared that right up, actually." I wasn't sure if her look was one of shock or discomfort. If anything, it improved her.

"I am quite close to Jeff, you know, Jack." She said this with something approaching pride.

"Well, your secret's safe with me." The thrust of this seemed to have hit her wrong. She folded her lips, making her beak even more prominent.

"What's that supposed to mean?" Ah, genuine anger. "If you're implying . . ."

"I rarely imply. I usually come right out and say it. Now, I've got a three or four hour trip to make and I need to pick up my stuff." I walked by her, carefully allowing my coat to brush against her so as to leave the greatest possible smudge. She did need cooling down. When I got back to the door, she was still waiting.

"You're not taking that dog with you, Jack."

"Why not?"

"You don't need him."

"Who's supposed to do the driving?" At this point, Rollo, his paws on the dashboard and his nose out the window, barked. "He can be pretty impatient but he's a wonder on the highway."

She gawped like a landed trout and shook her head. I closed the door and ran through the rain to the car. I didn't know what to say to Rollo, so I pushed him aside and got in. With luck, she was probably calling Jeff about then.

* * *

"All I want's fair justice. That's all I want."

He was a sight. Not overly tall, Harry Popowicz had a swirl of white hair that topped a face ravaged, in turn, by wind, scowls, a dribble of chewing tobacco and, probably, a fair bit of booze over the years. It was a pudgy face, even one that could have been called cherubic, some fifty or so years ago. Now, the ravages of time, toil and no small amount of verbal combat had taken their toll. His eyes lay like blue stones, sunk deep into a wallow of red-lined flesh. His nose might have been broken more than once, although I suspect one good smash might have done that much damage. The mouth formed a permanent scowl enhanced by a lower lip that jutted out like the prow of a ship. He continually chewed something. I hoped it was nothing he wanted to spit at me. Four hours of driving and a pretty shabby conversation with Rollo and this was what I got.

"So, what I want's fair justice. That's what. Can you do that for me, Mr. Prince? Can you get me fair justice?"

"Is there any other kind?" It seemed a good question.

"I don't want none of your smarty lawyer talk. I just want fair justice. It ain't right what they did to me. Whaddaya think?" He shifted in the client chair, thoughtfully left in the witness room. It looked like something that washed up during the Pleistocene Era.

"Well, Mr. Popwicz, I'm not really sure what went on here. I have the statements that the police—"

"All lies. Them cops don't tell the truth. They're just out to get me."

"Well, why don't I just go over what they do say and you can tell me where it's wrong. Okay?"

He shook his shaggy white mane and sucked on his upper lip. "You can just go right ahead. It won't make no difference. Them's all lies anyway." The chair creaked as he settled back in it.

I took a breath. "Well . . . it says that on the thirtieth of June of this year, you went to the local police station to make a complaint of being harassed by Tom Wold, the local bylaw officer. When you got into the police station . . ."

He snorted at this. "Police station. More like a bus station if you ask me, all them Indians just sittin' around, drunk proba'ly."

"No doubt. Anyway, when you got into the police station they say you were talking to someone named Constable Whipple and you got a little excited . . ."

"Excited? That sawed-off weasel don't listen. He just starts tellin' me, 'Harry, you gotta do this an', Harry, you gotta do that an', Harry, we don't have to take none o' your bullshit. He tells me he don't have to take none o' my bullshit.'"

"Did he use that word?"

"What word?"

"Bullshit?"

"I donno. Something like that."

"No, not something like that. Did he use the word, bullshit?"

"Yeah, I'm pretty sure he did."

"Oh. So then what happened?"

"Well he starts tellin' me he don't have to listen to none o' my bullshit no more an' I hafta get outta the police station."

"It does say, 'Popwicz was asked several times to leave the station after he became abusive to the member.' Do you remember anything about that?"

"Abusive! I go in there to make a complaint just like any other citizen. I got a right to make a complaint, don't I, Mr. Prince?"

"I would guess so."

"Well, I sure would guess so, too. I know my rights, you know."

"I'm sure you do. I'm just interested in what you may have said to this Constable Whipple."

"I told him that I wanted to make a complaint against that worm, Tom Wold. He's been doin' stuff to me, damagin' my property, givin' me tickets for nothin'. He an' them other guys is out to run me outta town an' I ain't leavin', ya know. I just ain't leavin'. No way!"

"Well, let's leave that aside for—"

"No, we ain't leavin' that aside. It's important. It's real damn important if you ask me. If you don't know nothin' about what them guys at the town a been doin' to me, then you don't know nothin'."

"Well, I hate to point this out to you, but they aren't on trial today. You are. Charged with causing a disturbance by using insulting language."

"Insultin' language. Hah! That's a laugh, if you ask me. Them guys a been insultin' me for years and I get charged. What a laugh!"

"If I can go on before we go in there. It says, 'Popowicz was asked several times to leave the station after he became abusive to the member. He turned and told the member, "You're just like the rest of them pieces of shit. You aren't worth nothin', you lousy, little weasel." At that point, the member warned Popowicz once more to mind his language and leave. When Popowicz did not do so, the member came around the counter and attempted to escort him from the premises. Popowicz resisted and was arrested and given his rights.' Does that sound about right?"

"'Mind his language,' that's a laugh. That cop was swearin' at me and laughin' an' he thought it was one great big joke. Mind his language! Hah!"

"So, when was it that he told you that he wasn't going to take any more of your bullshit?"

"Whaddaya mean?"

"You told me that he said he wasn't going to take any more of your bullshit."

"Yeah."

"Well, when did he say that to you?"

"What's that got to do with anything? They're tryin' to railroad me. You know what that means, Mr. Prince? Do you? They're tryin' to railroad me out of this town and I ain't leavin'. No way!"

"You may if you get convicted of this."

"Whaddaya mean?"

"If you get convicted of this, you can go to jail, you know."

"Hah!" I'd never really heard it said like that before. "I don't got no record. They can't send me to jail if I ain't guilty an' even if I am, I don' got no record."

"I have a CPIC printout here that says you were a found in at a bawdy house, what, twenty three years ago? Is that right?"

"Yeah but that ain't nothin'."

"According to this, you had to pay a $200 fine. That's something."

"You gonna represent me, Mr. Prince, or am I gonna hafta get someone else?"

"Well, I'll do my best."

* * *

"All rise! The Provincial Court sitting in the town of Moskilsippi is now in session. The Honourable Judge W.C. Senuk presiding." A tiny figure entered with this and launched himself onto the chair at the front of the court. He must have had some sort of springboard up there because one second he was barely visible and the next he was comfortably and precariously perched in a chair, his head several feet above the bench. He matched my client for wisps of snowy hair and had a rather less damaged cherubic face. He peered down at all of us standing there.

"You may take your seats." Then, a look of concern came over him. "Perhaps, I should rephrase that. You should sit down, not take your seats. I don't want to be understood as encouraging anyone to take their chairs away. You might get charged with stealing them and I wouldn't want to be responsible for anyone being charged with anything."

I looked over to the Crown prosecutor. She was a tall, willowy creature with horn-rimmed glasses who looked too young and too serious to be a real lawyer. Besides, she ignored me.

His Honour unclipped a pair of half-framed glasses and reviewed the information before him. Something was concerning him. "Miss . . . I mean Ms Couture, is it?"

My opposite number rose. "Yes, Your Honour?"

"I'm concerned about this Information. It seems to be somewhat irregular. I wonder if counsel would like to look at it. Clerk, would you please show this information to counsel?"

Both the prosecutor and I rose and marched up to the clerk's desk where we were handed the long sheet of paper outlining the charge. We both looked at it. Since I had no idea what was bothering His Honour I just continued staring.

"I'm sure counsel have noticed what I did this morning when I reviewed the information."

"Ah, yes, of course." All right, so it was a lie. To a judge. In court.

My opposite number wasn't quite so deceitful. "I'm afraid I missed it, Your Honour."

"The jurat, Ms Couture. The jurat. Surely, you see that the Justice of the Peace has signed it below where it says 'Justice of the Peace' and not on the line where he should."

"Mr., uh . . ."

"Prince, sir. John Prince from Yamnuska Centre Legal Aid. For Mr. Popowicz."

"Yes, of course. What do you have to say about this error?"

"It seems somewhat serious."

"Yes, I quite agree. Very serious. How can we proceed on a defective information such as this? Well, Crown?"

"Your Honour, it appears that the Justice of the Peace has written something just after his name."

"How does that help you, Ms Couture? This is an information." If he had said it was the Ten Commandments, still steaming from a quick trip down Mount Sinai, I doubt he could have given this rather smudged and ink-blotched sheet much more significance. "Mr. Popowicz is charged with a serious matter. His liberty is in the hands of this court and he is entitled to be treated with all the respect and fairness that this court can show him. Instead, he is faced with an information that may well be defective. What do you have to say, Mr. Prince? Does this not require an immediate inquiry into the propriety of this official document? If it is that, I mean?"

"Well, as I was saying, it seems somewhat serious..."

"More than somewhat, Mr. Prince. I think this goes to the very root of the justice system. We can't have just any old piece of paper being used to send a man to jail... and I don't mean to imply that I have already decided this case. Mr. Popowicz, you should be assured that when I say you are being sent to jail, what I mean is that, if you are convicted of this offence after a fair and impartial trial, I could send you to jail, on top of a lot of other penalties, but you should be assured that I haven't decided that you are guilty or that you would go to jail if you are found guilty. It's important that you understand that, sir. Just to be clear."

The scowling Harry Popowicz rose. "I understand that, Your Honour. All I want is fair justice. Fair justice, that's all."

"Of course, sir. That is what we are trying to do for you. And you shouldn't expect anything else." He paused at this point and poured himself a glass of water. "Well, Ms Couture, what do you have to say about this?"

"Your Honour, it seems to me like a harmless error that can be remedied by a simple amendment or I could have the police officer re-swear it before the court. He's right here." She pointed at the constable beside her who was slowly seeping beneath the table.

"Ms Couture. How can you even suggest that I take an oath from the very police who are prosecuting Mr. Popowicz and attesting to the truthfulness of this document and then turn around and give him a fair trial? How would that look, Ms Couture? Try putting yourself in Mr. Popowicz's place for a moment. The prosecution just using this court as a rubber stamp right in front of him." As opposed, I suppose, to doing so behind his back. "I won't have it. You can have fifteen minutes to remedy this egregious error."

At this, he slipped from his perch and fairly bounced from the room. Harry was in his element as the Crown hunched over the table trying to explain to the court officer how he was going to fix his terrible mistake. Or that of some anonymous JP.

* * *

Lunch intervened. If you can call French fries drenched in gravy lunch. Well, they were the highlight of The Jerry Can, a haunt run, it seemed, by someone named Jerry Cann. The name of the place was about as original as the decor and food. The last time the hamburger was part of a cow, she was busy dying of old age. Even the lettuce was deep-fried. Rollo turned *his* nose up at it. The Jerry Can had the sole advantage of avoiding the prick of a syringe when injecting cholesterol directly into the vein. Still, it made for an interesting break and I was almost finished ignoring the last vestiges of something passed off as "homemade pie à la moode" when my learned friend, as we lawyers derisively call each other, approached my table.

"Mind if I sit?"

"Would it matter?"

"Pardon?"

"Nothing. I'm digesting. I get cranky."

"I just wanted you to know that we've got a new information."

"Is he always like this?"

"Who?"

"Judge Senile or whatever you call him."

"He's a local legend."

"The kind you scare your kids with so they'll go to sleep?"

Ms Couture was severe. "We like to think of him as a classic judicial figure."

"Oh, the kind my mother used to collect in Wedgewood china. But she went in more for the cute bunnies and fairies in their final agony."

"Scoff all you want, Mr. Prince, but we are very proud to have a man like Judge Senuk here. I think that if you took the time to look it up, you'd find that he has authored important legal decisions that have found their way to the Supreme Court and been held up there."

"Ah, yes, those nasty bandits, the supremes."

"Well, if we have nothing more to talk about . . ." She was getting up when a rangy sort, over-dressed in a World War I great coat, its collar turned up to protect his sparse beard and acne, sidled up. You didn't see a lot of sidling up going on in Moskolsippi, so I took him for the local eccentric or a lunatic. In a town this size, they probably couldn't afford both.

He put his head down and eyed the room. "Want some weed, man? It's *primo*!"

There was a time in this fair land, as the song goes, that marijuana was strictly forbidden. The mere possession of a single joint could drop you into jail for six months, four if the judge was in a particularly good mood. Times have since changed, what with modern politicians who like to avoid that unhappy knock on the door and a tax-funded chauffeuring to the local clink. And this was during those halcyon days of yore.

He continued with the furtive eying and repeated himself. "*Primo* weed, man."

"Do you have any idea who this is?" I hissed as I motioned towards my learned friend, Ms Couture.

"Sure I do, man. How ya doin', Claire?"

Claire, as I now knew her, leaned back and smiled. "Not too bad, Tommy." Her smile became a grin.

"So, you're going to sell me on high tea in . . . what's this place called?"

He laughed out of the side of his mouth, like a machine gun. "High tea. Hnnhn, hnnhn! I like that. That's pretty good. Hnnhn, hnnhn."

"I've got a million of 'em, Tommy, is it?"

"Yeah, Tommy, like in tommy gun."

"How original. Do you know who I am?"

"Sure. You're that lawyer guy from Yamnuska Centre up with The Popper."

"Popper?"

"Harry Popowicz. Sure, we know all about you." This last trailed off, sing-song-like.

"And you seem to know Ms Couture, too? Claire, I mean."

"Yeah, Clair, hnnhn, hnnhn!"

"Well, don't you think it's a bit risky, you know, selling weed to me with her here?"

"Naw. Claire's cool, ya know."

"Almost icy, if you ask me. But she is a prosecutor. You know, someone who works with the police who, if I'm not mistaken, still arrest people for selling . . . you know . . . *primo* weed, as you put it."

"Don' worry man. Claire don't care. The feds prosecute drugs, man. Don' you know nothin'?"

"Apparently not."

"So, hey man, it's my last bag. You can have it for fifty bucks. Split it with the lady, hnnhn, hnnhn."

I checked the room for prying eyes. No one looked much like a narc as they slurped what passed for actual food, so I pulled two twenties and a ten out of my wallet and slipped them under the table to him. He grabbed the cash, pulled it out to make sure I wasn't cheating him and tossed the baggie onto the table. "Hope you get lucky with the lady, hnnhn, hnnhn!"

By this time, Claire Couture was standing. "I'll see you in court, counsellor."

Since I didn't much figure to carry a bag of marijuana with me into a courtroom, I made a pit stop at the car. Rollo was eager to see me so I took him out to water the trees and bushes of Moskolsippi before returning him to the car. I tossed the baggie under the driver's seat.

"Take care of it." I didn't know that dogs can roll their eyes.

* * *

The afternoon did not go well.

If my fame had preceded me, Harry "The Popper" Popowicz's had fairly washed about the place for several years. Constable Whipple got up and told us all about The Popper's carryings-on in the police station in the clipped, carefully worded style so fashionable among the police.

"Mr. Popowicz attended at the local detachment at approximately 15:23 hours on the day in question in regards to a complaint he had against Bylaw Officer Tom Wold. After being told to take a seat and wait his turn, Mr. Popowicz aggressively pushed his way to the counter where I reminded him of the rules and regulations that we have in the detachment. When asked to leave, Mr. Popowicz called me a 'fucking bastard' and made a licking motion with his tongue that I found highly insulting and suggestive."

"Did he say anything beyond what you have already told us, Constable?" My friend—as we legal types fictitiously refer to each other; it is called a "legal fiction"—probably had a certain number of questions she had to ask in order to get paid. With Tom Wold, she'd never make quota.

"Other than calling me an 'ass licking, bum buddy' of Bylaw Officer Wold, he also referred to the police and courts as being nothing more than 'standing there with our mouths open, waiting to do service'."

"And how did this make you feel, Constable Whipple?"

"Objection!"

The gnome on the bench peered at me. "And what is your objection, Mr. Prince?"

"Actually, I have several."

"One will do."

"Well, it's self-serving, prejudicial and irrelevant."

I was about to be schooled at the feet of a local classic. He favoured the Socratic method, named after Socrates, the fascist philosopher of Athens, and much beloved of law types for ages. It consists of withering questions, posed, no matter what you say, in an attempt either to sharpen your thinking or leave you despairing. At the end of a good round of the Socratic method, you're the one ready to gulp down the nearest hemlock. "So, how is it self-serving, Mr. Prince? Hmm?"

"The question is intended to curry favour with the court, sir."

"Curry favour or curry flavour, Mr. Prince. The only curry I enjoy is on my tandoori chicken. I do not find the question so tainted." Well, maybe not that Socratic. "What else? Prejudicial?"

"Yes, it's designed to demean my client's reputation in the eyes of this court."

"Highly unlikely. Mr. Popowicz is considered innocent until I convict him, Mr. Prince. And by that I do not mean to suggest, Mr. Popowicz, that I consider you guilty or that I will necessarily be finding you guilty, only that you can be found guilty only when I do it. Based on the evidence, I should add."

"Irrelevant?" I ventured.

"Highly relevant, Mr. Prince. How he made this officer feel goes directly to the question of whether he was disturbed. It speaks for itself, wouldn't you say?"

"Highly disturbed, Your Honour."

"I beg your pardon."

"I was saying that I am sure the witness will tell us he was highly disturbed. And based on what we've all just heard we all should have been."

"And what do you mean by that, sir?"

"I think the evidence speaks for itself."

We got to hear more about how The Popper left them all stunned at his outburst and how they then took him into custody.

"You may question the witness, now, Mr. Prince." I thought it good of him to point out the procedure that I had long been familiar with and made a point to note it for him.

"So, Constable Whipple, did you ever utter the word, 'bullshit,' to Mr. Popowicz?"

"When would that be, Mr. Prince?" He was one of those cops who believe they are being burdened by actually having to give evidence and feel obliged to tell defence lawyers that they know better.

"In the detachment."

"When was that?"

"On the day that you say that Mr. Popowicz said all these dreadful things to you."

"Oh, he said them. You can be sure of that."

"On that day, Constable Whipple, did you utter the word, 'bullshit,' to Mr. Popowicz?"

"I'm not sure I follow you."

"Come now, Constable, the question isn't that complicated, is it?"

The Crown now came to his aid. "Your Honour, I'm not sure I understand what Mr. Prince is trying to get the officer to say." Frankly, in her case, I didn't much doubt it.

"Your Honour, this witness is simply not answering the question."

"What question is that, Mr. Prince?"

"The one I've tried asking him twice."

"Well, maybe you should ask him."

"I have. Twice."

The Crown seemed to be getting in the swing of things here and rounded back. "Mr. Prince is hectoring the witness, Your Honour. You can't let him do that."

I decided to ignore her. "Constable Whipple. Did you use that word to Mr. Popowicz in the detachment that day?"

"What word?"

The Crown rose and almost shrieked. "Objection!"

"Bullshit," I replied to Constable Whipple.

"There's no need to insult counsel, Mr. Prince."

* * *

I did finally get Constable Whipple to admit that he had, indeed, used the offensive term. By the time I had, things had fully deteriorated. The constable left the stand well satisfied that, if he had done any damage to the defence, all was well.

Of course, we couldn't do without my client's taking the stand. Actually, I thought the least he could do was to confuse things some more.

I thought I'd keep things simple. "Mr. Popowicz, could you tell us what happened that day at the police detachment?"

Harry sucked at his dentures a couple of times. "Well, I went in there to complain about the problems I've been havin' with them people at the town hall."

So far so good. "And what did you tell the police about your difficulties with the people at the town hall?"

"Objection. Surely, that is hearsay." Ms Couture did a fair imitation of a slightly peevish twelve-year-old, I thought.

"No, it's not." That's how I usually deal with twelve-year-olds—when they aren't in reach, that is.

"It is, too." With arguments like this, the years were shedding from us like a snake's skin.

His Honour felt he should intervene before we started heaving pails of sand at each other, I suppose. "Mr. Prince, here in Moskolsippi, we usually let the judge make the determination of questions of law."

Before I could utter my next thought, he proceeded to lecture me at some length about what was and was not hearsay. And besides, how was it relevant?

"Part of the narrative, Your Honour."

"What narrative is that, Mr. Prince? We are all quite familiar with Mr. Popowicz and his difficulties with the authorities."

"So, you don't want to hear about the basis of his complaints with the local town authorities?"

"I don't think I need to."

"Wouldn't it be better to put the evidence out there so we could see where it leads?"

"Mr. Prince, I can take judicial notice of any fact that is notorious to any person knowledgeable about the affairs of this community."

I'd heard about judicial notice and he did *seem* quite sure of himself. I just wasn't sure what people's sex lives had to do with it. Still, I didn't think it wouldn't hurt to cover all the bases as it were. "Wouldn't it be wiser just to put his evidence on the record?"

"Why would you want to do that, Mr. Prince?" This last seemed more like Judge Morceau. Maybe, they swilled from the same trough at judges' conventions or something.

"Oh, I don't know . . . to make the record clearer." And then, almost without thinking, "For the appeal."

"Mr. Prince, your suggestion is not only improper, it is scandalous!"

Well, it *was* that sort of day.

* * *

We had Harry tagged and bagged before sundown. I can't say who gave the longer speech, Judge Senuk, when he called Harry everything from obtuse and arrogant through recalcitrant and stultifying, all the way to verbose and yammery, which I wasn't even sure was a word.

Harry, for his part, having been told that he could address the court, launched into a rant of heroic proportions. He stood in his place, finger-pointing dangerously about the place, like some Old Testament prophet looking to smite local Jezebels, hip and thigh—or thereabouts.

"I come to this town three years ago to help my uncle with his bus contract. You know that. And when I come here I was willin' to work hard. Real hard. An honest day's work for an honest day's living, that's what I say. And then them thievin' crooks at the town hall, they just up an' took our buses. They don't have nothin' to do with them buses but they up an' took 'em with not even a skinny rat's ass of a reason and just put us outta business. Well, they say 'You can't fight city hall,' that's what they say, but I say, 'Yeah, but you can fight town hall' and I been fightin' ever since. All them thievin', lying skunks that sit on what they call town council, they're nothin' but chickenshits and whiners."

He went on like this for the better part of half an hour. The gist was that he and his uncle had lost their buses and it was all the fault of some local bureaucrat named Chuck Windsor, who was variously referred to as "Chuckles Windsor," "Chuckie Windsock" and "Upchuck Windsore." I think it was somewhat accidental when Harry wound this up with the following gem. "An' I ain't gonna rest, I ain't gonna stop complainin' and making complaints, until I break Windsor. No way! You can be sure of that!"

Despite the lack of any record, other than being a "found-in," Harry was carted off to jail for forty-five days. I retired to my lonely government car and a rather put-out Rollo.

He had a *curious* look in his eyes—glazed and furtive. He would have fallen out when I opened the door if I hadn't levered him back to a semi-sitting state. I shoved him aside as I tossed my briefcase in the backseat. And then, it hit me. The smell of quality pot.

I looked around—first, outside and then in the car. There was nobody about, so I swept out the shards of what the police are fond of referring to as a "green, leafy substance with a distinct and characteristic odour." Rollo, having had nothing better to do for the afternoon—instead of sleeping, instead of slurping up the dish of water I had left for him, instead of playing his favourite country music station—had chewed open a fifty dollar bag of perfectly good weed. Not satisfied with that, given the few stems and pieces lining the creases of the front seat, he had wolfed it down.

And he just sat there. Grinning.

I was more than a bit miffed. I mean this was going to cost me a fortune in dog yummies.

I used a snow brush to sweep out what I could see in the interior but the smell was pretty overpowering. When I was done, I looked guilty and he just looked stoned.

I didn't have any idea what a quarter ounce of *primo* marijuana would do to a dog but I had the sense that it wouldn't be something I'd like to share with the good folks of Moskolsippi, especially given my role as the chief defender of their chief nutcase. They'd probably think I'd dope up Harry and set him loose.

I made it well past the outskirts of the fine burg when Rollo regained what one might call semi-consciousness. He tried to sit up, then flopped against the passenger side door, rolling ingloriously to the floor. This had the effect of causing him some considerable stomach upset. He was well into spasm by the time I'd swerved to the side of the road, narrowly missing the mailbox of someone named Bogdesavich. I rammed the gearshift into "park" before the wheels stopped turning and ran to Rollo's door. I almost made it. Fortunately, most of it wound up on my shoes and the ground. By the time Rollo was empty, all that remained of fifty of my worst-spent dollars—all right the $1200 I spent for wedding rings wasn't that wise an investment, either— was a lumpy pool of yellowy-greenish swill following the slope of the ditch to its bottom.

Of course, right then, help arrived. It came in the form of a mostly white car with a roof rack of flashing lights. A young Mountie alighted from the driver's side and reefed his belt of dangerous tools until it was square with his line of walking, even if the yellow stripes down the sides of his pants arced rather sharply somewhere around his knees. He'd squared his hat so that it mostly shaded his eyes. You could still see traces of stubble where he'd steered his razor to avoid pimples.

"Good evening, sir. Something the matter?"

"No, no, officer. Just a little car sickness, I'm afraid."

"You all right, sir? Should I call an ambulance?"

"No, no. It's quite all right. The dog had a . . . a little . . . uh, accident, I guess you'd call it."

Constable C.M. Winehouse, or so his nameplate described him, was a careful soul. There's no telling when some confederate of mine might leap from cover and spray us all with an Uzi. He put his hand to the butt of his gun. "I'd ask you to stay where you are, sir, while I check things out." I made it a point to keep my hands on the car roof as he inched around it, flicking his gaze between me and the passenger side of my car.

"This your dog, sir?"

"Yes. His name's Rollo. He's a very intelligent dog."

"I'm going to ask you to come around the front of the car. Keep your hands where I can see them at all times and restrain this animal, sir." There was something distinctly menacing about his monotone. It put me in mind of John Wayne in some of his lesser pictures, say, *Big Jim McLain*. At least he didn't say, "I keep my warrant in my shoe." Well, not yet, anyway.

I raised my hands just like they do in cowboy movies and started around the engine compartment.

"No need to hold them up, sir. Just keep them where I can see them."

"How's this?" I started shaking them like I was in some sort of religious frenzy.

"That's not necessary, sir. I need you to restrain this animal."

I looked at Rollo. He looked like he needed artificial respiration a lot more than restraint. I got him to the sitting position. He just swayed blissfully about and spasmed one more time. Constable Winehouse went for his gun again, then relaxed. Slightly.

"Just a little burp."

Winehouse leaned over the remainder of Rollo's spew and curled his nose. "Smells like weed to me, sir. Have you been using a narcotic tonight, sir?"

I was mostly honest. "No, Constable. I certainly have not. I don't approve of such things."

"Then, how do you explain this, sir?" He held up a ganja bud, dripping with yellowish-green ooze.

"It's Rollo's—he's my dog—it's his."

"Sir, I do not like being treated with contempt. I didn't just fall off the turnip truck this morning. Where did your dog get a dangerous narcotic like this from?"

I decided not to opine that his vegetative fall might just have been last night. "Actually, I'm afraid Rollo suffers from glaucoma. Look at his eyes. You can see it, can't you?"

Winehouse actually pulled a flashlight from his surgical supply cupboard of a belt and flicked it in and out of Rollo's eyes. "Yeah. I can see it." Well, one of us should have. "What's that got to do with anything, 'specially a serious narcotic substance like cannabis?"

"His vet gives it to him."

Constable Winehouse looked at me. "What? What for?"

"Glaucoma." I said it as if it were obvious to even a small child. "Surely, officer, you've heard that medical marijuana is available for the treatment of certain intractable conditions such as glaucoma. I don't know how it works but with Rollo it's been an absolute blessing. His eyes have come back to almost 20/20."

"Don't they give him some sort of card for that?"

"What's the point? Rollo can't read. The glaucoma."

"That's amazing, sir."

"It's a wonder. I can't say how truly thankful I am to Dr. Perkins for finally restoring his sight to him. It's been, I don't know, a true blessing."

"But how come he's all puking and stuff?"

"That's the wonder of it. They don't know the right dosage for dogs. I mean, you can't just give them a joint to smoke."

"Yeah, I can see that."

"So, we feed them enough that they just throw up and it heals them. When they have too much, they throw up the excess so they don't, you know, overdose."

"That's amazing!"

"Yes, I love my Rollo and I wouldn't have him with me anymore if it weren't for the wonders of modern veterinary science." I sniffled at this point.

Constable Winehouse had a bit of a hitch in his voice as he bade us a good night and drove off into the dusk. Rollo just turned to me with that look. If he could have spoken, I'm sure he would have quoted Constable Whipple, of recent memory. "Bullshit!"

APPEAL TO NOBLER MOTIVES

The worst part about having a job is mornings. And the worst part about mornings is waking up. Nothing spoils a day quite like the sounds of singing birds and cheery television hosts. At least one of them should be made to die in extreme pain. Slow poison works. I'm just not sure how to deal with the birds.

I've found it helps to set the alarm so that the TV comes on about fifteen minutes before you actually want to get up. That way, the fleeting buzz of sleep is etched away until you're conscious. After the news, even a cold shower is welcome.

Our trip from Moskolsippi hadn't ended well and Rollo was curled in the corner, moaning and issuing the occasional belch. That would have been disconcerting enough if not for the dulcet tones of one Jolly Jeff Wooster gorging the tiny speakers of my television. I'm not sure how these things happen but someone had gotten the idea that nothing would so stir the masses as a weekly visit from our MLA, now burdened with the title of Legislative Secretary to the Minister of Justice. He wore it well. He'd put on a few pounds since from the campaign. Maybe just a little jowly.

The interviewer looked like he'd just stepped out of elementary mortician training. He might have been the deceased—except he talked.

"Ah, Mr. Wooster, I . . . uh . . . understand that your government is considering some changes to the court system in this province."

"Well, yes, Walter, that's quite right. The new Conservative government feels that for far too long, far, far too long, things have been allowed to slide under the previous government. Standards, that should have been set, haven't been and I'm sure we all remember the disastrous calamity of the court strike of last year."

This puzzled the sepulchral Walter. Perhaps, he'd been boning up on advanced embalming or learning that special corpse comb-over effect. "Oh, yes, of course. Right. You have some ideas in this area?" At least enough to hold us through to the next commercial?

Not that he needed to have worried. "I'm glad you asked that, Walter. Yes, your new Conservative government has been studying this problem quite thoroughly since we came into office. Quite frankly, the mess the last government left us with is quite amazing. I am almost surprised there are any courts even left in this province with the chaos of the past several years."

"Chaos?" I wasn't quite sure if Walter was referring to the courts or some premonition of hell. Still, it was the most journalistic thing he had done so far. This was riveting television. Just ask Rollo. He'd even stopped burping.

"Yes, chaos. Lawyers out of control. Clerks misfiling papers. And the legal aid plan is something beyond belief. We've had to root out hundreds of so-called lawyers who haven't been doing anything for years, just sitting on their backsides moaning about the rights of criminals. It has to end." Well, I, for one, hadn't sat on my backside moaning about anything. I try to save moaning for an entirely prone position and the only moaning that goes on . . . well, you get my point.

"I understand that you have a proposal."

Wooster half turned to the camera. "Yes, Walter, we owe it to the many hardworking, law-abiding taxpayers of this province to make sure that they get the justice system that they deserve. We've got a five-point crime-reduction plan that we will be implementing in the next one hundred days. Our plan will streamline the system and give folks in this province a justice system we all can be proud of." Well, maybe, things were looking up. I could think of a couple of judges we could "root out."

"How are you going to put this plan in place?"

Walter had obviously jumbled his cue cards. Jolly Jeff winced and forged on.

"I think I can say that our five-point plan will give this area a real jump-start that will make them all proud. Very proud."

"So, your plan will be put into place in the next hundred days or so?"

"That's right, Walter. We believe that in only one hundred days, we can start to turn this around. In that time, I assure anyone who's watching today you'll notice the difference we've made."

Walter checked his watch. He didn't look happy. So, he threw out a Hail Mary to see if Jolly Jeff could run under it and score the big touchdown. Or maybe just run out the clock.

"These five points . . . are you in a position to share them with us?"

Jeff Wooster drew himself up and shook his head with that smile. "Heh, heh! Now Walter, you wouldn't want me to break cabinet secrecy, would you?"

I'm sure it was accidental but at that point Rollo whimpered, then broke wind. Walter broke for a commercial and I, for my shower. Appropriately enough, it was cold.

* * *

I didn't make it in on time and when I got there, Gail, my secretary, stole my coat, handed me a stack of papers and took Rollo to my office. She had two words sure to curdle my blood.

"Library. Meeting."

"Good of you to join us, Mr. Prince." I looked up. Carrie Anne Bloodworth stood there, nose erect as ever.

"I know but think nothing of it. Not much on the plate for today, I'm glad to say."

The library was replete with youngish women, all penned and padded, ready for the fray. Actually, there were five of them, four if you don't count Carrie Ann. They all looked young, eager and well-coiffed. Each wore the same basic ensemble of pantsuit, lacy shirt and patent shoes. Clearly, not Catholic school girls at the dance, although the pantsuits more or less precluded any reflected glories. Each had already scratched out a few notes. Completing this array was a young guy, bespeckled and clearly suffering his first day on the good ship Yamnuska Centre Legal Aid. A bit seasick and we were still in port, or so I thought. I knew a couple of them by sight but not name.

"I was just introducing your new colleagues to our office and reminding them of the importance of being on time."

"Yes, none of you young ladies wants to be late."

Carrie Ann smiled. It was the smile you get from a Rottweiler just before it rips out your throat. But, of course, with one notable exception, our learned leader was not particularly doglike. Well, maybe, the nose.

"As I was saying, from today onwards, punctuality will be required of each person in this office. And I'm sure Mr. Prince can tell you all what I mean by punctuality." Her glare would have flayed a leper.

"I'm guessing it's not knowing where to put your commas and apostrophes." Given my previous comment, I thought it wise to avoid any mention of periods. It looked like we'd all learn far too much about them, far too soon.

"Mr. Prince does like his little jokes. I'm sure we're all entertained by them but we have several critical matters to discuss." She motioned to one of her acolytes to pass out some faun- coloured folders with the provincial crest and an embossed title, "Protocols, Procedures and Paradigms: The Legal Service Plan."

"I haven't seen that many *p*'s all in one place since Boy Scout Winter Camp."

Someone tittered. "I beg your pardon, Mr. Prince."

"It's called alliteration, isn't it?"

"I'm not sure we have time for your clever comments, Mr. Prince. We have a long agenda and some pretty tight timelines."

"You didn't think it was something risqué, did you, Carrie Anne? I was just admiring the alignment of three words all starting with the same consonant. Alliteration?"

"Yes, how droll."

"They call that sarcasm." The young guy stifled a chuckle, then looked down at his yellow pad.

After a suitably heavy sigh, our legal director began her proclaim of all the new policies. She was almost proud. "We, at YCLA, have been given the great honour of being the first office in the system to pioneer the new protocol for Legal Aid in this province." There were gasps and a spontaneous round of applause from the lawyers. And the young guy.

"The goals of this plan are to provide legal services in a cost-effective and professional manner to all of our client base. You will notice that each type of offence has been allocated a set period of time. You are to complete each file within that period of time." Sure enough, the various types of offences were listed and a number of hours was set out beside each.

"Excuse me, Carrie Anne."

She looked at me. If her eyes rolled upwards any faster I would have worried about brain damage. Or, maybe not. "Yes, *Mr.* Prince?"

"Does this mean that we have to do everything for our client within the time set down here?"

"Yes. Is that a problem?"

"Not if we plead them all guilty."

"I beg your pardon."

"Gladly given and no need to beg." All right, so it didn't improve things. "It's just that five hours isn't enough to do a proper job on, say, a minor theft."

"The department has done time and motion studies that indicate that the average minor theft takes 4.3 hours to complete from initial interview to conclusion in court. Surely, even you won't need any more than the very generous 0.7 extra hours. Now, if we can continue..."

"That's the average. I don't know. Doesn't that mean that there are some that take maybe about an hour and some that take ten hours?"

"I'm sure I can't say, Mr. Prince."

"As am I." I paused for effect. There was none. "Well, let's look at it this way. It takes thirty minutes to talk to a guy for the first time, you know, ask him how old he is, how many kids he's got, maybe, I don't know... did he do it? And then, you sit in court for half an hour to make his plea. If his plea is guilty, that takes ten minutes to half an hour if you've got a slow prosecutor or a judge with a speech impediment. So, what's that, an hour and a half? But if the guy is pleading not guilty, there's the date setting, looking for witnesses, the trial. That could run you eight to ten hours."

"Mr. Prince, I don't know who you think you are representing. The people we represent are guilty. They aren't paying for this service and it's costing the government millions every year. We don't have the time or the resources for your Cadillac trials. That may be how things were before, but we're all in for a change."

"As the baby said to the child molester."

"I beg your pardon."

"I already told you, no need."

"Do you have any other questions?" As in, "I'll wait for you to catch up."

"Yes, can we at least take the time from the quick ones and apply it to the slower ones? You know, if I have three guilty pleas that only take an hour and a half, can I take the leftover time for something else."

"Mr. Prince, you will be assigned a certain number of files, based on the time available and the expected duration of those files, the Allocated File Formation, Execution and Completion Time, the AFFECT, as it were. The AFFECT time will be calculated to fill your day. If you have time left over, you will be expected to ask for further files. We will not have idle hands in this office. Am I clear?"

"Oh, quite. And will you be handling some of these files? Just to check out these time and motion studies and their . . . what is it, AFFECT time?"

"Mr. Prince, I am a very busy person. You, as much as anyone, should appreciate the time it takes to administer this office. Much as I'd like to, I simply can't spare the time. It just wouldn't be fair to our clients." Then came the shark smile.

Not wishing to chum the waters further, I replied, "I'm not sure I could agree with you more."

Things continued. If her enthusiasm was infectious, I'd had the shots.

We concluded with a television screen being hauled out and a disc plopped into the player. And lo, I was in the audiovisual presence of Jolly Jeff Wooster for a second time that day. Like chocolate, it was just too much of a good thing. On this occasion, he had thoughtfully left the cadaverous Walter to bone up on intermediate cosmetology or wash the hearse. The voice was well modulated and sincere. I checked for my wallet.

> "I would like to introduce all our fine staff in the justice system to changes that we think will make all the important work you do for the fine people of this province so much better.

> "Since the terror attacks, the world has changed. Things we all accepted as normal have been turned upside down in an instant. Innocent people have been bombed, shot and maimed. Many have been killed. No government can stand for that. Public places and public spaces are the targets for these evil people and we have a responsibility to the good people of this province to make sure that their public business is conducted as safely and securely as it can be.
>
> "Our courthouses have long lagged behind those of other provinces and all fifty of the American states in terms of security. In the last ten years, attacks on judges have risen a startling sixty-two per cent in the US and a similar amount in this country. Our courthouses are often many miles from police detachments and people come and go without ever thinking what might happen if just one maniac armed with a bomb or an automatic weapon decided to take justice hostage."

I flashed to an image of Morceau bound and gagged, an AK-47 pointed at his head by a wide-eyed, bearded creature in a turban, shrieking curses and verses from the Koran. A man can dream.

> "In its first hundred days, the new Conservative government will be adding layers of security to all of the court houses in this province. All these provisions will be set out in our new *Court Administration and Secure Housing Act*. In it, we will outline just what can and can't be

> brought into this most important part of our justice system.
>
> "Is this necessary? There is no doubt. Have there been any problems? No, but that isn't any reason to believe that there never could be. Proper preparation prevents poor performance."

What was it with the letter *p* and these guys?

> "But you play an important part in this process. You are our eyes and ears. You know who comes to court. You know who shouldn't be there. It's your duty to watch and warn of any potential disturbances so that the law can be administered in a fair, impartial and appropriately stern manner in circumstances of extreme safety."

Carrie Ann hit the stop button. "Any questions?"
"Just one." She sighed. Surely, she expected it.
"Yes, Mr. Prince."
"Are we supposed to report all suspicious people or only the ones who are criminals?"
"What do you think, Mr. Prince? I thought it was fairly obvious."
"You're right. We can't have criminals hanging around the courts."

* * *

I had just returned from a sumptuous lunch, high in cholesterol, sugar, salt and preservatives. Even if I don't live forever, what remains of me will. I was met at the door by Carrie Anne.

"Mr. Prince, you have court in twenty-five minutes."
"Oh, where's that?" I'd checked my calendar and mostly I had planned for a quiet afternoon, pretending to work

and considering—and mostly rejecting—the possibilities of an undetectable murder. Nothing there about court that I recalled.

"Here." I didn't know if she meant in Yamnuska Centre or "here is the file" as she handed me a folder. I took it so as not to seem ungrateful. Inside, it was spattered with hieroglyphics that I could recall as Scottie's and faintly make out as stating that Russell Lewkowicz was charged with assaulting his good lady, common law spouse and mother to his three, no doubt snotty-nosed, children. He was pleading guilty. Probably a good idea, all things considered.

"You will be an example to the others so I am sure you will demonstrate your professionalism in all respects."

"Others?" On cue, my five colleagues of the morning emerged, scrubbed of face and eager of countenance. I was moved.

"You mean that during the last two weeks when I've been off on errands throughout the province, not one of them has been to court?"

"Of course not, Mr. Prince. They were undergoing orientation at Legal Aid Central."

"So, does that mean everyone is re-oriented? Were they disoriented before?"

I'd seen that look before and I wasn't quite sure whether it was bewilderment or gas. I smiled, considered my posse of eager beavers and otherwise, and called to them, "Well, saddle up, then." Ignoring her digestive distress, once again, I smiled even broader, nodded and quipped, "We're westerners, you know."

My four young maids, or not, all turned out in the new, official Legal Aid uniform, and Chuck, never Charles, Ewanchuk trooped down the sidewalk like the mentally challenged on a school field trip. Chuck tried engaging me in war stories—my biggest trials, my hardest cases—but I ignored him and began the grand tour of Yamnuska Centre.

Pointing to an alleyway, I advised them of the lurid goings-on that pervaded the back lanes and dark underbelly of our supposedly peaceful city—drugs, midnight beatings, the occasional murder—and, for the not so dainty, the shocking history of Yamnuska Centre and the white slave trade. That sustained a murmur of offence and outrage for a number of minutes while I blathered on about how to get to the police station and avoid all the perils, as it were. I doubted many of them would make it to any of the local Chinese restaurants for months.

Less than a block from the court house was an old tree that had somehow escaped Dutch elm disease. It featured a stout, mostly leafless branch some thirty feet above us. I stopped and considered my flock.

"I don't know how many of you are familiar with the history of this province and Yamnuska Centre." None, apparently, me included. I pointed to the branch. "YC wasn't always the quiet place we all now know." All right, so I'd just contradicted myself. I wasn't in much danger of being unmasked and I wasn't going to add "except for white slavery, of course."

"This was a lawless area, mostly populated by renegades from the US. Its isolation and similarity to the southern plains made it an ideal place for these people to 'hole up' in.

"It was a frontier town where murder was an everyday event. So, the people here had to band together and take things into their own hands. *This*," I said, pointing to the elm, "was the *hanging tree*."

Necks craned. Mouths whispered. Chuck even ventured a "holy shit!"

I pointed to some abrasions on the branch. "That's where the rope went."

One of our flock ventured, "I can almost *feel* the evil!"

"Well, it's a terrible thing to kill a man."

"Yes. That's why they got what they deserved." She was quite firm on this. I hoped she was one of our leading lights in family law, where the death penalty still exists in this country, but only when it's preceded by years of financial and emotional torture.

I was wrong, of course. Once we reached the courthouse, she and the others all recoiled when I located Russell Lewkowicz, a straw-haired soul with an expression of pure sadness about him. Scottie used to say, "There's bu' three things ye need ta know ta be a defence lawyer, lad—whar's yer court, whar ye stand, an' who's yer clien'." One out of three's not bad.

It appeared that the Crown was making her debut, as well. She was long of leg and blond of hair. *Her* three piece pantsuit was pinstriped and featured a rather fetching pin made up of crossed handcuffs. Once regaled to stand, identify ourselves and otherwise act according to the customs of the place, I pleaded poor Mr. Lewkowicz guilty as charged to what appeared to me to be a relatively minor bit of spousal grappling.

"Ms Shouldice?" Morceau was unduly solicitous to my learned friend. Maybe, they shared quiet reflections as they scrubbed the gore from the instruments of the auto-da-fé.

The prosecutor flipped to her Prosecutor Information Sheet, which I had, as well, and we all read along. "Ah, yes, Your Honour. At 2135 hours, police were called to 4532 Trudeau Way on the complaint of a neighbour that Mr. Russell Lewkowicz"—with this, she pointed a red-tipped finger nail in the general direction of the defence table—"and his common law spouse, Wanda Wiebe, were involved in a domestic disturbance. Constables Venale and Poirier arrived at 2147 hours. After ringing the doorbell and getting no response, they feared for the safety of the occupants and had to *force* their way into the residence." At this point, she paused, as if to summon the courage to go on. "As they entered the home, the found Ms Wiebe in the kitchen, *sobbing*." Ms Shouldice's shoulders rose and fell in sympathetic imitation. "She had a *deep and angry* red mark on her wrist where she said that she had her arm *cruelly twisted and torn* by the accused, who was standing there, *enraged*." Here, she paused once again and lowered her voice. "There was a *terrible* mess on the floor where one of the children, a baby named Winston, was seated. He was playing in sugar and cornflakes that must have been flung about during *this terrible beating*. We allege that the child was a witness to the entire attack." At this, Ms Shouldice slipped, almost formless, into her chair, her head bowed.

"Are the facts, as alleged, admitted, Mr. Prince?" For Morceau, it was almost even-handed.

"They are to the extent that they reflect the charge." I detected some murmuring behind me. I had brought my own claque, it seemed.

"Then, a conviction is in order. Ms Shouldice, on sentence?"

She rose and drew a breath, almost in pain. She hauled out a new sheet, all typed. "Your Honour, the incidence of spousal assault in this community is *truly appalling*. It is restricted to no socio-economic stratum. It is found in the homes of the rich and poor alike. It is estimated that in this province *one* in *three* women is the victim of spousal abuse. Eighty-four per cent of all spousal assaults are believed to be unreported. Yet, children and spouses are *repeatedly* subjected to *attacks* by their partners, spouses, husbands and dates that leave a trail of *shattered lives and tortured bodies* in their wake." She looked up from her reading to see if Morceau was getting all of this. He was hunched on the bench, his pen at ease in his hand.

Shouldice started pacing firing statistics at will. "Fifty-five per cent!", "One out of four!" and "A frightening six hundred and thirty-two out of every ten thousand children in a recent study in the state of Iowa." We heard about cohorts of this horror and percentiles of that maltreatment. All while Ms Shouldice marched, prodded, and otherwise drilled statistic after statistic into our mouths like a crazed dentist. She was beginning to redden and sweat as she reached her point.

"This man, Your Honour, *this man!*" She slashed at us once again with vivid fingernails. "This man is yet another one of these pathetic *beasts* who treat their wives like walking punching bags, absorbing *abuse after abuse*! He must be told, Your Honour! He can't continue to walk the streets of this community. His wife and children *need* protection! They *cry out* for protection! They *demand* protection! *And the Crown demands it, too!*"

By this time, she was doing what I would call the Dying Swan. I almost expected her to swoon, collapsing to the counsel table, the back of her left hand to her fevered brow. I was only slightly disappointed.

Morceau was at a loss. "So, you're saying I should send Mr., uh, uh . . . Lewkowicz to jail?"

She almost hissed. "Yes, Your Honour. Absolutely!"

"For how long?"

"Six months. That's what the *Code* says."

"Are you alleging a record?"

"No, Your Honour. Mr. Lewkowicz has no record . . . that we can determine." She almost winked with that, as if my twenty-year-old client were a terrorist travelling under an assumed name and lifestyle.

"But you're asking for the maximum penalty?"

"Yes, Your Honour. The Crown's office is taking a zero tolerance policy on this sort of thing. We believe that unless Mr. Lewkowicz and people like him are jailed for as long as possible, he, and those like him, will never learn."

"Oh." I was flabbergasted. Morceau rarely settled for a one-syllable word like "oh" when a five-syllable one suggesting rapine excess would do. "Mr. Prince?" It was almost a plea.

"Yes, Your Honour. Mr. Lewkowicz is twenty and the sole support of the complainant and their three children, twins age two and young Master Winston, the young devourer of Captain Crunch . . ."

"It was *Corn Flakes*." This came from Ms Shouldice, ever the stickler for precision.

"I stand corrected, Your Honour."

"Yes, Corn Flakes." Morceau made a careful note in his judge's book, in case this undoubted error led to an appeal.

"As I was saying, Mr. Lewkowicz is the sole support of this young household, working as he does as a day labourer at various construction sites." I went on at some length about his lack of sophistication, his minimal education and, obliquely, at his and Ms Wiebe's appalling ignorance of birth control. I pointed out that the usual tariff for such as he—young, without a record and a crime on the lower end of things—was a fine and, maybe, some probation.

I hadn't made it to my chair before Ms Shouldice was up, crying havoc and letting slip the dogs of war. "The Crown strenuously objects to the characterization of this matter as minimal. No attack on a young woman such as"—and here she rustled through her papers—"Ms Wiebe should be subjected to unprovoked and cowardly attacks such as this. The Crown *demands* jail! *And justice demands it, too!*"

Well, if it was going to be like that, I should just slink out of there and not be bothered.

But, it obviously did the trick. Morceau tempered his mercy and only gave poor old Russell a relatively paltry four months in jail. Russell shook my hand and said thanks before he was led out. I didn't know where to look or much of what to say. My claque fairly melted in admiration and joined Ms Shouldice in the hallway.

I checked my watch. With no preparation, I'd brought the file in with two hours and twelve minutes to spare if I went straight back to the office. Well within the full AFFECT.

When I got there an hour later, I was met by a sobbing Wanda Wiebe. She'd already been seen by Social Services.

They had come to court and were considering apprehending her children, what with the assault, and the cornflakes, and all. But they couldn't help her with any money until the first of the month. And only if she brought a child support application against Russell.

It's great to be pro-family so long as you don't have to have too much to do with them.

QUESTIONS OTHERS WILL SAY YES TO

People think that laws make us good. Just pass a law and everything will be all right. It won't, but it makes everyone feel better. A little kid gets run over by a dump truck and somebody says, "There oughta be a law." The kid's now vegetable mush but a law would sure make things better—well, next time, maybe. Some guy runs off on his wife and family: pass a new law. That'll sure slow him down the next time he lusts after his secretary. We'll just stack them all up in some jail cell. Then we'll all feel so much better about things.

And, it's not as if we don't have some fairly clunky laws already. There's an absolute prohibition against waterskiing by night. That can get you six months in jail. Just you and your driver. By the time you get out, you'll both have to skate. And let's not forget blasphemous libel. Even if God doesn't—or, possibly, can't—get you for something you said, you can still go to the hell of some penitentiary for up to two years.

Of course, it's a bit harder to pass laws than come up with them. So, we get *rules*. There's no law against being obnoxious, but there sure are a lot of rules. Never mind that the people you're obnoxious to are usually brain-dead klutzes who couldn't fall down with the benefit of gravity. You just can't say harsh things about them. There's bound to be a rule against it somewhere. If not, give me a few minutes and I'll make one up.

And you've got to have signs: large, well-painted signs threatening a painful eternity or trouble with the police work best. Particularly tasteful are references to non-existent crimes.

So, I wasn't the least surprised when I reached the office one fine morning to find a stark reminder that "Rudeness is abuse!" in bold, upper-case letters, all black. This was plastered not only on the window of our front door but reiterated within in bright black-and-white, with a bit of red thrown in for flavouring, I suppose:

> "Rudeness is abuse! This office has zero-tolerance for any rude or abusive behaviour. This includes shouting, swearing, using off-colour language or any other words or actions that could threaten the safety or security of our staff. Offenders will be asked to leave and the police may be called."

Well, that ought to end it right now. Anyone looking for someone to keep them out of jail may just find himself staring at extra time, compliments of his own lawyer!

I guess some of our clients would get a bit testy when their fourth appointment was cancelled because somebody forgot to check her diary. Somehow, telling Gail that one was a bit miffed didn't seem that awful. *Not* telling Ms Stockard that she resembled a Guernsey cow in looks and temperament seemed to me a culpable failure of perception. Then again, there was a sign against it so it had to be treated as something just short of insulting the Queen but well beyond acceptable free speech.

I admired the sign for a few seconds while Rollo considered its possibilities as a fire hydrant.

"Is this for real, Gail?"

"Oh, yes, Mr. Prince. Ms Bloodworthy wanted it placed in a promising place."

"So, this comes from on high, then?"

"The highest."

"Come on, Gail. Even a Catholic girl like you should know that the Pope isn't against a bit of abuse . . . so long as it isn't self-abuse."

Gail giggled. Ms Stockard, looming about, as always, like a transitory ischemic stroke, did not. "That's just what the sign's for, Mr. Prince. Dirty words like *that*!"

"Which ones, Pope or Catholic?"

"You know what I mean, Mr. Prince. And don't think I don't, neither!"

"Perish the thought, Ms Stockard . . . or any thought for that matter."

"Don't you keep up them smart-ass comments, neither. I got my eye on you, an' that sign refers to you, too."

"Everyone in the office, then?"

"A course, Mr. Prince, everyone."

"Then, let me be the first to report someone for such appalling conduct."

"An' who'd that be?"

"You, Ms Stockard. A word like 'smart-ass' is so demeaning that I am shocked, utterly and completely shocked, that it could ever pass your lips. And I'm so disturbed by it that I have to go to my office to try to pull myself together." I sniffed a bit and took a deep breath. "So, whom do I report this to?"

She glowered. Actually, it was a bit hard to tell. "I'm designated as the monitor. An' I know when I been put on, Mr. Prince, so you watch it!"

I turned towards my office but looked over to Gail. "Not even an hour goes by before we have the first outrageous assault against our abuse-free zone. When will it end, Ms Deare? When will it end?"

Rollo sneezed and I made my exit, stage left, to the office.

* * *

I was making my way through the assembled clutter when the calm of the day was burst. Carrie Anne simply waltzed into my office, oblivious to the closed door, beyond opening it, I suppose. I didn't look up. Rollo's whine was enough.

"Suppose I had been involved in something personal and private in here, Carrie Anne." I flipped over the page of a letter from the ever-more chatty Bobby Cherry, suggesting that Clarence Caron, alleged pilferer of ladies undergarments from various stores in town, might want to lift the load of guilt from his soul and make an appropriate plea; in return for which Bobby thought a month in jail and lots and lots of counselling might just get young Clarence back on the road to one of the more usual perversions misassociated with human reproduction.

She ignored me. "I have three matters to take up with you, Mr. Prince."

"That's a relief. I thought you might have developed an unfortunate desire to intrude on the privacy of others. That said, I doubt you'd see anything you hadn't been close up to already. Oh, and if you do, let me know. I've been looking for a new pick-up line."

"That's the first thing, Mr. Prince."

"What is?"

"Your constant efforts to turn everything into some sort of joke. I'm tired of it."

"Good," I thought, "maybe, you'll stop." But I just raised an eyebrow and smiled.

She ignored me. "I heard about your encounter with Ms Stockard this morning. Our policy against this sort of rogue abuse is serious. It has to end."

"Which?"

"Which what?"

"The abuse or the policy?"

"*That's* just what I was getting at."

"Ambiguity?"

"Then, there's the matter of Mr. Popowicz."

"What matter is that? I thought he went to jail."

"He did and he has now been released. Now, he's charged with some more offences—an assault or something. I want you to deal with it."

"What? There are no other lawyers in the system."

"None of quite your . . . *calibre*."

"I thought I warned you about ambiguity. It's catching, you know."

"I don't have time to sit and quibble with you, Mr. Prince. Get the file from Gail and get on with it."

She turned to go. So I took up the slack. "And the other thing?"

"What's that?"

"You said you had three things to tell me and you've only yelled at me about two . . . so far."

She reddened. The cords of her neck strained. "I have not yelled at you at all, Mr. Prince. I will not have you doing that . . . ."

"What?"

"That horrible thing you do. Putting me down in front of people."

I looked about us. "Rollo? He'll never say a word. Trust me. Besides, he's probably thrilled."

"That dog cannot be covered under the *Service Animals Licensing, Training and Exemptions Act*."

"Oh?"

"Yes, I had some research done."

"Really?"

"Yes, and according to it, in order to be a service animal, it must have some ability that makes up for some failing on your behalf."

"Failing? Doesn't that breach some sort of human right?"

"What do you mean?"

"Surely, you're not saying that blindness, or should I say visual impairment, is a failing. That's so insensitive!"

"You know very well what I mean, Mr. Prince. You do not suffer from any handicap and that . . . *thing* is not a service animal."

"Isn't that just the way, Rollo? Not half a minute ago she thought you were human and now you're nothing but a thing. Sounds abusive to me."

"Just what *handicap* do you suffer from, then, Mr. Prince? Aside from being a flippant, arrogant, sexist Neanderthal with an abusive temperament?"

"You mean that's not enough?"

"Your handicap, Mr. Prince!"

"I suffer from temporomandibular joint dysfunction with secondary arthritic peliorithic oscansular nephralgia."

"We'll see, Mr. Prince. I want a note from your doctor with that diagnosis in it."

I shrugged. "Okay."

She had reached the door. "And another thing. I want you to have the staff refer to you only by your title, Mr. Prince."

"Lord of All He Surveys seems so, I don't know, overwhelming, don't you think?"

"That's just what I was referring to, Mr. Prince."

"Actually, you know, you said you had three things to discuss with me and I think that makes five. I've got work to do." I put my head down and she left with far more heat than I thought necessary.

It was an important thing to say, though. Carrie Anne's a bean counter and if she starts confusing three with five, who knows what havoc might result?

* * *

Harry "The Popper" Popowicz had filled out a new application for legal aid. On it, he had listed a home phone number, a cell phone number and a fax line. Of course, there was no work number. I was wondering about this when Gail called to inform me that a "Mr. Popplewinch" was calling.

"Ah, Harry, I was just about to call . . ."

"Well, it's about time. Them guys are tryin' to set me up. That's what they're tryin' to do. Set me up."

"Set you up how?"

"You know. Them guys'll accuse me of murder the next thing ya know. That's what they'll do. You can just mark my words about it, you can. They'll stop me for somethin' and search my car and the next thing ya know, I'll be charged with murder."

"Well, I suppose the good news is that it isn't murder this time, Harry."

"Well, it will be the next time, you just watch. It'll be murder. That's what they'll do. Next time they got a spare body, it'll be a murder charge. You just watch and see if it isn't so."

"Come on, Harry. They don't have the time to spend worrying about you. You're just a minor irritant for them."

"That's what you know. That's what you know, Mr. Prince. They're just waitin'. Waitin' and watchin'. First time they get a chance, they'll prob'ly charge me with murder. They won't need no body. No way. It'll just be me charged with murder, goin' away forever."

I was starting to see the other side's point of view in all this. "Look, Harry, if we could just try and focus on what we've got here. They say you're charged with assaulting Charles Windsor."

"Hah! That's a laugh! Never did nothin' to old Chuckles Wimpsore. No way! He's nothing but a liar. A godamned liar! That's what he is. Assaultin' Charlie Windsore. That's a laugh!"

"Well, good. Maybe, we can all have a few chuckles with Chuckles and then go home more or less happy."

"That's a good one. I never did nothin' to Charlie and he damn well knows it. No way!"

"It says here that you were parked outside of the town hall in your van with some signs on it."

"Yeah. What's wrong with that? I gotta right to put whatever I want on my van and Charlie Windsor can't do nothin' about it."

"It says here that he came out and went over to your van and politely asked you to take the signs down. So?"

"So what? He can't tell me to take no signs off my van if I wanna put them there. No way! This is a free country an' I can put anything I want on my van and no half-assed piece o' donkey shit like Charlie Windsor is goin' to stop me either! Don't I have that right or has this country just turned into Communist China or somethin'."

"Well, I'm not sure." Considering what I'd seen lately. "Uh, Mr. Popowicz, maybe I'll just read you what they're saying and when I'm finished, we can go over it. Okay?" Despite the strangled comments from the telephone, I continued. "When Windsor requested the accused to remove the signs, the accused exited the front seat of the van and faced him, pointing a finger at him and calling him an 'empty-headed piece of crap' and a 'cocksucker.'"

"I didn't call him nothin' like that."

"Did you call him anything?"

"Maybe 'garbage breath' or a 'puffed-up piece of peacock shit.' Nothin' too bad." Ah, the alliteration was coming right along. It was p's, too. With Harry's talents for sign painting and his mastery of the p's, he had real potential working for this government. Maybe, that was how he could afford all the phones.

"I'm sure he's been called worse."

"O' course he has. I called him lots o' things."

"That day?"

"Yeah."

"Like, maybe a piece of crap?"

"Sure. An' he is one, too." This was going well.

"Just to finish this off, then, Harry, it says 'The accused moved towards Windsor in a threatening manner and he put up his hands to keep the accused away. The accused spit at Windsor striking him on the left cheek.' Is that about what happened, Harry?"

"I didn't spit at him. There's no way I spit at him. Maybe it was rainin' an' he felt a drop on his cheek but I didn't spit at him. There's no way that happened. No. Way."

"So, you want to plead not guilty to the spitting."

"Damn right I do."

"So you want a trial?"

"What I want's fair justice. That's all. You tell me this. Can someone just come and tear down your signs offa your van? You tell me, is that right? Charlie Windsor ain't got no right to take my signs offa my van just 'cause it's parked in fronta that town hall and he don't like it. Well, I say tough. Yeah, tough. He can't just tear the signs offa my van an' nothin' happen to him. You tell me. Is that right? Is that fair justice?"

"Why were you parked there?"

"Whaddaya mean?"

"Why were you parked in front of the town hall?"

"I can park anywhere I wanna park and there's nothin' Charlie Windsor and that bum boy o' his, Tom Wold, can do about it. I read the Chartera Rights."

"So have I and I don't recall bum boys or parking in front of town hall being mentioned. Maybe, I should have another look."

"You do that, Mr. Prince. I got my rights, an' I want fair justice."

* * *

So, nothing would do but I made my way back to the fair metropolis of Moskolsippi for another tilt in the lists of Judge Senuk and another chance to plug my arteries at The Jerry Can. All things considered, I brought Rollo along.

The door to the courthouse was emblazoned with a sign. It seemed familiar:

> "Rudeness is abuse! This building has zero-tolerance for any rude or abusive behaviour. This includes shouting, swearing, using off-colour language or any other words or actions that could threaten the safety or security of our staff. Offenders will be asked to leave and the police may be called."

It made me hope that the original author had kept his copyright and was collecting royalties. And that Harry could get full-time work and off Legal Aid. Besides, I was impressed that any building could have zero, or any, tolerance for anything besides wind and rain.

I made my way to the courtroom to discover my client already in attendance and Judge Senuk busy consigning some poor soul to Senuk's version of the fifth circle of hell. Said soul went by the name of Simon Dart and was a walking negation of his name. Neither swift nor particularly sharp.

"Now, Mr. Dart, is there anything you would like to say before I sentence you? You can say anything you think might reduce the sentence that I am about to pass. This is not to say that I have decided my sentence but I am going to give you a chance to influence my sentence, which is not to say that I am necessarily subject to any improper influence, you understand. I understand that you do not have a lawyer. A lawyer would have said something on your behalf or should I say might have said something on your behalf, but you don't have one. So, you'll just have to do as well as you can, under the circumstances. I'm not sure why you say Legal Aid wouldn't give you a lawyer, by which I mean appoint one—since lawyers aren't given away like so much candy on Hallowe'en—but I mean appointed, of course."

Good old Simon was pretty much at sea. After that, so was I.

"Well, Your Honour, I don't know."

"Say something you think will help you."

"Well, Your Honour, I got a wife and three kids, ya see."

"And what sort of example have you set for those children? And your wife, of course, is the victim of your crime."

Simon gulped and bowed his head.

"Is there anything else, Mr. Dart?" The words seemed kindly, but impatient.

"I gotta a job, ya know, workin' at the sawmill. I don't think it'll be there if I go to jail."

"You don't think it will or it won't?"

"I, uh, don't know."

"You don't know..." The judicial head bobbed down and considered the assembled papers before him.

Simon was quite confused. "I usu'lly got a lawyer for this stuff. They just wouldn't give me one this time." The effect was to make Judge Senuk purse his lips and grunt. So, Simon Dart did the only thing he could think of. He walked forward and fell to his knees, his hands raised, as if in prayer.

"Don' send me ta jail, judge! I got kids. I gotta job. Don' send me there no more!"

Senuk leapt up, his eyes wide. "Mr. Sheriff! Seize that man! Seize him!" The judge ducked down below the level of the bench and ran, crouching, for his door. He shot a quick look in the direction of the now weeping accused. "Put him in custody! We'll deal with him later... We're adjourned." He flailed for the door, pulling on it and peeking back to see if any further danger lurked. The door wouldn't open. I wanted to tell him that he had to turn the knob, but his face, red and lined with fright, didn't seem to be taking much in.

At the front, the police had gathered Simon Dart and were hauling him in the other direction, towards the holding cell. All the while, Simon continued his now weeping cries, "Don' send me ta jail, judge! I got kids. I got a job. Don' send me there no more!"

***

It was fifteen minutes before the Court was once again ready. His Honour Judge Senuk had returned, even if his colour had not.

"Harry Popowicz." At this, Harry trundled to the front, lower lip firmly pouting. I followed and found my place at the front. Senuk continued, "I see you've got counsel, Mr. Popowicz. Mr. Prince, is it?"

I said it was and we began. This time he had no difficulties with the information but with his sitting.

"Madam Crown, would you agree that since I sat on Mr. Popowicz's last trial, I should recuse myself on this one?"

My somewhat learned friend was not sure and said so in the usual Crown way. "I'm not sure that your sitting on this matter would necessarily offend any reasonable apprehension of bias or not." She was, no doubt, training for her moment on the bench.

"Mr. Prince?" He said this in a hopeful "Save me from my fate of not getting in nine holes today" tone, although he didn't strike me as the golf type. More, invigorating hikes and yodelling.

"I couldn't agree with the Crown more." At least, I didn't mutilate it.

Judicial sigh. "Well, if you're both satisfied that there is no apprehension of bias, let's get started." He hadn't asked that. If he had, I would have said there was. Simply having Harry and a judge in the same room was grounds for bias. The Popper was a walking appeal on the point.

The Crown's case was really quite simple.

Community Constable Thomas Alva Wold testified that he had been parked at the town hall when he noticed the defendant's van across the street, festooned with colourful signs. "I put on my glasses so's to be able to read them and was very offended by their content."

"Do these pictures accurately portray those signs?"

"Yeah." It was almost a question in response. I waived any objection and the pictures went in.

"And what did you do then?"

"I went into Town Hall and found Chuck, I mean, Mr. Windsor and I told him to look out the window."

"What happened then?"

"Well, um, Mr. Windsor went across the street and him and The Popper... I mean, the accused got into it real good."

"What did they do?"

"They was yellin' at each other and then the accused, he just up an' gobbed at Chuck, I mean Mr. Windsor."

That was it for the Crown. So, I stood up. I looked at the good constable. He was a bit of a mouth breather and he had that trapped rat look. I don't know why. I hadn't asked him anything. Yet.

"So, you went and told Mr. Windsor about the signs. Is that right?"

Gulp. "Yeah."

"And you did this because you thought he should see how well he was thought of by Mr. Popowicz?"

"Well, no."

"Oh. Did you think seeing these signs would make him happy?"

"I don't know what you mean."

"Sure you do. You wanted to cause a problem between Mr. Windsor and the defendant, didn't you?"

"Not really." More gulps and a look about the witness box. "It's just... you know..."

"You wanted Mr. Windsor to get the message."

"Well, no. I mean yes. Sort of."

At this point, calm enjoined us, compliments of His Honour. "Mr. Prince, I think that the signs speak for themselves. I mean 'Windsor Not' with a hangman's noose. 'Upchuck Windsor Is A Puke.' I think you'd agree with me that these objects were not offered as tokens of friendly esteem by your client. Hmmm?"

"That seems a reasonable view, sir."

"Yes." He paused. "So, just what is your point? I note that the Crown hasn't objected but I felt that I should... clarify the issue, as it were."

"The point, Your Honour, is one that will become clear all too soon, I'm sure." When in doubt, lie obliquely. Frankly, I didn't have a clue but I was enjoying the ride.

"Well, get to it."

"Thank you, Your Honour." Always a pleasure. And be sure to get your parking validated on your way out. "So, Mr. Wold..."

"Constable Wold." It was the Crown correcting me.

"You do me a great honourific and I am beholden to you." It confused her, which shut her up for a while. "*Constable* Wold, then, can you tell me where you were when you say that the defendant expectorated on your boss, Mr. Windsor?"

"Hunh?"

"Spat, Mr. Wold." It was His Honour, this time. "You know, Mr. Prince, resorting to large, often obscure words prevents the witness from having the clarity to respond accurately and weakens your cross-examination. Most witnesses can process only about six words at a time and that speed is often reduced by unfamiliar language and constructions. I'm sure you'll keep that in mind, won't you?"

"Thank you ever so much, Your Honour. I will keep that in mind. Now, Mr., er, Constable Wold, where were you when you say my client, Mr. Popowicz, *spat* on Mr. Windsor?"

"I don't say it. It's true."

"What is?"

"That The Popper gobbed on him."

"But that doesn't answer the question, now does it?"

"Hunh?"

"I asked you where you were."

"I was in the town hall."

"Not across the street with Mr. Windsor and Mr. Popowicz?"

"No, but I know it happened."

"How is that?"

"Well, Chuck, he told me and he was wipin' his face at the time, like right here, beside his nose."

I couldn't think of anything else that was of much help. Harry had other ideas. He insisted on dragging on my arm and intoning sweet nothings in the general direction of my ear. I should have been relieved he didn't spit, I suppose. None of this escaped judicial notice. "Would you like some time to confer with your client, Mr. Prince?"

"Not really, Your Honour. I have no more questions for this witness." The Popper took this as his clue to bang on the table, scrunch up a piece of paper and generally indicate his displeasure with me.

"Very well. We will take a break now. Fifteen minutes."

Harry used this time to follow me about with insinuations of my competence, masculinity and allegiance. I was in the bathroom, busily relieving myself without much relief.

"You didn't ask him nothing about him and Chuck Windsor stealin' my contract from me. An' I didn't hear nothin' about the time him an'—"

"Quite frankly, Harry, I don't care about those things. They aren't relevant."

"Aren't relevant? You crazy? Man, you gotta get on this stuff better'n that."

"Harry, if you don't think I'm doing a good enough job, then fire me. I'll go home and you can have all the fun of defending yourself. And you can ask all the questions you like. Okay?"

"Don't think I won't, Mr. Prince. Nothin' I'd like more."

"Then do it and leave me to pee in peace, okay?" At that point, the toilet in the stall next to us flushed and a red-faced Mountie emerged. Otherwise, I might have been forced to "assault" my client with whatever I had at hand, as it were. But then, I was about out of ammunition.

Charles B. (for Billingsworth) Windsor was the last of the Crown's witnesses. Yes, he had been upset by the signs. He felt threatened by them and the only way to stand up to a bully was to face up to him. He'd been the town administrator for twelve years and never had so much as had a complaint against him until Harry Popowicz came to town. Now, it was nothing but complaints and insults, and even the occasional threat. So, when he saw Mr. Popowicz's van all tricked out with those signs, he knew he had to stand up to Harry as the bully he is. It was all very grandiloquent.

On cross, he turned to me like some despised minor nephew at the wedding who'd gotten tipsy and a bit out of hand.

"So, you were upset by the signs on the van?"

He paused, considered his answer and ground out the words with evident distaste. "I found them not only insulting but threatening, as well."

"Is that a yes?"

"You have my answer."

"But not *the* answer."

"You have *my* answer."

"So, you walked across the street?"

"I've already said that."

"Angry?"

"Who says I was angry?"

"You were upset and angry, weren't you?"

"I don't choose to answer that question."

"I don't think you have a choice. You were upset and angry, weren't you?"

"If you say so, Mr. Price."

"It's Prince and I do. Do you?"

"You have my answer."

"Did you say something to Mr. Popowicz?"

"When?"

"When you walked across the street, angry and upset?"
"I didn't say I was angry and upset."
"Did you say anything to Mr. Popowicz?
"I may have."
"You may have said, 'Popowicz, I'm gonna break your fuckin' neck, you piece of shit?'"

His Honour couldn't resist. "While we often hear language in this room that reflects the commonality of experience in the community, I require some warning of it. That language, Mr. Prince, is not what I expect of a member of the bar in this or any other courtroom. Or anywhere else, for that matter."

"I was trying to keep in mind that resorting to large, often obscure words prevents the witness from having the clarity to respond accurately and weakens my cross-examination. It stood to reason that more common and well known expressions would strengthen it." He gave me a "watch out" sort of look and grunted. I turned back to the witness. "So, did you?"

"What?"
"Say that?"
"Say what?"
"I can keep repeating it and His Honour can keep getting upset until you answer. I don't care but I expect he does."
"I may have."
"And did you start ripping the signs off his van?"
"What else could I do? I was being viciously slandered!"
"Libelled, if anything."
"What?"
"Never mind. Did Mr. Popowicz try to stop you from clawing these signs off his van?"
"He tried but I managed to get one of them off when he spat at me."
"You mean that some spittle flew from his mouth and hit you while he was calling you names?"

"No, he reared back, hocked up a big gob and spat at me. I think he was aiming for my eye."

Harry didn't improve things when he took the stand. He insisted in regaling the court with tales of municipal evil doings going back to his first encounters at the town hall, some three years before. Of course, there was the report of the lost bus contract and other yarns of other mistreatment at the hands of Mr. Windsor, whom he insisted on insulting with every reference. All in all, it took a good hour to get out of him that he hadn't deliberately spat at anyone, much less, Chuckles Windsock, as he put it.

She didn't need to do it and, quite frankly, she didn't do it well. Nonetheless, the Crown did not feel our day complete without an hour of rehashing most of The Popper's testimony on cross. By this time, Harry had dug a hole right to bedrock.

Judge Senuk wasn't brief either. The judgment extended for another forty-five minutes with digressions on the duty to tell the truth, admonitions on neighbourliness and a peroration on the dignity of public officials. Shock of shocks, he convicted Harry.

Sentencing was even worse. "I consider what you did, Mr. Popowicz, to be a particularly brutal assault. Your lawyer has argued that it was nothing but spitting, that spitting is pretty minor when it comes to an assault, no bruising or bleeding. But I do not agree. I find that what you did was not only grossly insulting and disgusting but extremely dangerous. You spat in Mr. Windsor's face. His face. That is a particularly sensitive part of the body. That is the part of the body that we show the world every day when we get up. It's what we smile with and what we frown with and what we cry with.

"I've heard that it struck him on the cheek. It might have hit his nose and he could have breathed it in. It might have gone in his mouth. Have you considered how sickening that would be? You might have hit him in the eye. He doesn't need your germs, your undigested food. And worse, we heard that you, how was it put, again? 'Hocked up a gob.' By this I take it to mean that you created a mound of green phlegm and used that as a weapon in your assault on Mr. Windsor. Yes, Mr. Popowicz, that mound of phlegm was your weapon. I must remind myself that you are not charged with assault with a weapon, only a common assault. Even so, I must take that into account, in sentencing you today. And no one has the right to put his saliva into another person's body without his consent.

"I take into account your record and what was said on your behalf but I am left in a position of absolute dismay. Your conduct was wrong, it was dangerous and it was a criminal offence. I am sentencing you to three months in jail and two years of probation."

He then listed off thirteen probation conditions, including orders that Harry not go to the town hall for any reason at all and that he not post any signs that referred to any municipal official on his car or elsewhere.

Harry was led away protesting that his rights had been violated. I was left to ponder at the power of signs. And droplets of mucus.

THE OTHER PERSON'S IDEAS AND DESIRES

"You *are* appealing, Mr. Prince. You do know that." It seemed nice of Carrie Anne to think so. And not that I had similar feelings for her. Maybe, she even meant it. I didn't want to seem unduly eager so I didn't say something like "Nice of you to notice."

"Oh, so what brought this on?" She had come into my office, unannounced, except for the briefest whines from Rollo.

"You will be appealing Mr. Popowicz's matter." It had seemed, for far too brief a time, a sudden chink in the armour of inhumanity that she wore so frequently. And well.

"I will?" Frankly, I hadn't given Harry two seconds' thought since he was hauled ungraciously away by two rather beefy thugs, masquerading as cops. The Popper felt that he should, at least, get a last few protestations in. Judge Senuk had help fleeing the scene so it was left to me, the Crown and a few railbirds to witness the expulsion. Then, I'd found a decent motel, a better bottle of Scotch and a liberally-minded patroness of the local bar to lick my wounds—many and sensitive they were, too—until about 11:00 the following morning. The drive back to Yamnuska Centre was pleasant. Late fall is a wondrous time to cruise lazily through cottage country. No one else seemed to. And I didn't want a speeding ticket.

"Yes, Mr. Popowicz has convinced Legal Aid Central that he was not given a fair trial. You are to write a report and then do the appeal."

"This report?"

"Yes?" Her eyebrow arched precariously close to the hairline. I'm sure it was a medical condition. If not, the pharmaceutical companies will invent one—and a drug that cures it, despite the many side-effects. "Don't take *Regardless* if you work with heavy artillery or need a decent night's sleep. Don't take it if you are pregnant, antagonistic, Presbyterian or plan to become one of these. In rare cases, patients have reported minor reductions in IQ scores and attractiveness, visions of the apocalypse, a blurring of their inner vision and a wholesale loss of self-respect. Tell your doctor if any of these conditions apply to you."

"What exactly is it supposed to say?"

"That Mr. Popowicz did not receive a fair trial and that he should be approved for an appeal?"

"Oh, is that all. Why don't you just write that up and I'll sign it?"

"Because you need reasons."

"Do they need to be true?"

"Why?"

"Because I need to know if I'm writing fiction. Harry got a fair trial and, aside from pissing off Judge Senuk, he got a reasonable sentence, as those words are now interpreted in the courts of this province."

"Then, I guess you didn't do a very good job of representing him." She was entirely too proud of herself.

"Were you there?"

"No, but Mr. Popowicz was and he is quite dissatisfied with your representation."

"So call the law society."

"I've considered and rejected it—at this time."

"Well, that's a relief."

"I'm sure it is."

"Not the law society. I had thought that this appeal might be based on some fact or original legal insight but, with Harry, we can pretty much count that out."

"He was very accurate and precise with me on the telephone, yesterday. You simply failed to raise important issues of evidence that were key to his defence."

"Like the whole bus business."

"Among other things."

"So, you're going to argue this appeal. You can raise all these important issues of evidence that were key to his defence?" I had hope. Besides, with careful instruction and a sympathetic taxi driver, she might just find her way to the courthouse.

"Oh, no, Mr. Prince, I thought I'd made it clear. It's like those pottery places . . . you know?"

"Oh, I stay away from anything that deals with pot. Trust me."

"You broke it, Mr. Prince. You bought it. By the way, an appeal such as this has a fifteen hour rating."

"Well, then I'd better get my creative juices flowing."

She grimaced. That's the word. Then, she flipped the file folder onto my desk. It hit the corner of a stack, bent ever so slightly downwards and tumbled into my wastepaper basket.

"Nothing but air! A three-pointer!"

She just shook her head, and left.

* * *

I was just starting to consider how to write something that would get past her and not unduly stain my credibility. Somehow, "incompetence of counsel" sounds so, I don't know . . . judgmental. I'd work on it.

I was considering how to attack the matter when Megan McCarthy walked in. (This time Rollo didn't warn me. I'll to talk to him.) She was the one so open to the gallows. She had added some flair to her basic business grey ensemble: a yellow shirt *and* handkerchief, flirtatious in a commercial sort of way. I allowed that the handkerchief could double as a tourniquet in the event of severe blood loss but was completely useless in times of surrender. She was confused. That was a start.

"Mr. Prince..."

"It's Jack."

"Carrie Anne has emphasized with us the need to keep things in this office on a strictly professional basis."

"Which profession would that be?"

"I beg your pardon."

"Never mind. You were saying something about keeping things, you know..."

"Yesss! Um... I was saying that Carrie Anne does not want us using Christian names in the office. She says it sounds unprofessional and creates a bad example for the staff."

"Well, how about nicknames. I could be "The Dog Boy" and you could be... I don't know... how about "Boomer"? Or, maybe, "Enchilada." That's Spanish. It'll give you an aura of foreign mystery."

"I don't think so."

"You could pick your own. I'm easy. And I'm not married to "Dog Boy," either, just so you know."

"I was told you could be a bit... uh... difficult."

"Me? I'm the sole of ease. Just ask Rollo. Hey, Rollo, am I not just the sole of ease?"

She noticed him for the first time and scrunched her nose. She didn't say "Eew!" but she wanted to. Rollo, for his part, didn't show his best manners, rolling over so his back was to her, sneezing and letting out a little whine. I wanted to tell him we don't whine in front of company but thought I could save the lecture until later. Public humiliation is not good for the young canine ego.

"Mr. Prince". She had summoned up her best business manner so as to get through this as best possible. "Mr. Prince," she repeated, "some of us in the office are in CASA. I don't know if you know what that is..."

"The Spanish word for 'house.' As in '*Mi casa es su casa.*' I still think you should go with "Enchilada." It suits you."

"As I was saying, many of us in this office are already members of CASA."

"Some."

"What?" She had started to panic. Never a good sign.

"First, you said 'Some of us in the office are in CASA' now you're saying 'many.' Just trying to be sure."

She sighed. "Fine. Some of us are in CASA."

"And that would be?"

"What?"

"CASA? I take it that none of you are homeless and it stands to reason, therefore, that CASA hasn't taken on its Spanish meaning... for you, that is."

She was at the point of frustration. "CASA stands for 'Citizens Against Spousal Assault.' You're obviously not familiar with it or its objectives."

"Oh, I don't know. How about, you are citizens who are against spousal assaults? Close?"

"Yes. That's about right. And we stand for the idea that spousal assault is the most pernicious and evil crime commonly committed today."

"More serious than... say... murder?"

"I'm glad you brought that up. Do you know that seventeen per cent of all murders are committed by men against their wives or common law spouses?"

"I'd heard that, actually."

"And one in three women is the victim of spousal abuse."

"But don't forget that eighty-four per cent of all spousal assaults are believed to be unreported." She seemed encouraged. "You know how they figured that out?"

She was on a roll, undeterred. "The abuse just goes on and on from assault to sexual assault all the way to murder."

"Don't forget about 'the frightening six hundred and thirty-two out of every ten thousand children in a recent study in the state of Iowa.'"

"What about them?"

"I don't know. I stopped taking notes at that point. You should have asked, Ms McCarthy. Now we'll never know ... unless we can find one of those six hundred thirty-two children in Iowa. Then we could ask him or her."

"You're making fun of me!"

"No, but I thought you were doing quite well all on your own."

"I didn't think that a primitive like you would understand. Some of us, at least, are ready to stand up for the victims of abuse, Mr. Prince, even if you are not!"

"I stand up for them on a daily basis, in court, where it counts."

"Then, you will want to join CASA and stop this terrible slaughter."

"Why?"

"Aren't you against spousal abuse? You said that you stand up for victims every day."

"Yeah, but I like to eat. Of course, I'm not against it. I'm for it, so long as the spouse being abused isn't me and her ... or his ... abuser is on legal aid."

"I should have known. Carrie Anne said you're nothing but a Neanderthal."

"Don't forget flippant, arrogant, and sexist with an abusive temperament," I called to the most quietly slammed door ever.

* * *

I have to say this for Chuck Ewanchuk: he knocked. I guess *he* didn't have a boyfriend in the police to teach him how to breach a door with a size twelve shoe. And he lacked Megan McCarthy's low-level burglary techniques—all the better to insinuate her into situations of high abuse, no doubt. I had just settled into the sort of mood where I'd be able to construct a passable fable. It had to be one that was just good enough to pass muster and not make me look like a complete boob. When it came, the sound was less a knock than a timid rap. The door cracked open and Chuck poked enough of his nose in that it would have been rude, not to say highly painful, to have turned him away.

"Uh . . . Mr. Prince—I mean Jack. I . . . wonder if I can, you know, uh . . . talk to you about something." It reminded me of the former Mrs. Prince, about two in the morning when she had slunk in to find me freshly asleep. Minus the wheedle, the whine and the promise of sultry sex—likely not the first of her night—that is. Not that I could hold that against him.

I sighed. "Why not? Come on in, Chuck. What's on your mind?"

He minced in like I'd said 'Take twenty baby steps' in some Legal Aid version of "Mother May I?" His head hung down and his shoulders folded back. He found his way to my client chair and sat. I don't think it was fair, but I caught Rollo rolling his eyes and letting out a defiant snort. Chuck jumped away. "Does he . . . bite?" He pulled a file he'd brought with him to crotch height so as not to offer too soft a target.

"Only on the most carefully considered propositions."

"Wha . . . ?"

"Never mind. You had to be there." Chuck checked down to his right where Rollo had taken to nuzzling himself suggestively and considered his words carefully.

"Jack . . . I don't know if you're the right person to come to on this." He fumbled with the file, dropping a yellow sheet from it. He reached down with one hand grasping for it on the floor, while keeping a weather eye out for any sudden moves from Rollo, who had curled himself into a ball.

"What's this?"

"It's, uh . . . a file . . . as you can, uh . . . see." I could hear his hand snatching at the carpet, finally trapping the offending yellow sheet and bringing it to eye level.

I leaned back. "What sort of file is it, Chuck?"

"My client is innocent and he's got court on Thursday, I think.... Yeah, it's Thursday and I don't really, uh..."

"What sort of client is he?"

"He's innocent and he's a white guy."

"That's unlikely."

"No, he's definitely white, I assure you."

"No, the innocent part. Maybe, he isn't guilty but innocent... nah!"

"Oh, yes he is!" This last was said with the sort of certainty that did credit to eight-year-olds everywhere.

"What's he innocent of?" I know that this was a longer list than what he might be guilty of but it might get us started.

"Uh... theft?"

"You're sure?"

This pushed him to go through his file in a frantic search to prove me wrong. He tore out a long sheet of paper and read it over carefully, moving his lips and nodding. There's a certain triumph to be found in certainty. "Yeah, it's theft!"

I smiled and nodded. "Over or under?"

"Huh?"

"What's the amount?"

"What amount?"

"Of the theft. If it's over $5000 it's always indictable. If it's under, it can be either."

"Either." This wasn't so much a question, more an admission.

"Yeah. The Crown can proceed by indictment or summary conviction. You know, like they taught us in law school."

"I... uh... didn't do too well in... uh... crim."

"Define 'too well.'"

"I got a D."

"A 'D' as in you just barely passed it?"

"They had a curve."

"Somehow, I think they weren't the only ones, Chuck. So, what did you take?"

"In law school?"

"Yeah, unless you want to tell me about high school."

"I took stuff like . . . you know . . . courses."

"In what?"

"Jurisprudence, Judicial Remedies, Legal Status Based on Sex—that sort of thing." He paused. "I liked to write papers."

"Oh? On what?"

"I wrote one on First Nations people and taxation."

"That ought to come in handy if we find a First Nations person around here who actually has to pay tax."

"But they don't. Not if they live on the reserve."

I considered briefly changing my name to "Snake Charmer"—in honour of my many days before Judges Morceau and Senuk—and moving onto the local reserve. Then, I recalled the sad wrecks they called cars and the shacks they lived in, five to a room, and thought I'd pass. "Anything else?"

"Well, I got an A for one called 'Differentiating Discrimination: Women, Race, Class and Sexual Orientation.' They were going to publish it in the law review but it got bumped at the last minute because it didn't fit in with the theme of the issue."

"Theme?"

"Yes, it was the spring issue on abuse."

I tried not to roll my eyes. "Of course. So, when did you article?"

"Last year, I split it between a non-profit organization—ever heard of Women and Children First?—and six months with the Commission on Equality. That's where I met Carrie Anne."

"And she hired you?"

"Of course! She and Stella—that's who ran WCF—are close friends and there wasn't a job there."

I nodded. This was going to take a while. "One question, Chuck . . ."

"What's that?"

"What if it's between women and children? Who goes first, then?"

"I don't get it..."

* * *

"I never thought I'd get to the point of hating to think about sex, Jack." Kathy was munching on carrot sticks and a pot of something that was supposed to ensure that her progeny were male. It was that sort of place. I wouldn't have been found dead there on a dare but it had two recommendations: Neither would her husband, Brian, and I wasn't paying.

No one looked up at this so I supposed the other huddled diners were engaged in at least as personal bits of conversation. "Sex or just thinking about it?"

"The thinking part. I'm not so sure about the sex part, either."

"You know what they say: What's better, sex or drugs?"

"No, I don't, but you're going to tell me, aren't you?"

"It all depends on your pusher."

"Ba-dum!"

"Nice rim shot."

"Thanks. When I started, it was so ... I don't know ... mysterious and forbidden. You had to sneak off into dark rooms at school or closets at house parties and let guys feel you up. Maybe, feel them up too—if you dared. You know. I'd touch them and they'd touch me, maybe, finger me and I'd make him come in his pants. Pretty tame stuff. And all you wanted to do was find out what *it* was really like. I mean everyone was talking about it and everyone was probably spending half their spare time thinking about it and masturbating but, of course, no one was doing it. Well, maybe some of them were. You know, the sluts.

"So, when I finally did it, I was pretty drunk and it hurt quite a bit. It didn't really feel like very much but I sort of liked it. Of course, I couldn't breathe again 'til I got my period, right? You know: 'I'm pregnant!' Ugh! And when people looked at you, you just knew they knew—they could tell.

"But that got me started and there were lots of times we'd do it and, well, nothing. He'd get off and I'd be stuck at the starting line. They never asked and I never told. So, I kind of got into oral. At least that way he keeps going until you come. And no worries about busted condoms or having them come off. You laugh—it happened a couple of times and I was absolutely terrified I was knocked up. But, sure enough, a couple of weeks later, I'd bleed and breathe again. Still, it was forbidden. And that made it fun, too.

"Then, I started going out with just one guy. I don't know, I guess I was seventeen. And he was—I don't know—maybe a couple of years older than I was. And all this pressure to have good sex. No condoms 'Who wants to wear a raincoat in the shower?' is how he put it. And I was *in love*. Still, I didn't want to get pregnant so I went on the pill. You know how hard it is to get the pill in a small town where the doctor is the same one who delivered you?"

"So, what did you do?"

"Went to the next town and gave the doctor a sob story about my periods."

"Did it work?"

"Sure. He was going to give them to me anyhow. I think he got a kick hearing whatever story I came up with."

"So, how long did 'love' last?"

"Until I caught him with my best friend at a party he wasn't going to when I was supposed to be studying for finals. I've gotta say, that I thought it was the best sex I'd ever had. I mean we were like a couple of rutting dogs. God! How my parents didn't figure out what was going on, I'll never know. But we were going at it three or four times a week. In his car, my place, his place, in the barn, in the boys' locker room after school. I think I liked that best.

"But that just got my appetite up. I spent my first year at university working my way through the guys' dorm. It was like I'd died and gone to heaven. I mean these guys really worried if I came or not. It was like an honour thing for them. I don't think I've seen that many pricks 'til I went to work for the government."

"You ever study?"

"You bet. I'm the girl who got honours. Besides, I liked the studying part, just not all the time. I tell you, university was the best seven years of my life and I never met a prick I couldn't make stand up when I walked into the room."

"Which one?"

She grinned. "You know." She dabbed a couple of carrot sticks into the mélange and chomped on them suggestively. "So, when I got out of law school, I went to work for a pretty big firm. You know Christianson, Richardson, Armstrong and Stoddart?"

I shook my head.

"They were the leading lights in all sorts of law. They didn't want to hire me because I was female and single and they thought I'd go off and get pregnant. And their wives were all worried I'd blow the bosses or something. I don't know. But I met Brian there. His dad was a potential big client and Brian could be quite charming. I was told to sell the firm and I did what I could."

"That include Brian?"

"In a way. I didn't mind dating him. Not for the firm. He was charming and fun and he had a lot of money. Besides, like I said, I like sex. It wasn't about getting ahead but I don't suppose it really hurt. Daddy went with Christianson, Richardson and I went with Brian. I wish I could say that it was because of me but I'm pretty sure Ron would have gone with CRAS anyway and Ron doesn't take Brian too seriously.

"Being married to him was great for the first couple of years. But I had to leave and get a job here. I could hardly be a farmer's wife and live in the big city. And I have to say, when he's sober, he can be a pretty good lover. For the first two or three years, we did it pretty regularly. But you know what they say. There are three phases to marital sex—tri-weekly, try weekly and try, weakly."

"So what happened?"

"Let's just say he couldn't satisfy my every need, especially when he wasn't there all the time. But now he wants a kid. I know he's got a little honey off somewhere but I made him agree to dump her in return for the kid."

"Did he?"

"Far as I know."

"And you have been quite faithful."

"You noticed?" She grinned. "Yeah, and that's the problem. Brian can be a pretty good in bed. He's just not—what can I say? Very imaginative. And now, while we're trying to make this kid, it's just banging boots every night. Well, every night he's home and sober and not doing the combining, you know. It's all thermometers and calendars and going to see fertility specialists. I've seen so many lab coats and glass tubes that I think I should do the bedroom over in white enamel. Or a board fence and binder twine. It feels like a cross between a laboratory and a breeding pen. And, every night, it's just Brian up there, going at it like he was hammering nails. Like I said, I never thought I'd get to hate sex. It's ironic, though."

"What is?"

"All those years rutting like a wild goat, always worried I'd get pregnant. Now, when I want to, I can't."

"He shooting blanks?"

"Eh?"

"You know, up to the task?"

"He's had the tests and they say he's got lots of little swimmers. They dive in. It's just they don't seem to want to swim to my end of the pool." She played with a main dish that was supposed to turn all those little tadpoles into Olympic prodigies.

I'd passed on it, myself. I didn't particularly covet nine months of morning sickness and hormones, although it might just put me in sync with my office mates. I'd asked for a cheese burger and was forced to settle for something tofu-esque. It sat on my plate, slightly nibbled at. I was hoping to run a blind taste test with Rollo. As usual, he'd probably wolf it down and never worry about what it tasted like.

"So, what are you up to, Jack?" It was a change of pace. I told her about my difficulties with The Popper and asked for advice.

"You should bring an application for his release pending appeal and maybe a stay on the probation order."

"You can do these things?"

"Of course. I'll send you over the precedents. Just don't tell anyone."

Breakfast may be the most important meal of the day, but lunch can come a close second.

TALK ABOUT YOUR OWN MISTAKES

"Psst! Jack . . . I mean, Mr. Prince! It's him." Gail Deare had breached the portcullis of Castle Prince, sneaking a look in the door that I had so carefully closed behind me.

"Who's him?"

"You know . . . him!"

"Which hymn is that? 'Nearer My God to Thee'? 'Amazing Grace'?"

"Not that hymn . . . him!" I looked at her. Her face was a cross between excited and wildly concerned. She checked behind herself. "Him! You know," and she bent into the door with this and hissed, "The Pooper!"

"Mr. Popowicz?" She nodded frantically, then checked again. "I'll be right out." This apparently was not soon enough because, before Rollo could even yawn, Harry forced his way in. "Good of you to come in, Harry. What's on your mind?" It seemed an obvious, if unfortunate, question. He considered it, chewed his gums a couple of times.

"You are." That was short. And to the point.

"So, what's the problem?"

He leaned over so that his forearm was propped on my desk and leered at me. "I'm thinkin' that that judge don't like me."

"Well . . ."

"I ain't finished. I figger that him and that Charlie Windsor are probably out to get me."

"Not Constable Wold?"

"Well, him too. Yup, the three of them and all them other ones at Town Hall."

"So, it's a conspiracy, then."

He thought a minute. "Yeah, a conspiracy. That's pretty good, Mr. Prince. Yeah."

"We aim to please." I once considered that as the motto of my bedroom—you know, a tasteful sign, just above the bed—but my then-wife nixed the idea. She wanted it for the bathroom, as in "Aim too, please!" It's little things like that that can sour a relationship. Not that Harry knew this or cared much.

"I've gotta know, Mr. Prince, are you for me or not?"

So many answers; so little time. I considered. "I *am* doing my best to see you get a fair trial." I left out 'in each case' since it seemed a bit redundant.

"Well, that's all I want—fair justice—nothin' more, just fair justice."

I was hoping this was his exit line and I could get back to my labours of the last three weeks—finding something appealable about his case, if not him. Not so, it appeared. He sat there chewing his gums and considering his next foray into jurisprudence, Popper-style. I thought I'd encourage his departure with a little subtlety. "By the way, I don't really mean to point it out, but aren't you supposed to be in jail? I mean the judge gave you three months, as I recall."

"They give me a day pass to talk to my lawyer."

"That's nice of them. I mean, if you'd called, I might've gone to see you. I know you've got my number."

"Well, I wanted to go to the doctor with Ada."

"Ada?"

"Ada Severn. She's the woman I live with. She's got a doctor's appointment at two."

"I thought you were single."

"I am. I just live with Ada. I don't, you know . . ."

Well, that certainly was a relief. The very thought that there was an outside chance of Harry's reproducing was the stuff of science fiction and nightmares. "So, you and she share living quarters, just not any undiluted affection."

"Huh?"

"It's nothing, really." I hoped.

"So, what's happening with the appeal?"

"Well, I have to determine what the grounds of appeal are and then write a letter to my people at Legal Aid Central. They approve it and then I can do my written argument." I tried to make it sound as important and legalistic as possible.

"What's the holdup?"

I had to raise my voice a bit. "You may have noticed that things here are a little busy right now, Harry. I don't have just one case like Perry Mason or whoever on TV." I pointed to the stacks of files now sliding off my desk onto what Shakespeare called "that small model of the barren earth" that serves as my floor.

He shook his head, quite violently. "There's nothin' hard about it. It's real simple. That Judge Senuk is out to get me and he believed them liars an' not me. It's one o' them conspiracy things, like you said." He was a bit hotter and louder, too.

"Maybe, I'll give you a bit of law school 101, Harry. We can't just say that the learned trial judge erred in that he believed them liars and not me and, besides, there's a conspiracy."

"Why not? It's true." He was exasperated.

"Leaving that aside, Harry, we have to appeal on a question of law or mixed fact and law."

"Sounds like a lot of bull hockey to me, Mr. Prince. Like a bunch of legal BS, if you wanta know. I want my appeal and that's that." He had reached about ten on the volume knob. "And I got some witnesses, too."

"We . . . don't . . . call . . . witnesses . . . on an appeal." I spaced the words out clearly and strongly. I was, by now, shaking my head.

"Why not? They called them liars at my trial. Why shouldn't I call some on my appeal? That's fair justice."

"Because it's a legal argument on questions of law, not a trial." I don't think I understood the word, apoplexy, till then.

Harry was shaking his head, in return. "That's just a lot of bull hockey and hooey! I wanta testify at my appeal an' I'm gonna. The only question is whether you're on my side or not? You don't sound like it, if you ask me."

I wiped his spray from my notes. "Well, if you don't like my representation, Harry, maybe you should call Ms Bloodworth and see if there is any other counsel who can do a better job." Carrie Anne couldn't force me to work for him against his wishes—just against mine.

"I might just do that. I might just do that." He added flailing arms to his performance. The lips drew into a sour pout and I thought we might just be done. He even stood up and he flipped me a folded sheet of paper. It was from the correctional centre.

"What's this?"

"My day pass. You gotta sign to say I come an' seen you." His voice had returned to its normal level. Well, as normal as it ever was.

I considered what he'd told me about Ada and the doctor. And I considered the difficulties of having Harry charged with being unlawfully at large. And I considered a whole host of legal troubles I could get into as a party to the offence if I signed. So, I forgot what he told me about Ada and the doctor. I signed.

We were done. I had some fiction to write. He had a doctor to see. He was halfway out the door, now open for all the office to see. He raised his voice again, flushed.

"An', Mr. Prince, I want you to know I ain't takin' no more crap from you or anybody else. I'm gonna get fair justice or you're gonna be in big shit, mister! Big shit!"

As opposed to deep, I suppose.

He smiled as he walked from the office, now silent.

* * *

I returned from four days on the road, of supporting the twin causes of perfidity and lust, to find my office strangely *neat*. Normally, there is an ungainly stack of files on my desk, several torturously piled so that the slightest breeze will knock them into a more confused mound and one or two, wedged into the detritus and stained through their use as trivets in my Mint Tea Ceremony. All were now stacked like SS battalions at a Nuremberg rally. It was a shock.

Perched decorously, mid-desk, was an envelope, emblazoned with the new Legal Aid trademark—which should have been a client held down and being force-fed pap—in the upper left hand corner. In handwriting on it were the words, "Mr. John Prince, Personal and Confidential." This did not bode well.

> "Dear Mr. Prince,
>
> The events of last Friday, the 3rd of December, between you and Mr. Harry Popowicz have come to my attention. You were heard by many members of the staff and some visitors to this office to have shouted at Mr. Popowicz. All of the witnesses relate that obscenities were used.
>
> You may recall that this office does not permit abuse of any sort. That policy specifically precludes the use of such language. Further, I interpret your demeanour and behaviour to have been both unprofessional and disturbing.

This is yet another example of your unsuitability for this office.

Because of your actions on that date, I have no choice but to reprimand you in writing. A copy of this letter will be placed on your file.

Any further incidents of this kind will be met with more severe disciplinary action. Please conduct yourself accordingly, in future.

Yours truly,

Carrie Anne Bloodworth

Legal Director, Yamnuska Centre Legal Services"

I considered smearing it with dog food and handing it to Rollo but she might have taken "poison-pen letter" rather too literally. So, I took the whole thing to her office. The door was closed but I knocked and went in. She was alone. That wasn't too much of a surprise. I imagined that her many acolytes were off selling out clients or having their consciousness raised—manually.

She didn't look up from her keyboard which she attacked with fury. I planted myself in a chair and waited, trying to figure out exactly how a Venetian blind works. She ignored me for a good five minutes, stopping only when I resorted to humming minor bits of pop songs.

"Oh, it's you." She tried to sound nonchalant, surprised to see me. She wasn't nearly as good a liar as she thought. She sighed which I took as my cue.

"What's this about?" I held up the letter.

"What does it look like, Mr. Prince?"

"It looks like a setup." I was starting to sound a bit like The Popper. Maybe, I should work in something about "fair justice."

"Call it what you want to. I have many witnesses to your outrageous conduct last week and I will not put up with it. You are supposed to be a professional, Mr. Prince. I suggest you start acting like one. All the rest of us do so."

"What about my right to reply?"

"Don't bother. I have lots of witnesses to your outbursts. There's nothing much you can say."

"That's your *professional* analysis, I take it?"

She coloured. "Just what do you mean by that?"

"I was just wondering what profession you might be referring to."

"Mr. Prince . . . !"

"I'll just be leaving while you try and sort this thing out, shall I?"

"You can't just barge in here and accuse me of unprofessional conduct!"

"I didn't . . . yet." I rose to go.

She wasn't finished, of course. She smiled. There was something of the hyena about it. "I still don't have your opinion on Mr. Popowicz's appeal and, by my count, you're out of time to file it."

"Oh, I save fiction writing for my evenings. You'll have your opinion tomorrow."

She smiled, satisfied. "I don't think that will be necessary, Mr. Prince. You're out of time and you'll never get the court to give you an extension. You don't have any grounds." She sat back, steepling her fingers and smiling a feral grin. "Another example of your *un-professionalism*."

So, I smiled back. It was the right thing to do. "I suppose you're right, Carrie Anne. I don't suppose I could get an extension of time, the courts being what they are and all."

"And the best part . . . Jack! The best part is you're going to be reported to the law society. They don't like sloppy work. I won't have to do anything but sit back and grin."

"Not two of your most highly-developed skills."

"Keep it up. You're only putting fuel on the fire. I just wonder what you'll do next, Jack."

"Oh, I wouldn't worry about it much, Carrie Anne. I'll be fine."

"While we're at it. I want that dog out of here today. I asked you for proof of your, so-called *handicap* and I haven't seen any. So, the dog goes—then you do." I was sort of hoping she'd do something truly villainous, like cracking her knuckles or cackling. But she shouldn't strain her skill set.

"You'll get your letter. It's just I've been rather busy out on the road for you."

"What's that supposed to mean?"

"Don't think that I haven't noticed. With the exception of Harry Popowicz, every file I've picked up as a conflict has been some poor sot whose vices are versa. Guys that like little kids, sheep, shoes, ladies' panties. Don't forget the guy down south with the eighty gig hard drive of naked women, all crucified. I guess your new lawyers don't have the stomach for it. So, don't get rid of me just yet. You need me."

She went back to smiling. "Don't worry, Mr. Prince. I don't need to do anything. You're doing fine all by yourself. Remember . . . *the law society.*"

I opened the door and was mostly out, when I turned. "I wouldn't worry too much about that, Carrie Anne. I'm sort of surprised at you, though."

"Why is that, Mr. Prince?"

"I thought you had spies everywhere. Apparently, none of them are court clerks. I filed the Notice of Appeal last week. So I didn't miss any deadlines. You should talk to Gail about more than what you think's going on in my office."

It sounded like a pen that hit the door behind me.

* * *

I thought about it for a while.

I had a file with a letter in it from a Dr. Valentine Hryhorchuk. I found the file and the letter in a matter of minutes. It was written on a white bond paper without any printed letterhead. I checked the font, then wrote this on my computer:

> "Ms Carrie Anne Bloodworth
>
> Legal Director
>
> Yamnuska Centre Legal Services
>
> Dear Madam:
>
> I understand that you have requested a medical letter from me with respect to Mr. John Prince, an employee of yours. Unfortunately, the pressure of my practice obligations has prevented me from providing this to you until now.
>
> Mr. Prince has consulted me in my practice as a physician and surgeon for certain conditions which he suffers from. These include temporomandibular joint dysfunction with secondary arthritic peliorithic oscansular nephralgia. Both conditions are chronic and treatable only with difficulty. Because of their nature, it is necessary for Mr. Prince to have regular rest and to use the services of a service animal. As I am sure you are aware, with such conditions, there is a danger both to Mr. Prince and to others in his vicinity should he not be able to have such an animal with him.
>
> I trust that this is of assistance to you.
>
> Yours truly,
>
> Dictated, not read
>
> Valentine Hryhorchuk, MD, FRCOGC"

I checked the phone book for a number for Dr. Hryhorchuk and dialed it.

"Dr. Hryhorchuk's office." I wondered if the people who are hired for doctor's offices all have that naturally tinny voice or whether they take training.

"Ah, yes, I'd like to make an appointment with Dr. Hryhorchuk, if I might."

"Are you currently one of her patients?"

"No, I'm a new one."

"Your name and health card number?" I gave her both. "Can I ask what this is about, Mr. Prince?"

"It's rather personal."

"I'm sure it is, Mr. Prince, but we need to know what you are coming in for before we can set an appointment."

"Well, it's difficult to talk about on the phone." Or at all, actually.

"I can understand that, Mr. Prince, but we do need to know."

"I'm not sure I can quite explain it on the phone."

"I think I can understand why you are seeing Dr. Hryhorchuk. Is Thursday good for you, 2:30?"

"Yeah, that should be fine.

* * *

I should have checked first. When I got to Dr. Hryhorchuk's clinic, it seemed to be full of women in various stages of pregnancy. And Kathy Markle.

"What are you doing here, Jack? Get careless?"

"Something like that."

"Do tell."

"I don't think so."

She grinned. "It isn't that secretary of yours, is it? What's her name, Gail Deare? Isn't she going with some guy who's six foot five and about two fifty? You know how to pick 'em."

"It isn't Gail." As if it were someone else.

Kathy grinned. "The boss! You sly dog! You did old what's her name! And you got her—"

"Shh!" People were beginning to stare and I felt somehow flushed.

I was rescued by a nurse who took me down the hall, took my blood pressure and left me.

Dr. Valentine Hryhorchuk was a middle-aged woman with an accent that suggested she was from somewhere in middle Europe. "I wass wonderinge why you have come to see me, Meester Preence."

"You are a . . . doctor?"

"Yess. I am a doctor. For ladies. I am a gynecologist. I have much medical training, Meester Preence, and I theenk you are not a lady."

"Good guess."

"So you come to see me why?"

I thought about why I might come to see her and a wild thought came to my mind. "I think I might be . . . um, you know, *sterile.*" This last was whispered. I felt the need to go on. A plausible story might just get me out of here without much difficulty. Maybe, it was the presence of Kathy Markle and her difficulties. "My girlfriend and I are, you know, trying to have a kid and I don't know if I'm just shooting blanks."

"Shooteeng blanks? I don't know this . . . shooteeng blanks." Then, she smiled. "I understand your meaneeng. You want to know if your sperm ees motile." With that, she handed me a plastic container, explained my duty and directed me to a small room, a lot like the one at the STD clinic. This one came with a few gamey magazines which were unnecessary.

I put the plastic cup into a little slot and emerged, smiling. I took my file from the slot outside the door and placed the letter I had written underneath it. On my way back to the waiting room, I put them on the reception desk which was vacant. With a quick nod and a smile to Kathy, I left.

Three weeks later, I received a belated Christmas gift. Dr. Hryhorchuk had added a happy face.

THE OTHER PERSON'S POINT OF VIEW

So, I came back from the Christmas break, somewhat rested and more or less eager for the fray. Time away has that effect on you. You forget all the trials and troubles and remember only the best.

Carrie Anne had clearly spent her Christmas not considering the many benefits given us by the birth of Our Lord and Saviour. She was tanned, rested and ready for additional mischief, after the better part of two weeks in some hot place or other. It seemed entirely appropriate to me. Of course, no new year could begin without a well-placed meeting and I had no excuse for missing this one.

I sat beside Chuck who regaled me with stories about two weeks of joy and bliss spent in the ever warming arms of his family who had a farm somewhere outside of Outlook, winnowing grain or chatting up the heifers—whatever passes for fun 'round Outlook way.

"I'd like to welcome everybody back for what I think will be a year of challenge and opportunity for us." The smarmers smarmed and I tried not to choke on my mint tea. Words like challenge carry an inherent curse. Grade twelve math is a "challenge." Having an IQ of twenty-five is a mental challenge, but no real barrier to successful careers in politics or sales. Of course, being The Popper's lawyer is a challenge. Two nights before, Harry had contacted me after getting himself arrested in Moskolsippi for breaching his probation. Not twenty-four hours after his release to the comfort, if not the arms, of Ada, he'd driven about the town displaying a new array of signs. These included but—as we lawyers are fond of saying—were not necessarily restricted to:

"Windsor and Wold Lied"; "Chuckles and Tom Tom: Demonic Duo!"; and my personal favourite: "Windsor Not, Wold Wild: Both Lied at My Trial."

When the police arrested him, they offered to let him go on conditions that he take down his signs and promise to be good. "They can't do that to me, can they Mr. Prince? I mean I got rights."

"Well, you've got the right to remain silent and I wish you'd take advantage of it."

"What's that supposed to mean?"

"Just an observation, actually."

"So, what can I do?"

"You could sign the undertaking and be released. That doesn't sound too difficult, does it?"

"But I got a right to my signs, don't I? I can put up any signs I want. That's freedom of speech, ain't it? I got a right."

"Harry, I don't know how to put this. You also have a probation order that says you're not supposed to put up any signs about anyone at Town Hall. You haven't forgotten that I trust."

"Nobody can stop me from putting any signs I want on my van and I'm gonna. They can't stop me. No way!"

"Actually, I think they just did. And hauled you off to jail. Otherwise, you wouldn't be calling me right now and interrupting the perfectly good movie I borrowed from the library. Now, I'm not even in the mood anymore."

"But they can't hold me."

"Oh, yes they can. If you won't sign the undertaking, they'll hold on to you until they can get you to court."

"How long's that take?"

"I don't know. It depends where the judge is."

"So, whadda I do 'til then?"

"You can sign the undertaking or you can spend the rest of the holidays in jail. Your call."

"It ain't right. No way! It just ain't right."

"Like I said, Harry, your call. I'm going back to *Ripping, Writhing and Wrestling: Sex and Pro Sports*. It's a fine documentary. I'm sure you'd enjoy it."

"Can't enjoy nothin' here, locked in a cell. Not gettin' my rights."

"Call Amnesty International in the morning. Maybe, they'll start a letter writing campaign." I made a mental note to change my phone number and hung up.

Now, we were all facing a *challenging* year ahead. It'd be good to share the load a bit.

Carrie Anne, having gathered her many chicks about her, now clucked to demand our attention.

"It is good to see all of you and perhaps I can start off by letting you all know that the rumours aren't true." Since I hadn't heard any rumours I was bound not to be disappointed. "You will all be glad to know I am not pregnant and never have been."

I, for one, was thankful. Nine months of trimester reports, hormone outbursts, Lamaze classes and female gushing is more than any sane man should have to endure. These were inevitably followed by the mournful predations of those who think babies are somehow cute, cuddly or otherwise to be desired, all set about with tales of stretch marks, midnight feedings, croup and teething. Those who take on the willing role of parent ought, in my view, to be locked up and until their offspring become teenagers. Then, they can coo and preen for the little monsters. Even though I think well of Kathy Markle, motherhood's an estimable madness that seizes otherwise perfectly rational women and holds them until they are no longer interesting.

But, if I'd expected to miss the gushing, I was disappointed. Apparently, getting knocked up out of order was quite fashionable in our circles. The chicks were all cheeping their deep disappointment at Carrie Anne's lamentable fate. They did drop one tidbit. Apparently, Ms Bloodworth had moved on from the weedy Wayne Venale and spent her Christmas flaked out on a beach somewhere with someone named Merv—no doubt, all tricked up with political connections and a backslapping acquaintance with Jolly Jeff Wooster.

Megan McCarthy had the floor now. Santa had been good to her. He'd brought her a nice shiny ring that promised some poor guy about five years of begging, wheedling and being nice before he gave up and started chasing Bacardi with beer and the most likely girl in the bar.

"I know I have spoken to all of you about CASA." Nods were noted from the sisterhood. "I was wondering, Carrie Anne, if we could institute a new policy at this office. Would it be possible to align ourselves with the victims of crime rather than, you know, always standing up for men who abuse women?"

Carrie Anne decided to poll the meeting. Caroline Crawford spoke up first. Unlike her mates, she favoured a flavour of yellow that put one in mind of washrooms in the gas stations of my youth. She was quite a bit cleaner than they were. "Well, I don't know about anybody else. I mean, like, just before Christmas I had, like, five clients all charged with assaulting their wives and these guys all had previous records for similar offences in the past. And I'm, like, 'what's going on here?' Like these guys just never quit. I think we should have something like a sorta quota for these guys. And if they like get too many charges then we, like, cut them off?"

"Off what?" I spoke before I thought. I hadn't even had a drink, other than my mint tea.

"Legal Aid!"

"Sorry, I misunderstood. I was still on the last topic."

There was considerable assent from the room and I felt out of place stating the obvious, so I didn't.

Carrie Anne was not to be denied the opportunity to expose my less endearing side. "We haven't heard anything from the men. Mr. Prince? I'm sure you have something to say."

"I thought I'd let Chuck go ahead. I imagine he's got a lot to say on the subject and I wouldn't want to hog the chauvinist spotlight."

Chuck stuttered something that seemed to accord with his A in "Legal Status Based on Sex." He continued with what he thought might be something new. "I . . . uh . . . don't know if you've considered this but, you know, once word gets around, *that* may make guys think twice, uh, you know, about assaulting someone?" There were further, positive murmurs.

"Well, Mr. Prince, what *do* you think?"

"Chuck, my boy, what a great idea! I never saw it coming. I mean, can you think of anything that's more likely to make a guy, pissed to the gills and mad at the old lady, say to himself, 'Whoa! Better not hit her. I've been to Legal Aid twice this year and if she remembers and tells the cops, even though I've threatened her pretty good and maybe broke her nose, and I get charged with assault, I won't get a legal aid lawyer. I better reconsider and not do anything 'til I'm good and sober and maybe not so pissed off.' Makes sense to me.

"And what better way to cut down on the workload around here? No guys accused of assault—that's what, maybe fifty per cent of our case load? Then, we can crack down on the sexual assault guys and maybe a few shoplifters and we can close the place down. Well, except for me and Carrie Anne. She has to administer things and I'll still have the Perv Patrol."

"What's that?" Chuck was endlessly gullible. It was his most endearing quality.

"Don't you know, Chuck? My clients have been elected the most likely to exceed."

"Huh?"

Carrie Anne decided to cut things off before I went into disgusting detail of my Top Ten. "We do all like Mr. Prince's colourful little jokes, don't we? Why don't I take your views to Jeff and see what he has to say?"

By the looks on some faces, I doubt I was the sole holdout against unanimous consent.

* * *

"Mr. Prince, I have the letter from your doctor."

"Oh, which one?"

"Dr. Hryhorchuk."

"No, I mean which letter?"

"Why the one involving your *dog*. What other one is there?"

"Oh, nothing. I get them all the time."

"Dogs?"

"No. Letters." I was sort of hoping the one about my fertility status hadn't been passed on, too. Especially with a roomful of putative mothers. They'd be on me like hot fudge on ice cream and I was trying to keep my Sundays free.

"You do have the other paperwork?"

"Of course." What paperwork she was looking for I couldn't imagine. She might be holding out for the sperm count. I mean, maybe Wayne and Merv were both running low on ammo, as it were, and she needed a little something. I tried imagining the Bloodworth-Prince spawn and all they promised, for the foreseeable future, were nightmares.

"Well, I need a copy of the certificate from the DHHS for the file."

DHHS sounded like one of those shots you plague your children with so they don't drop stone dead in the Safeway parking lot some Saturday afternoon and hold up traffic. I'd check with Gail.

"I have it at home. I'll have to have a look for it."

She passed from my office like the Ghost of Christmas Yet to Come, complete with sepulchral scowl, graveyard manner and the beginnings of *rigor mortis*.

* * *

My next order of business was Harry's appeal. It takes a while for these things to happen. It's all very easy to prepare a Notice of Appeal. You can say just about anything in it. If you like, you can make reference to the learned trial judge's affinity for necrophilia or small dogs. If the Crown doesn't like it, they can always apply to strike the grounds of appeal. They never do. Why would they? It's a lot more fun to watch defence counsel squirm on the many hooks proffered by a bench too soon bored by plucking the wings off flies and watching evidence tapes of police chases.

You have to back up what you're saying with reams of argument and bundles of case law of dubious provenance and relevance. *That's* what takes so long. I'd fought with myself as to what I could say about The Popper and his green gob special. Judge Senuk had believed Windsor and Wold and not believed Harry. That was pretty much it. So, after careful consultation, I opined that even if Harry were not *believed*, he might just be *believable*. It's an old dodge but one which dresses up a lying client in the rented clothes of respectable "might have beens." Besides, Kathy Markle had slipped me some cases that raised the question. A silent Harry Popowicz could mean the outside chance of not being completely embarrassed.

Just because Harry wouldn't be happy without a mention of the Charter, I threw in some stuff about freedom of expression. Quite frankly, in my view, Harry was a bit too free in his expression.

Finally, I stated that the sentence was unreasonable. This was actually my strongest argument.

> "However justified the sentence, if the accused deems his conviction and sentence to be unjustified, he cannot be constrained to change his behaviour simply because the authorities attempt to compel him. The threat of prosecution and punishment, even incarceration, is irrelevant to this appellant's view of his situation and the facts of this offence. As such, specific deterrence is irrelevant in this case."

That's law talk. No ordinary human speaks like this. It requires years of training. However true, my argument was, it would not go over particularly well in an appeal court. It *looked* good, though. Harry insisted on getting a copy so *he'd* be prepared for the appeal. I told him, once more time, that he had nothing to say.

None of this mattered much to Harry's case: he'd already finished his sentence, except for probation. And he'd already breached that.

And then, a curious thing happened. The date for Harry's appeal was set for a Monday in late February. His trial for breaching his probation by displaying the signs was set for the next day.

Mr. Justice Gerard D. Aylesworth was not a man to be trifled with. That he made clear in his opening remarks. He sat on the bench like a tombstone with glasses and a thatch of grey hair. His mouth never moved, even when he talked. He blinked only occasionally. His face was frozen in a rictus of disdain for any and all who might come before him. And then, he spoke.

"Counsel, I have read your briefs." It came from beyond the grave. "Mr. Prince, who is this seated beside you at the counsel table?"

Harry had made the trip down from Moskilsippi, in spite of my lavish suggestions that he not do so. He wanted to make a good impression on the court, he said. I asked him, since he was doing impressions, if he might try *The Invisible Man*. Apparently not. He had descended on the court charioted in a lime-green van of indeterminate vintage, still decorated with a display of his judicial opinions. When I offered that he might not want to do so, he went on about his right to his opinions. This was quenched by a small, brown-haired woman who alighted from the passenger side, painfully

"Now, Harry, why don't you listen to the lawyer? He's got your best interests at heart, dear." She turned to me, smiled and said, "Hi, I'm Ada Severn."

Harry, unprotesting, quietly removed the sign from his dashboard and went around the truck, plucking others, and a fair amount of paint, from the van.

But now, he sat beside me, eager for the fray and constantly elbowing me with suggestions. Ada sat pale and quiet in the body of the court.

"This is the appellant, Mr. Popowicz, my Lord."

"We don't do that anymore, Mr. Prince. Didn't you get the memo?" It was a monotone, barely audible.

"Which is that, my Lord?"

"We don't do the 'my Lord' thing anymore. Smacks of an aristocracy or something. Your Honour is quite sufficient."

"Thank you . . . uh . . . sir."

"I've read your and Mr., uh . . . Cherry's briefs quite thoroughly. Let me tell you I'm quite unconvinced about much of your argument. However, there are two points I'd like you to address." He continued, his voice barely above an ordinary speaking level. It was almost lost in the cavern of the room.

This was going to be shorter than it should have been. Harry was beside himself and—unfortunately—me. He was busy digging his elbow into my thigh and whispering admonitions. I tried to ignore him. The judge did not.

"Mr. Popowicz, you have quite adequate counsel representing you. He cannot do so to the best of his abilities if you are forever distracting him. Do I make myself clear?" His Honour was still quiet, still controlled.

"Yes, Your Honour. It's just I don't want him goin' off sayin' things that aren't true an' sellin' me out."

"Mr. Popowicz, I am sure that Mr. Prince has told you how this proceeding will take place." It was the kindly voice of quiet reason.

"Well, that don't make it right, your Honour. It ain't right."

"Mr. Popowicz, Mr. Prince has the legal training to act on your behalf. I think it would serve you very well if you let him do his best for you."

Undeterred, Harry popped in, *sotto voce*, "And that ain't too good, if ya ask me."

"What was that, Mr. Popowicz?" This was barely louder than Harry's comment.

"Nothing, Your Honour."

So, I plunged on. It was like diving into a pool of green slime. As soon as you think you've freed yourself from one greasy frond, you find yourself strangled by another. I was glad that I was up there taking all the judicial abuse. I didn't have to watch my learned friend, Mr. Robert Cherry, Esq., gushing disdain in his queenly way for his queenly client. But, after twenty or thirty minutes of slashing, mashing and discomfiting, His Honour, summarized things. Neatly, I thought.

"What you seem to be saying, Mr. Prince, is that your client is so unorthodox in his dealings with others that he should not be judged by the same standards as the rest of us? Mmm?"

"It might be put that way. I prefer to say that his demeanour is such that it prevented the learned trial judge from assessing his credibility properly."

He turned to the Crown. "Mr. Cherry, I don't need to hear from you on any of the issues except the probation order. Should Judge Senuk be able to tell Mr. Popowicz what he can and can't say on his signs?"

I have to say that Bobby was suitably affronted by any limitation on judicial discretion. "Your Honour, it is obvious to any fair observer of the facts that it was these appalling placards that led to the appellant's outburst and disgusting displays of aggression. I mean, if it hadn't been for these terrible signs, Mr. Windsor would never have been lured out on the street into a confrontation with the appellant. And I remind you that it was that confrontation that resulted in Mr. Popowicz flinging phlegm at his victim."

"And I thought he spat at him."

"Well, yes, I suppose that might be more accurate. But that is quite beside the point. The signs in question are in very poor taste and may even be slanderous."

"Isn't that a matter for another court?"

"I'm sorry?"

"Isn't that a matter for the civil courts? If Mr. . . . what is it?—oh yes, Windsor—is so offended and these signs are—how did you put it?—slanderous, surely his recourse is to the civil courts. Why should I worry about it? And why should Judge Senuk use a probation order to restrain the appellant until there has been such a finding? And, I suppose, I should ask if he even has the jurisdiction. Hmmm?"

Bobby strove mightily on. I had the impression that all resistance was futile but I give him points for staying on his feet when I would have sat down, happily, and stared, dazed.

At last, the *auto-da-fé* ended with a dismissal of my appeal, with the sole exception that the term about signs was deleted as being contrary to the Charter of Rights. Then, Paylesworth, as I now thought of him, made a fatal mistake. "Is there anything else, gentlemen?"

Never one to miss a cue, however lightly given, Harry was on his feet. "Your Honour, I've got some things to say."

I thought I heard Ada, moan, "No, Harry, no."

But Harry was up, fully loaded. "Them guys in Moskolsippi are a conspiracy. You don't have ta take my word for it, Mr. Prince'll tell ya." I coloured and looked for cover. Bobby Cherry had broken into a Cheshire cat grin. "Charlie Windsor an' all them other guys is just a conspiracy to cover up what them guys is up to." He held forth for a good twenty minutes while I looked for a bolt hole, Bobby kept grinning and Ada moaned, "No, Harry, no." Only Paylesworth sat there rigid, unblinking, the rictus never flinching. Until Harry paused for air.

"Mr. Popowicz." It had no effect. "Mr. Popowicz!" Still, nothing. "Mr. POPOWICZ!"

"Uh, yes, Your Honour."

At that moment, I didn't know which to fear for more: judicial wrath or judicial stroke. Paylesworth's colour came back to his face and he was immediately animated.

"We are adjourned!"

None of us made it to our feet before the bench was deserted and the door to judges' chambers slammed shut. I turned to The Popper.

"I doubt you'll be mistaken for the risen Christ and I would never have taken you for any other sort of miracle worker, Harry, but I think you've just raised the dead."

* * *

The next day's proceedings did not start until the afternoon. That was just as well. Looking at Harry's van and Ada, it was an open question whether either of them would make it back in time, or at all.

When I got there, I found new signs. Quite frankly, between Harry and whoever the province was hiring, I was getting tired of words written on walls. But these ones on the courthouse door advised us that no one, absolutely no one, was to have in his possession—presumably on pain of death or grievous bodily harm—any cell phone, tape recorder or weapon while in the precincts of His Honour Judge Senuk. It seemed a curious list of forbidden objects so I asked the sheriff.

"What do a cell phone, tape recorder and weapon have in common?"

He seemed an amiable soul. He just scratched his head and said he didn't know.

"Well, maybe, you can help me with this. What's a weapon?"

He reeled off a list. I think he'd memorized it. "A weapon is any object that can cause harm or can be used to threaten any person with harm and includes any knife, scissors or other object that is sharp."

"So, I'm left at a disadvantage then."

"How do you mean, sir?"

"I can't bring my wits to court but the Crown can."

"I'm afraid I don't understand, sir."

"I'm not surprised."

In court, Judge Senuk padded to the bench and launched himself onto it as the clerk, a new one, rather pretty announced his presence. I smiled. It was at the clerk but I think Senuk misunderstood. He nodded at me and Claire Couture, who was our prosecutor *du jour.*

It didn't take the Crown long to put its case in. Constable Fleury had "h'observed da h'accused on da street wit' his car, an holder model van, green in colour."

"And what did you see on the van?" I don't object to leading the witness when he is a child, not very bright or has nothing particularly surprising to say. In this case, two out of three aren't bad.

"De h'accused, he 'ad some, how you say, pictures."

"Pictures?"

"Ah, yes, you know, wit' words on dem."

"And do you have these with you?"

At this, we embarked on a show-and-tell of five neatly lettered signs decrying the many conspiracies and supposed malfeasances of various officials, including but not limited to Messrs. Windsor and Wold and, dear Lord preserve us, His Honour. It accused *him* of running a "Kingaroo Kourt." Thank goodness, bad spelling isn't an indictable offence.

"Objection, Your Honour. The sign is prejudicial and provocative. Besides, so far as I am aware, the probation order makes no specific reference to the court."

"Maybe it should, Mr. Prince. Hmph! But I'll sustain your objection. The sign in question will not be considered in my assessment of the evidence in this trial. While I am aware that I have seen it, Mr. Prince, I will put it out of my mind and I can assure you that I already have. Continue, Madam Crown."

That was all the Crown had to ask, so it was left to me to try to think of something to ask this witness. "Constable, when you saw these signs, were you aware that Mr. Popowicz had appealed his sentence?"

"I was not h'aware of dat."

"Objection, Your Honour." Ms Couture was on her feet. "What relevance is it?"

"Mr. Prince?"

"Only that the Court of Queen's Bench found only yesterday that your probation order was defective in that it breached Mr. Popowicz's freedom of speech."

"That very well may be, Mr. Prince. So what?"

"So, the order that Mr. Popowicz is accused of breaching is null and void. It was unconstitutional. It was as if it didn't exist."

"But, you would agree with me, wouldn't you, Mr. Prince, the order was in place when your client was found displaying these placards?"

"Obviously."

"And the order was that he wasn't to do what he did—put signs like these on his van?"

"Yes, but the order breached his Charter right to free expression. It was a nullity."

"I don't think so, Mr. Prince. You can't say that he wasn't bound by the order. He was. And the fact that it might have been unconstitutional is quite irrelevant until it is so declared."

"But it has been so declared, as you put it."

"As I put it, he had a sign that was forbidden . . ."

"By an illegal order."

"That doesn't matter. Your attack on the order is collateral and a collateral attack cannot amount to a defence in matters such as this. Do you have any defence beyond that or should I proceed to sentencing?"

I didn't, so we did.

"Mr. Popowicz, we had a term for you when I was in the army. Do you know what that term is, Mr. Popowicz? It was *incorrigible*. You, sir, are *incorrigible*. You disobey court orders at will. If people can't rely on court orders, we'll end up with nothing but chaos. *Chaos!* Do you know where people who disobey court orders end up? They end up in *chaos*. *Chaos*, in your case, is a very small room in a very big prison. Three months!"

Ada came and hugged him before he was dragged away, yet again. I went to talk to the clerk. Her name was Cindy.

DO IT SINCERELY

Just as my father started each day in prayer and silent reflection, we at Yamnuska Centre Legal Aid seemed to begin ours in meetings. And with no lesser deity than Carrie Anne Bloodworth, too. "Oh God, Our Help in Ages Past" was now replaced by "Oh God, Now Help as Ages Pass" and our prayers now frequently invoked some darker angels. At least they didn't pass the collection plate. Yet.

So, I was relieved when Gail extracted me from the midst of our meditations on the importance of neatly kept offices with an insistent summons to the telephone.

"It's Eighty!" she hissed.

"Eighty?"

"You know, The Pooper's wife."

"I have it on good authority that they are in no way sexually entangled."

"I know. It's his wife!"

I took the call in my office and noticed it had fallen far below the acceptable government standards of efficiency and decorum. "Ada, what can I do for you?"

Her voice sounded ragged and a little tired. "It's Harry, Mr. Prince. I just don't know what to do with him."

"Well, the last time I checked, he was still in jail. He can't get into too much mischief there."

"Oh, I'm not so sure, Mr. Prince. He just keeps a-cryin' and a-moanin' about his rights and all. He says he's going to show 'em all. That's what he says, 'I'm gonna show 'em all.'"

"Ada, that's nothing new. You and I both know he talks a better game than he plays. Which is probably just as well."

"Whaddaya mean by that, Mr. Prince? My Harry's a pretty good man. He takes real good care o' me, if ya ask me. Real good care."

"I'm sure he does, Ada. It's just that he leaves a lot to be desired as a rabble-rouser."

"Mr. Prince, I won't have you callin' my Harry a rabble-rouser. He's got real good reasons for makin' them guys all upset. You shoulda seen what they done to him."

"I've heard, Ada. So, why doesn't Harry just sue them, take them for a bunch of money and just leave them alone? That's pretty simple, isn't it?"

"And what'll that do, Mr. Prince?"

"At the very least, it'll give him some money and a chance to get on with his life."

"You don't know Harry, Mr. Prince. You don't know 'im at all."

"I would've thought that after, what, four trials, I'd have a pretty good idea."

"He ain't like that, Mr. Prince. Harry's a proud man! Real proud!"

"I'm sure he is, Ada, but surely he's got to get over all this stuff about Charlie Windsor and whatever the town cop's called."

"Tom Wold."

"Yes. Why doesn't he just take some money and leave Moskolsippi?"

"He's proud, that's why."

"Yes, real proud."

"You're not making fun of my Harry, are you Mr. Prince?"

"Never! I would never make fun of Harry. That would be beneath me as his lawyer and counsel."

"That's more like it." She sounded mellower now.
"So, is that it?"
"What?"
"You called me, Ada. Out of a very important meeting. I was wondering if there was something more. I've got critical government business to get back to. Your call has been very important but I'm in the midst of some very important considerations right now."
"Well, it's Harry."
"What is?"
"My problem."
"I thought we agreed he was in jail and that he wasn't getting into any more trouble."
"It's just I'm sure he will, Mr. Prince, and I need you to do something about it."
"I'm not sure what I can do. Harry pretty much does what he wants. I come along and try to help him out afterwards."
"That's just what I'm aworried about, Mr. Prince."
"The trouble?"
"The afterwards."
"Lately, he pretty much just winds up in jail."
"How long can that go on, Mr. Prince?"
"Quite a while, Ada."
"That's what I mean. He's just gonna get himself in more trouble, isn't he?" She started to cry.
"I'm afraid so, Ada. That's what he does. Why doesn't he just stop doing what he's doing? Maybe, he won't get into trouble anymore."
"You're just like them other guys! Just like 'em!"
"Ada, I . . ." It didn't matter. The buzzing in my ears made it clear she wasn't there anymore.

* * *

"Good of you to rejoin us, Mr. Prince." Carrie Anne does sarcasm remarkably well. You could almost hear her eyes roll back in her head. The others were looking down at their yellow, legal pads. Some were actually pretending to make hurried notes.

"I hadn't realized I'd been missed. It actually makes me feel wanted around here." I put on my most counterfeit smile and sat, pen poised.

"This entire meeting was devoted to organization and quality of service, Mr. Prince. Those are two areas where your standards are woefully below all other staff in this office."

"Oh?"

"Yes, I've looked at your office. It is confused, cluttered and contemptible."

"Straight C's. That's a pass mark."

"Mr. Prince, studies have shown that a cluttered office reflects a cluttered brain and a cluttered brain is an inefficient brain."

I smiled at the others. "I think you're supposed to write that part down." A couple of them coloured. No one even tittered.

"You are taking this very lightly for someone whose work suffers from a lack of focus and organization."

"I seem focused and organized enough to have run seventeen trials including four for Harry Popowicz without any problems."

"And lost all four, Mr. Prince. Not a very good average, if you ask me. This office runs on results."

"I'm confused."

"That doesn't surprise me."

I ignored her. "I've run seventeen trials. How many have you done in the same period of time?"

"I am an administrator. I administrate. Do you know what that means, Mr. Prince?"

"Apparently, not much to do with representing clients and running trials."

"Quite right, Mr. Prince. It does not. I am beyond that stage in my career."

"That's a lot like being past it, isn't it?"

"I beg your pardon!"

"You don't do trials because you're past doing them."

"My function is to make sure *you* do them . . . properly."

"Is that it?"

"Is what it?"

"Is that your only function?"

"I also have a leadership function, Mr. Prince. You do know what leadership is?"

"No, but it's obviously not something that's done by example."

"Mr. Prince, I've had about all of your impertinence as I'm going to take today."

"Then, I'll store some up for tomorrow, okay?"

She turned to her desk and tossed a wire-bound booklet my way. It was entitled *Multi-Individual Network Computation and Time Use Systems*. "While you were off gossiping with one of your girlfriends, we have been discussing our new time-keeping system. It has its own name, MINCTUS. As you can see, it records all the time spent on a file so that we can ensure that no one exceeds the designated maximums for any file. It requires you to input the file name, your function and the machine will keep track of the time spent on each matter and function. It would appear to be fairly simple. Do you think you can handle that, Mr. Prince? Or do you need to call your girlfriend again?"

"It looks pretty simple. But I do have a question. How many hours are we expected to bill in a day?"

"All of them, Mr. Prince."

"All seven and a half?"

"Yes, Mr. Prince. All of them. It's all in the book. Look it up. These will be monitored on a regular basis so I expect compliance and no difficulty from anyone."

I checked the inside cover. I thought I recognized the name of Gavin Turcotte among the authors. He was a chartered accountant unless CA stood for something more low-brow. A man could dream. He was surrounded by a flock of QCs and a number of those so deprived of a designation it must have shamed their mothers.

"If there's nothing else, I'll see Mr. Prince and Mr. Ewanchuk after the meeting."

The others had fled; Carrie Anne restarted.

"I've kept you back, Mr. Ewanchuk, to ask you to help me and help this office." Chuck fairly beamed at this. He sat that little bit straighter and sneaked a glance at me. "You may have noticed that Mr. Prince is having some trouble adjusting to his duties under the new administration. I know he's trying to do his best but . . . let me be frank."

She, paused, wheeled and stared at me. I decided to let her be whoever she wanted to be. If multiple personality disorder was her problem, I couldn't help her much. I'm not a shrink.

"Mr. Prince, you are a substandard employee. You are undisciplined, inefficient, thoroughly confused in your work and out of date in your thinking." She turned to Chuck who was morbidly taking all of this in. If it had been an accident, he would have parked his car by now and gotten out to take blood samples from the injured and dead. "Ordinarily, this might result in his being fired but we have to *accommodate* him, Mr. Ewanchuk. Am I being clear?"

Chuck didn't have much to say. His mouth was too far open. So, I thought I'd take over for him. "What was the one after inefficient?"

Carrie Anne ignored me. "Mr. Ewanchuk will try to help you find your feet, Mr. Prince. I only hope you can learn something from observing a fine, young lawyer like him. Chuck, do you have any trials coming up that Mr. Prince could help you with?"

"Darren Powace is coming up in two days."

"There you go, Mr. Prince, the Darren Powace matter. You will help Mr. Ewanchuk with it. Any questions?"

"Yeah, what's he charged with?"

"I think it's doing an indecent act."
"Can you do it, Mr. Prince?"
"Do what?"
"Help Mr. Ewanchuk with the indecent act?"
"If he holds still . . . sure."

* * *

I poured over the MINCTUS handbook for about an hour. Gail had already put most of my client names into it but I added a few more. If we were expected to account for our every minute, it only seemed fair to add in "Government Business" for meetings, "Miscellaneous" for making tea and "Bathroom Break" for quiet times without uncalled for disturbances.

Chuck brought me the Powace file and directed me to review it. Chuck told me to come to see him in an hour to review our strategy. I clicked on Darren's name and the icon for "Review of File Materials" and started the timer. I was done in about ten minutes, six of which had been devoted to trying to decipher some cop's notes. I called several friends and drank some tea.

The file revealed that Darren had told Chuck that he had been in a blue jeans store, shopping for pants. He couldn't find any he liked, so he left. He was arrested outside. The statement of the complainant, a young lady named Janice Worthy, said that Darren had come in and shared a bit more of himself than his waist and leg sizes. He had peeked around the curtains of the change room with the one eye he had that he definitely could not see with. This, Darren strenuously denied.

I clicked my time off at fifty-five minutes, three seconds and noted that MINCTUS, thoughtfully and predictably, rounded everything up to an hour. I gathered some note paper, a copy of the Criminal Code and a couple of pens and made my way to Chuck's office, stopping only to click onto an icon called "Conference With."

Chuck was in Lawrence's old office. Gone were the plastic orange fittings. Now, it was all blond wood and computer gizmos. Chuck spent his time wisely, looking up the law on everything. He announced his position to me before I could settle comfortably into the client chair. "This is hopeless. I'm just going to plead him guilty and see what he gets."

"Sounds like a plan. What does the Crown want?"

He flicked over a letter from the stack he had extracted and piled in the upper left quadrant of his desk. It said something about three months and listing poor old Darren on the sex offenders' registry.

"He got any record?"

"No. But this is hopeless."

"Have you told Darren that yet?"

"Well, no. He's a pretty big guy and I, you know, wouldn't want him too mad at me. I thought you could do that."

I resisted the urge to get mad at Chuck and asked, "What if he won't?"

"I don't know what to do. You don't think he, like, you know, knows where I live, do you?"

"You in the phone book?"

He was hyperventilating by now. "Yes." It was more a croak than any form of human speech.

"I wouldn't worry about it. He probably can't read. You just have to hope he doesn't get anyone at the correctional centre to look it up for him."

"Oh, God!" He had his hands over his face so I couldn't see if he was actually whimpering.

"Don't worry about it. Maybe he has a short memory." This didn't improve things so I made a final sally. "You can always put on a really good show in court and maybe he'll blame it on the Crown."

* * *

I went back to my office after half an hour of listening to Chuck plot various ways of getting out of town. We considered and rejected having him wear a bag over his head for the trial and bringing a Charter application for delay. I was here to learn from a "fine young lawyer." I never thought it would involve a change of name application.

I snapped off the "Conference With" icon and snapped on "Government Business." I called Rollo and told Gail I'd be gone for an hour or so.

My first stop was an optometrist's. He had a fine display of sunglasses, including some fairly expensive looking wrap-around ones. Once I'd bought them, I considered a career in law enforcement.

We stopped at a pet store and I bought a leash for Rollo, one with a solid handle at the top. Rollo gave me a look. He didn't do leashes. I put it back in the bag. "We'll talk." Carrie Anne's rolling her eyes is one thing. She, at least, talks.

My last stop was the drugstore. I approached a teenager who was obviously working his way through grade ten. For the third time. Evidently, his sex life hadn't perked up much as I caught him trying to extract a pimple from around the stubble of his chin.

"Try shaving. It'll cut it right off." That startled him leaving him red enough to cover any leakage.

"Yes, sir. Can I help you?" he croaked, suggesting that his skin might just clear up when his voice changed.

"Psychiatry and drugs haven't so far. Give it a whirl!"

"I'm sorry."

"So are my parents. And yours, no doubt." I was obviously going way too fast for Zitto so I continued. "I'm looking for a cane."

"A cane?" The very idea seemed quite foreign to him but since we'd gotten this far in English I wasn't about to resort to my ropy French.

"Yes. A cane. You know, what guys wave about in the old folks' home when they want a nurse or get pissed off at their ungrateful grandchildren."

"Oh! A cane." I knew English had been a good idea. "What do you need a cane for? You don't look crippled to me."

I decided to avoid the story about waving it at ungrateful store employees and said, "My uncle. He's getting on. Can't see too well. You know."

"A cane." He started nodding like a bobble-head doll and made his way down an aisle past feminine hygiene products and family planning aids. That's what it said. If people actually planned their families, their children would be intelligent, pleasant and moderately good-looking. All available evidence is to the contrary. Nobody really plans his family: they just happen. Either that or they plan families like the military plans invasions: the first hours are well thought out; the rest is unrelenting chaos. I didn't share this with Zitto. I thought it might strike too close to home.

We got to a rack of canes: wooden, metal, plastic and titanium; knotty, straight and extendible; brown, blue, black and sort of an ochre colour. "You wouldn't have any white ones, would you?"

"White?" I was beginning to stretch the limits of his vocabulary. Next, I'd be teaching him to sit and fetch.

"Yes, white."

"They're for blind people, aren't they?"

"My uncle. Can't see a thing. Runs into walls all the time. He's done it so much, his nose is flat. Like a pig's."

"Ohhhh!" He rooted about for a while, then left me for the back. He came back with a plastic effort, specially priced at only $59.99. I handed him the money, including the tax and left him considering how I could possibly have calculated it.

Rollo was outside. We entered into negotiations as to whether he would wear the leash-harness. I explained it all carefully to him. In the end, I got him down and torqued the thing around him until it was on. Together, we walked to the government offices. He whined. Constantly.

I put on the glasses and took the cane in my left hand. I remembered to ignore the listings and approached the commissionaire sitting at his table. He looked at me and went back to his paper so I rapped on the table leg with my cane. "Excuse me, sir."

The commissionaire rattled his newspaper so I cleared my throat and pretended to be Ray Charles—except that he's dead and I'd look pretty silly lying there, not breathing. "Excuse me, sir."

The newspaper went noisily to the table. "Can I help you?" It was the whine of a particularly rusty door hinge.

"Yes, I was looking for the office where you register a service animal under the *Service Animal Licensing, Training and Exemptions Act.*"

"Third floor. Down the hall to the left, through the green doors. You'll see the sign."

"I beg your pardon."

"Third floor. Down the hall to the left, through the green doors. Look for the sign."

"I'm sorry."

"You deaf, buddy? I told you. Third floor. Down the hall to the left, through the green doors. There's a sign—right there."

I would have encouraged Rollo to express my outrage in his special, liquid way but I remembered that government offices all had security cameras. Part of the "Anti-Abuse Campaign" I guess. So, I deliberately ran over several tables and chairs, carefully swearing each time. I barely missed tripping over Jolly Jeff Wooster as he made his way, like the QE II at full throttle, tossing off quotes to some reporter trailing in his wake. He growled at an aide as he passed, "What's that dog doing here?" I thought Rollo was going to throw down at that point. He didn't and we made our way, unassisted, to the third floor and the office.

It was run by a guy far enough away from his pension to be considered young but old enough to have been with the government for a while.

"Excuse me. I'd like to register my dog as a service animal." I was careful to look off at the wall. It allowed me to watch the guy roll his eyes and make hand motions suggesting my capacities were minimal enough to require a human handler, maybe some diapering.

"A what?"

"Service animal."

He looked through a number of forms until he found one. "You'll have to fill this out."

"I beg your pardon."

"Fill this out and sign it at the bottom." He twirled a long piece of paper at me and stood back.

"You want me to fill out this piece of paper?"

"Yeah. If you want the certificate."

"Am I missing something?"

"I don't know. Are you?"

"Does this mean anything to you?" I held up my white cane.

"I'm calling security, sir."

"I am holding up a white cane. Does that mean anything to you?"

"If you hit me, sir, the police will be called."

"A. White. Cane."

"I can see that, sir. But I'm going to have to ask you to leave or I'll call the cops. You gotta go."

"It means I'm blind."

He stood there for thirty seconds. Considered. He moved very slowly and quietly to the left. "I didn't know."

"So."

"Like I said. Fill out the form and I'll get you a certificate."

"How am I supposed to do that?"

"Don't you have a pen?" He leaned forward and slapped a pen onto the sheet of paper.

"I can't see. How can I fill out a form?"

He considered a bit and said, "Oh." He asked me my name, where I lived and other trivial stuff.

"Name of dog?"

"Rollo."

"How do you spell that?"

"Like the candy." He misspelled it. Probably more of a Lifesavers guy.

"Breed of dog?" At this, he leaned over and considered Rollo quite a long time. Rollo was doing his part, sitting up smartly, ears pricked. "I thought he was supposed to be a German shepherd or a Lab."

I let a few seconds go by. "You mean he isn't?"

* * *

We got out in time to trip over Jolly Jeff Wooster making his way back in, cursing out his aides for making him put up with "an asshole like that," meaning, I suppose, the member of the press he'd been sucking up to for the last forty or so minutes. I gave him a whack as I went by for Rollo's sake and got to the street.

We dumped the harness-leash in an alley. Rollo didn't miss it.

On the way back to the office, I stopped at the drug store. The young clerk was there. He was still in the family planning aisle, possibly speculating. I handed him the cane.

"I'd like my money back."

"What about your uncle? The blind one?"

"He didn't like the colour."

THE SWEETEST SOUND IN ANY LANGUAGE

Darren Powace's trial came up two days later. Since my role was to watch and learn, I became the native bearer of what seemed an awful lot of material. Chuck had packed ten cases, six pens of various colours, five legal pads, three criminal codes, and two copies of an evidence text book. I vainly searched the bag for a partridge in a pear tree, then shouldered it in best "bwana" fashion.

Chuck made a couple of extra trips to the bathroom after he combed his hair. He was on his way back when I grabbed him and steered him in the general direction of the front door. Gail looked up. "You're not going to appear in front of that Judge-and-More-So, are you Chuck? He's really mean, isn't he, Jack?"

"Maybe, the Prozac'll kick in today, Gail. You never can tell. It's got to, some time." Chuck's complexion suggested the imminent onset of lividity.

They say that animals can smell fear. I'm not so sure. It sounds something like elephants never forgetting and cats curing cancer. Rollo only seems to respond to urine on hydrants, canned dog food and sultry little numbers of the cocker spaniel persuasion. And I wasn't going to run him over Chuck as a "dread detector." If I had (and Rollo were talented), I'm sure the mutt's eyes would light up, his tail, wave like a flag in a gale and his body, go into full rictus.

But I grabbed Chuck by the elbow and guided him to the door and down the stairs with encouragements I'm embarrassed to use on a three-year-old.

We got to the court and went on an excursion to find Mr. Powace. Since I didn't know what he looked like, I wasn't much help. Chuck kept hiding behind bits of furniture and peaking about, half-hoping, half-fearing that his client wouldn't show up. "What if he doesn't come, Jack? I mean, what will we do?"

"You could ask the judge to get off the record."

"Will that work? I mean, will I be in trouble with anyone? I mean, what would Carrie Anne say?"

"Don't worry. I'd get blamed."

"Do you really think so, Jack? Really?"

"Pretty much, I'd guess."

Our discussions were interrupted by a spindly creature with hunched shoulders and a pocked complexion. He was only slightly smaller than Chuck and a bit less threatening than Rollo—asleep.

"It's him! It's him!" Chuck was hissing and pushing himself farther into the corner. I walked up to Darren, held out my hand and introduced myself. Darren shook it, all the while looking down. I winkled Chuck from the corner and hauled client, counsel and carry-on baggage into the courtroom.

There was a new prosecutor at the Crown table, or, at least, someone I hadn't encountered since my tour of the province in support of child molesters, exhibitionists, bum-feelers and, of course, Harry Popowicz. Things change: one must adapt.

I walked up to him. He was tall, fairly young, and had made up for premature baldness with a suggestive ginger beard that he stroked—maliciously, I thought. "Hi, I'm Jack Prince. My colleague, Chuck Ewanchuk, and I are here for Mr. Powace."

He didn't shake my extended hand, just looked at it as if I had leprosy or bad hygiene. So, I smelled it thoughtfully, smiled and said, "I understand."

He just continued staring at me. Either he thought we were a couple of boxers at some well-published weigh-in or my witty repartee had demolished him. "You are . . . ?"

"Shepherd." It was uttered with almost metallic grace.

"First name, German?" I turned, while he processed this, and guided Chuck and Darren to their appointed places.

I plopped myself between them, then turned to Chuck. He was furiously rooting through his paperwork in search of some pearl of great price. He hadn't found it and was now starting to mutter. Tears were welling in his eyes. He finally extracted some notes, well-blotted, more like hieroglyphics. He smoothed these out, obsessively.

He was still doing this when His Honour Judge R. M. Morceau launched himself onto the bench in great, walloping strides, like a dressage horse. He nodded at me, almost friendly, and started out. "Counsel."

No one leapt to his feet to challenge this assertion so it appeared everyone was satisfied. Morceau turned to the Crown, "Mr., uh . . ."

The Crown creaked to his feet and allowed that his name was "Shepherd. First initial, *G*."

"I knew it." This was mostly whispered but caught the judicial attention.

"Mr. Prince. So good to see you. Perhaps, you might introduce your colleague."

"To my left, Mr. Ewanchuck, first initial *C*. To my right, Mr. Powace."

He snickered. "So, are you admitting identity, Mr. Prince?"

"Only my own, sir. It's the only one I'm really sure of. The person I know as Mr. Ewanchuk will be conducting the defence. I am here to watch . . . and learn."

Morceau sighed. "As I am sure you will, Mr. Prince. As I am very sure you will."

* * *

The Crown managed to get things back in line in fairly short order. They called their first, and—we were promised, only—witness, Janice Worthy.

A slight, puckish figure, a young woman with short, brown hair, came, in answer, and sat in the witness chair, only to be told she had to stand. She was asked if she would prefer to swear or affirm. She wriggled and allowed that she didn't know, batting her eyes appreciatively at the learned trial judge.

There are some things I never remember. I can't recall my mother's birthday or my ex-wife's, for that matter. I often forget my Social Insurance Number and even my sister's name. My wedding date, on the other hand, is etched with acid on my consciousness. The last memory I will have as I sink into despondency and Alzheimer's, probably the last I have before God has His last laugh and shuts out my lights, will be that day. The other thing that I can never forget is the sense of someone I have slept with. Maybe, not their faces and often not their names, but I always have a sense of them. As soon as I saw her, I felt a burning, quite inappropriate to the time and place and recalled my thirty days of abstinence.

She sat and was immediately under the Crown's careful direction. He asked her name, where she worked and what had happened on the 30th of January, last, at The Jean Pool, her place of employment.

"Yes, I was working that day. I was working alone in the store."

"Let me just stop you there. What sort of store is The Jean Pool?"

"It's a clothing store. We stock all the better brands of jeans and other denim clothing as well as several lines of designer wear." Publicity you can't purchase for any money.

"Carry on."

"What? Oh, yes. I was, you know, working." Here, she gave one of her little grins and seemed even to wink at His Honour. There's no telling. Morceau might go for that sort of thing. His wife seems normal, all things considered.

"And what did Mr. Powace do?" At this, Morceau wheeled to look at the defence.

I elbowed Chuck in the ribs and hissed, "Object!"

He turned to me, hurt. "What?"

"Object!"

"Why would I do that?"

So I pushed him up and, since he had nothing better to do, said, "Objection, Your Honour." It was like a dog walking on his hind legs: not so much done well as at all.

Morceau considered what was happening and cleared his throat. "Yes, of course. Mr. Shepherd, the question is leading."

"Your Honour, I don't think it is leading."

"Well, it is. Carry on."

"Your Honour, I am thinking of a case. I can't quite remember it but it was in front of Judge Bertram last year in Sunareka, and he said—"

"I don't care what Judge Bertram may have done last year, Mr. Shepherd. The question is leading."

"But *I* don't think it is leading, Your Honour." His face and extended forehead both coloured to the shade of his beard. I was hoping he wouldn't seize the judicial pant leg in his teeth or pee on the carpet. I didn't fancy his getting swatted with the bench copy of the *Yamnuska Centre Clarion*.

"Carry on, Mr. Shepherd."

"I'd like an adjournment to find that case and present a full argument on the point, sir." At this point, Morceau was looking to the defence for help. Chuck was beavering away into his books so I stood. "Mr. Prince, I thought you were watching and learning."

"Oh, I am. And already I've picked up some real pointers." Before His Honour could ask "Where?" I continued. "If the issue is critical to the Crown, I am sure it can be addressed again before he closes his case."

Morceau looked at me as if I had somehow stumbled into respectability or mere sanity. Either way, he seemed shocked. So, I assured him that I'd picked up a lot from his bother Judge Senuk, smiled and sat down.

"Ah, yes, Wilbert. We were classmates, you know, Mr. Prince." Well, *that* figured.

All the while, Ms Worthy was staring at me. It seemed she had a worse memory for faces and other body parts than I. After all, her recollections were probably even more extensive than mine. Her brow had furrowed; the puckish grin, gone.

"If you could continue, Ms Worthy."

She picked up the thread of the narrative. "This man came in." She looked up at our client, smirked, and went on. "He asked to see some of our high-end jeans." Here, she stopped and looked at me again, some recognition but no sure thing. Then, she giggled.

"Something funny here, Ms Worthy?" It was Shepherd, first initial, G.

"No, it's just . . . Never mind."

"This is a serious business, Ms Worthy." The prosecution beard was, by now, trembling. Janice put her head down and looked at him through her eyebrows. There was a trace of a smile.

"I'm sorry. Just something I thought was funny." Now, she had turned her head sideways and was working on the pixie look. She sighed. "He came in and went into one of our dressing rooms, you know, to try on the pants."

"These dressing rooms. Can you describe them for the court?"

"Sure." She was all business now, her hands on her lap. "The business is in the mall and we have dressing rooms that are little booths and on the front of them, we have curtains, you know, made out of, like, denim. So, when customers come in, they get their clothes to try on and they go into these change rooms and pull the curtain shut so they can, you know, change." She squared herself to him and pulled her legs primly together.

"So, what happened on the 30th of January?"

"Well, he came in and he asked to try on some jeans. So, I gave him some and he went into one of the booths and he pulled the curtain behind him. Uh, he was, I don't know, in there a long time so I asked him if I could do anything for him." She looked at me at that point. I smiled. She remembered. Her smile stopped.

"What happened then?"

"He asked me for some more jeans and when I went to give them to him, I opened the curtain and I could see his thing."

"What thing is that, Ms Worthy?"

"You know, his thing."

"Does it have another name?"

"Yes."

"So what is it?"

"His man thing." She was trying to look anywhere but at me. And failing.

"Do you know any other names for it?"

"Yes."

"And what would those be?"

She blushed. Deeply. "His . . . cock." Her head was down and she almost whispered it.

"I beg your pardon?" Shepherd was one of those guys who needed to get every last grim detail out.

"His COCK! HIS PRICK! I don't know what *you* call it."

Satisfied, for now at least, Shepherd sat.

Chuck got up, fumbling. "I . . . uh . . . wonder about identity, Ms Worthy." And don't we all? "Are you sure you identified the accused as being the person that you saw in The Jean Pool on the 30th of January?"

"Yes." His first question of cross-examination, and a thing of beauty, too.

"How can you be so sure? I mean you didn't have a very good look at him, did you?"

"I saw more than enough of him." She tittered

Chuck flipped over a few more pieces of paper, looking for that "killer" question. "Um, you say you saw him well enough to remember him, is that right?"

"Yes."

"And you are really sure of that? I mean with everything that was going on and all?"

"Yes, it was something that was pretty hard to forget."

"Oh." Chuck checked his notes again. "But you didn't get a really good look at his face, I mean, did you?"

"Yes, I saw him. I saw his face. I saw his . . . man thing. I remember it. It was . . . horrible." She started to whimper at this point. Chuck got a bit red, checked his notes again and sat down.

Morceau looked at me. "Since you're just observing, Mr. Prince, I don't suppose you have anything to ask, do you?" He was sounding pretty sure of himself, so I couldn't resist.

"Maybe, a couple of questions, sir." I stood. The look I got from Janice Worthy was pure hate. "Ms Worthy, you've told us that you were the only employee in the store that day."

"Yes."

"Were there other customers there?"

From beside me I heard Chuck mumble, "Good question." I nodded and smiled.

"A few."

"What? Three? Four?"

"Something like that."

"You were helping them, weren't you?"

"Of course."

"So, Mr. Powace wasn't all that you had on your mind."

"I wouldn't say that."

"Oh, but his display of himself, was that for everyone or just for you?"

"I don't know what you mean."

"Well, was his showing himself just to you or to the world at large?"

"I can't really say. I can say that what he did was absolutely shocking to me."

"Oh, you've never seen anything like it before?"

"I don't know what you mean."

"Well, you know, a naked man?"

She blushed. The good Shepherd rose to her aid. "Where is this going, your Honour?"

Morceau shrugged. "I don't know. Maybe we should watch and see."

"Well, Ms Worthy?"

"Well, what?"

"Haven't you ever seen a naked man before?"

"I suppose."

"But you were shocked?"

"More like . . . startled."

"Oh, startled?"

"Yes, you don't expect to see anything like that, you know, in a place like, you know, a store."

"You mean a place where people go behind denim curtains, to take off their clothes and change?"

"Well, no. I sure don't just take my clothes off anywhere."

"Really?"

Shepherd was on his feet growling some more. "What's that supposed to mean? Does defence counsel know something that I don't?"

"Probably, but I have no further questions." I sat and waited.

The Crown closed its case at that point. Morceau turned to us. "Gentlemen, I don't know which one of you I should be talking to. Are you calling any evidence?"

Before I could stop him, Chuck was on his feet. "I'd like to call the defendant, Mr. Darren Powace."

"No, you don't."

Morceau was confused. So was I so it must have been really baffling. "Which one of you is handling this defence, Mr. Prince?"

"I suppose I'd better. I won't be calling any evidence."

Shepherd was up. "But he called the accused." He pointed to Chuck. "I want to cross-examine him."

Before I could think of anything to say, Judge Morceau put us out of our misery. "He seems to have changed his mind, Mr. Shepherd. Submissions?"

Shepherd restated the evidence and sat down.

At that point, Chuck whispered to me, "What should I do?"

"Try arguing the case."

"But my defence was identity. I didn't think she'd point him out."

"She's the kind that never forgets the important things, Chuck."

"Huh?"

I stood up. "Your Honour, the charge before the court is one of committing an indecent act. The case law indicates that this charge requires prurience."

Morceau leaned forward. "And what do you say is prurience, Mr. Prince?"

"According to the dictionary—carnality or lasciviousness."

"And why do you say the Crown has failed to prove it?"

"Because all the Crown has proven is that Mr. Powace, in the context of changing his pants, exposed himself to Ms Worthy. There's nothing more than that."

Morceau sighed. "You seem to have become quite the expert on indecency, Mr. Prince."

"Years of experience, sir." He winced.

"You are quite right, of course. There is no evidence of anything beyond mere nudity. The Crown has failed to prove the charge laid so the accused must be discharged. Is that all we have for this morning?" He was up and gone like a wisp of smoke before anyone got to his feet or was even told to do so.

"What does it mean?" Janice Worthy was on her feet and after the good Shepherd.

He tried to break it to her gently. "It means that we had to prove more than that he showed himself to you." He was turning red.

"You mean, I should've said he was all horny and, you know, squirtin' stuff? He got his gunk all over the merchandise."

I didn't feel too charitable. "It won't be the first time you've wiped it off your pants, Janice."

"You, you . . . pig!" She rounded on me and had to be restrained by Shepherd.

"Calm down, Janice. It's all right. We'll get you home. We can talk about it later."

"I don't have anything to say to . . . losers." She launched herself out of there like the unguided missile she was. He just stood there, the lonely Shepherd.

"Aw, don't worry about it. You should get yourself checked out, though."

"For what?"

"I'd start with the bite wounds and move down from there."

"You're disgusting!"

"Yeah, well talk to me in about ten days."

I smiled and turned to Chuck. "I thought that went rather well, don't you?"

"My first win! My first win! I'll never forget this, Prince!"

He was still celebrating when we got back to the office. By then, the brilliance of his cross-examination was well-settled and he was rehashing it like a long ago fishing trip. Carrie Anne approached with her warmest congratulations for her latest conquering hero, legal division.

"Well, Mr. Prince, did you learn something today?"
"Indeed, I did."
"I'm so pleased. And what was that?"
"So many things; so little time."
"Such as?"
"Such as winning and losing are mere trifles in the greater march for justice."
"What's that supposed to mean?"
"Justice comes at the oddest times, and in the oddest ways."
"How about something a little less elliptical?"
"Never send a boy to do a man's job. If you do, send a man with him, one who's already been there."
"I don't have a clue what you're on about. Go turn your timer off. I don't want you cheating MINCTUS by over-timing the Powace matter."
"I'll just leave that to Chuck, okay?"

I went to my office and timed off Powace. Then, I clicked the "Bathroom" icon and typed in "#2."

DON'T CRITICIZE, CONDEMN, OR COMPLAIN

I wasn't quite basking in the glow of my recent win on behalf of Darren Powace. I didn't look at it as tainted by Chuck Ewanchuk's claims but, if I'd been keeping score—and I have no doubt *he* was—it would have gone into the "win" column and counted for two points.

It had ended my streak of however many losses in a row with The Popper. Having Harry as a client was a bit like having the coach's son on your team. You had to play him and you couldn't just put him in when you were three up. Otherwise he'd complain to his mommy and the coach would wind up on the couch with the dog. Or worse, the dog would have the couch to himself. No, he had a regular shift, during which he'd be sure to fall down, trip your leading scorer or score himself—into his own goal. And there was precious little you could do about it.

I *was* basking in the warm glow of an early spring sun on the steps of the local Roman Catholic Church. To escape the irony of it all, it was half a block from my office and a handy place to meet Kathy Markle, whose office was a block the other way. Rollo liked it too. It was full of sacramental smells and footprints. Besides, he could leave one of his special messages on any of a dozen handrails, guardrails or plant pots.

"So, are you going to the wedding?" Kathy opened the top of her "California Pasta Salad" and dipped the plastic fork in.

I yawned and let the sun bask on my face. "I'm trying to give them up."

"What? Weddings?"

"Yeah. The last few I've been to haven't turned out so well, starting with my own. I feel like a Jonah."

"A what?"

"Haven't you read *Moby Dick*?" I aimed my pop can away from her and managed to splash Rollo a bit. He yawned, licked at it and went back to sleep.

"Is that a joke?"

"I said *Moby*, not mouldy."

"I was an English major. Of course not. Have you?" She took a forkful, careful to scrape a bit of green pepper off on the rim.

"No, but I dated a few of your type in undergrad."

"A few of what types?"

I looked both ways, then said, conspiratorially, "English majors. You know, pulled back hair, glasses, well licked fingertips from all that page turning."

"All right, I'll give you the glasses. What about *Moby Dick*?" A trickle of "Three Cheese California Pasta Sauce" dribbled onto the step and she tried to grind it into the concrete with her shoe.

"They're always going on about a sailor who brings a ship bad luck. They called him a Jonah. Like the guy in the Bible."

"You mean the one that got swallowed by a whale."

"It was a 'big fish,' as I recall."

"I suppose you dated a theology major, too?"

"Yeah, sure, if you count a ministerial candidate for the United Church of Canada."

"A what?"

"That's what they call them. Of course, I did. All of the guys in her class were gay or married so someone had to teach her the divine service."

"You are a pig, you know, Jack." She was shaking her head and smiling at this. She took a swig from her juice box.

"It's not all felt boards and 'Jesus is cool!' posters, you know. They have needs, too." My Philly cheesesteak sub was getting cold, sun or no sun.

"As all women do." She pulled out a load of pasta, considered it then levered it into her mouth. "So, did *she* teach you about Jonah and the really big fish or did you actually crack open the Bible?"

"No, I think I heard about it in church between trips to the bathroom." The Philly cheese had more or less congealed and what steak there was left was not worth chasing through the industrial goo.

"You? In church? I can't believe it."

"Oh, ye of little faith!"

The local cleric of this fine establishment came out at this point and smiled, apparently pleased either with the day or my Biblical allusion.

"Hi there, Father Ron."

"And how are you today, Kathleen, my child?" It wasn't an Irish accent. Otherwise, every other cliché was there.

"Oh fine, Father. Uh, this is my colleague, Jack Prince. We were just discussing the Bible and Jack was telling me about Jonah and the whale."

"It was a big fish, Kathleen, not a whale. There's a lot of theological significance to that, you know. A fish is a Christian symbol while a whale is just a large mammal, a cetacean, I believe".

"So Jack was just pointing out." She looked down at her salad, now mostly gone.

"Well, I hope to see you and your Brian in church this Sunday," said the priest. He considered me, no doubt consigning me to the status of useful heathen. "I'll not be keeping you much longer. It's a fine day and I'm off on my pastoral rounds."

"So, who's getting married?"

"Bobby Cherry."

"Bobby Cherry? Who's the lucky girl?"

"Oh, Jack! You're so old-fashioned. We have same-sex marriage in this country now. Surely, you've heard?"

"Yeah, but I didn't think they really meant it."

"Come on, Jack. You're not one of those who thinks that marriage is only for one man and one woman."

"I was sort of hoping to limit it to that, actually."

"Marriage is an institution that has evolved and should encompass all members of society."

I turned to Rollo, now licking himself as only he could. "Don't get your hopes up."

"Be serious, Jack. Gay people, lesbian people, they can love each other exactly the way straight people do."

"Not quite."

"I'm talking about love, Jack, not just sex."

"I don't really care if they do, so long as I don't have to try to imagine the wedding night."

"It's not *all* about sex."

"I've been married. You can be sure of that."

"Well, Bobby is getting married, just like you."

"I hope not, considering how that turned out."

"Well, his getting married is just like everyone else."

"So . . ."

"So what?"

"His sex life is all behind him now?"

"You're awful!"

"True. But who's the blushing bride or groom or whatever?"

"Myron Horschewicz."

"The MLA guy."

"He didn't get elected."

"I didn't vote for him. Did Bobby?"

She blushed. "Yeah, but Myron's still a politician, trying to screw the electorate."

* * *

I got back to the office to find Gail in the process of installing some sort of headset onto my telephone.

"What's this?"

"Ms Bloodworth says that it will improve your productablility."

"My productability?"

"Yes, you can do more of whatever you do, Jack."

"Is she giving me permission or just hope?"

"I don't get it."

"Don't worry about it. I think I do."

She gave me that look and showed me how to make it work. I thanked her and she left. But it wasn't more than five minutes before my phone made some sort of groaning sound.

"Gail? What's wrong with my phone?" She peeked in the door.

"What's wrong?"

"It's making that sound. I don't like it. Is it safe?"

"Don't be a silly, Mr. Prince. It's supposed to make that sound. It's normal."

"I can't get used to what's normal, Gail, but if you tell me that, I won't worry."

"Just press the green button on the side and you can talk to Mr. Popoffawitch."

"What do I push if I want to talk to somebody else?"

She gave me a look so I put on the headset and pressed the button. "Harry! What can I do for you today?"

He just started. "I'm real upset, Mr. Prince, real upset."

"Oh?"

"Yeah. It's Ada. She's real sick, real sick. Doctor says she aint' got no more 'n six months, eight at the most. It's real bad."

I clicked on the MINCTUS computer icon that stood for Harry. I'd changed it from a telephone to a clown. It seemed the right thing to do. "What's real bad, Harry?"

"Ada. Don't you listen to me, Mr. Prince? Like I said, she's real sick."

"And it's bad." I leaned back into my chair. A slash of sun met my face. It felt good

"You're not makin' fun o' me, Mr. Prince, are you? I mean this is real bad. She's only got maybe six, eight months."

"So what's wrong with her?"

"Doctor says something about leukemia or somethin' like that. It's real bad, real, real bad. I says to him that if I had my way I'd wish it was me, not Ada."

I let the break in the conversation go without noting—out loud—that I finally agreed with him about something.

"Mr. Prince?"

"Yes, Harry."

"What can we do?"

A very good question. Pray? Sue God? And what's this *we* business? "I'm not sure, Harry. What do you think?" When in doubt ask a question.

"Well, I'm thinkin' them guys're gonna do something to use this against me. That's what I think, Mr. Prince. They're gonna use it against me."

"How are they going to do that? What do you think they can do to you?" I sat back in my chair. Obviously, I wasn't going to have to take any notes.

"I dunno, Mr. Prince, but I'm thinkin' they'll do something, maybe do something to stop her from gettin' her medication or somethin' like that, Mr. Prince. Them guys don't care a bit about Ada. An' they'd do anything to get me."

"Harry, they aren't going to do anything to Ada. Don't be silly."

"Who're you callin' silly, Mr. Prince. You don' know what them guys are capable of. You don't. You're just some smart-alecky lawyer who don't know nothin'. Them guys'll do anything."

There wasn't much point in popping his delusion balloon. "So, what do you want to do, Harry?" The sun was now shining fully on my face.

"I don't know. You're the lawyer. You're the guy with all the smart-alecky ideas. You tell me. But them guys're out to get me, you can be sure of that, Mr. Prince. And it don't take no smart-alecky lawyer to know that them guys'll do anything. I wouldn't put it past them to hide some dope on me and get me charged with sellin' it to kids just so they can get me."

I sighed. "What do you want me to do?" I flicked a piece of paper off my desk so I could put my feet up on it. This would take a while.

"You tell me that, Mr. Prince. You're the smart-alecky lawyer guy. You tell me. What can I do about Ada, eh? She's sick and you can't tell me that them guys ain't gonna do nothin'. I know them. They're always doin' somethin' underhanded. You can't trust 'em. No way! They already got me charged with bootleggin', I can tell you that and I wouldn't be surprised if they wind up chargin' Ada, too. An' when them guys are finished, I'll be in jail for twenty years. Just watch."

"You don't get twenty years for bootlegging. At most a couple of grand fine."

"Yeah, an' you told me I wouldn't go to jail for no disturbance charge, neither. I remember that, Mr. smart-alecky lawyer. I remember that real well. An' what did I get? Couple of months in the slammer..."

"As I recall, it was thirty days."

"Well, I ain't been in no trouble before I came to this town and them guys ain't gonna make me leave either. Them guys may think they're smarter'n Harry Popowicz but I ain't leavin'. No way! They're gonna have to carry me out on a slab. That's what I say. They're gonna have to carry me out dead on a slab."

My eyes started to sting, so I closed them. Visions of The Popper, covered by a blanket and being hauled off on a sheet of rotting plywood. I was doing well until it broke under his weight, and he got up and started cursing them. I think I smiled.

Harry continued. "Them guys'll take me out one way or another and they won't rest until they do it. But I won't let them, Mr. Prince. They ain't heard the last of Harry Popowicz. No way! You know that? They ain't heard the last of me. You can be damn sure that's the way it's got to be. An' you know what I'm gonna do?"

"Not a clue, Harry, but I'm sure you're going to tell me."

"Damn tootin'. Damn tootin', Mr. Prince. I'm gonna run for town council. You know that. Then, they can't keep me out of the town hall, then. You can be sure of that, right?"

"Uh huh." I was quite comfortable.

The rest is a bit of a fog. I don't remember saying much after that. I really don't remember much until I woke up. Harry was still at it.

"An' then them guys are gonna listen to me. I'll straighten 'em up like they've never been straightened up. Damn straight, if you ask me! Damn straight!"

I checked the timer on my computer. MINCTUS read 34:52 and continued to roll. So did Harry. I yawned. Rubbed my eyes. Rollo was in the midst of one of those dreams that I best not know about. He's young. "Harry . . ."

". . . Straighten 'em right up. An' then they'll know they don't know nothin'. You understand me?"

"Harry, I hate to break up this wonderful encounter but I know you have a lot to do and I should get on with my day, too."

"You do agree with me, don't you Mr. Prince?"

"Damn straight, Harry! Just keep it up."

I disconnected the line and checked the time: 35:59. I could imagine what Carrie Anne would say when she saw that. All Harry had was a bootlegging charge and I needed all the time I could get to do the trial. Besides, there was no icon for "Nap Time".

I shut things down, punched in "Bathroom Break" and entered "#1." MINCTUS never sleeps.

When I got back, there was a message on my screen from Carrie Anne. "Wonderful call from Mr. Popowicz. He's thrilled with your efforts. I was wondering if I should assign him to Chuck. Please see me."

BE GENUINELY
INTERESTED IN OTHERS

Sometimes, Rollo is a bit too much like a wife. I leave aside the fact that he thinks he's entitled to the whole bed. Or the fact that he snores and won't admit it. And there are times when he is insanely jealous of whoever I might be sharing our bed with at any given time. Whine, whine, whine! And there's the way he just *looks* at them if they stay for breakfast.

But like my ex-wife, Wendy, he doesn't have any sense of time. Not that either one is ever early for anything. No, they both have that passive-aggressive habit of having just one more thing to do before we leave. It doesn't matter—a trip to the bathroom, maybe that final touch up on the face— probably something that just *needs* to be done.

So, it wasn't much of a surprise that we were late getting on the road for Moskolsippi. Even with the occasional bending of the speed laws, we cut it pretty tight. I left him in the car with a pan of water and a stiff lecture on the importance of punctuality. Louis XV of France referred to it as the "courtesy of Kings." Or so I told Rollo. He just rolled his eyes and looked bored. Which was better than the lamentable Wendy, who would probably have spit—or gone off to prowl. Come to think of it, maybe she was more cat-like.

I made my way around Harry's van outside the courthouse. It was a type referred to by police as an "older model" and by used car lots, as "parts." It was still bedecked with placards and posters: "The Crown Takes a Pay-off," "Tom Wold and Charlie Windsor Are Liars and Corrupt!" and "Windsor a Wimp and a Wipe-ass." There wasn't a lot of space between the van and the car beside it so I might have ripped the last one a bit on my way by. I hoped Harry wouldn't mind.

Once inside the courthouse door, I was directed around the airport scanner. The sheriff's officer grimaced and advised me, "Judge Senuk's order. Members of the bar exempt." Then he took my briefcase and put it through an X-ray machine, jiggling the toggle switch back and forth a couple of times to make sure that the clip that bolted my papers together couldn't be pulled out, stretched to its full two inches and used to slash the judicial throat in a moment of uncontrolled advocacy. Satisfied, he returned the case to me and I ascended the stairs.

Harry was there along with a fair number of the unwashed masses, eager for the fun to begin. One thing you could say about Harry, he brought in a crowd. They seemed more or less evenly divided, too. Like at a wedding: half on the prosecution side to cheer and moan; half on the side of those who feel that anarchy is something best not left to bearded bomb-throwers and other Bolsheviks. Nothing would do, of course, but that I would have to spend some small morsel of my life being enthused by my client who steered me unwillingly to a side room for a bit of a pre-trial pep talk.

"They're settin' me up, just settin' me up, that's all. I gotta right to live in this town and them guys ain't gonna make me leave. No way! You understand."

I thought a bit of light should be injected into this. "Harry, they're charging you with selling a bottle of Golden Apple whisky to one, Bernie Befus. You know Bernie?"

"Yeah, I know him. He's just a scummy little liar like all them guys. Don't you see what them guys is doin'. They're just usin' this to get at me, to put me in jail and shut me up. You think that's right?"

I ignored the last point. In jail, his long distance calls to his lawyer would be free. It was one of those rights that none of us noticed until the Charter was upon us, I guess. Along with gay marriage and Sunday shopping. You can't just pick and choose rights like peaches at Safeway. You were bound to get some squishy ones. "Harry, he says that he bought a bottle of Golden Apple from you and that he paid you a hundred bucks for it. What do you have to say about that?"

"Pfshh! They can't prove nothin'."

"That all depends on Mr. Befus, don't you think? I mean, if he's telling the truth, here, there isn't a whole lot you can say about it."

"They're just tryin' to set me up. Next thing you know it'll be a great big bag of cocaine or that heroin stuff." He pronounced it like the female version of hero so I doubt there was much likelihood. "An' then they can stick me away in some hell hole for twenty years."

"I don't think they care that much, Harry. You're just a pain in the neck, an itch that just needs scratching every once in a while."

That might have been unfair. It certainly was unkind. He turned on me, his face, scarlet. "I ain't no itch and I ain't no pain in the neck. You don't think I'm good enough for you and your kind, Mr. Prince, then I'll just hafta do this whole court thing myself."

I thought about it briefly. It was just what Carrie Anne would want: me insulting a favoured client. "I don't think that would be the best plan, Mr. Popowicz. The judicial system can be extremely challenging."

"Well, that just may be, buddy, but I ain't gonna have no lawyer tell me I ain't good enough for him."

"I didn't mean it that way . . ."

"Well, it sure sounded like it to me. So, you apologize to me, Jack Prince, and we'll just head in to court."

Sincerity has never been difficult for me. Whether I mean it or not. I told him I was sorry and we headed out. The hallway was now more or less clear of people who had been invited in for the big show. A couple of stragglers were consulting in the corner and a sheriff sat on a table beside the courtroom door. I stopped for a drink, straightened my tie and made sure my fly was fully secure. It can be quite distracting to feel a southern breeze in the midst of a serious submission.

I got to the door and would have opened it except for the sheriff, who had now drawn himself up to his full five feet six—that's a hundred and sixty-eight centimetres for the metrically adept—and blocked my way. "You can't go in there, sir."

"I have to. I'm a lawyer."

"I'm sorry, I can't allow you to do that. Judge's orders!"

"I'm sure he might think it's more convenient but my client is entitled to have me there with him."

"I don't know anything about that but it's full up in there. You can't go in."

"It's a public courtroom! Why can't I go in?"

He pointed to a sign etched in red, apparently by the fire marshal. "'Cause it says so. And I'm going to have to ask you to lower your voice, sir. Court is in session."

"I know very well that court is in session, you nin—I mean sir." I caught sight of the sign warning me of intemperate language and the possibility of spending a night in a cell. Who would explain things to Carrie Anne? Who would keep Rollo from going nuts in the government car? I checked my pocket for the keys.

"Keep your hands out of your pockets, sir. I want to see them at all times."

"What?"

"And don't roll your eyes at me, either. I don't like it."

"I really don't care whether you like it or not. I've rolled my eyes at everyone from Fortune 500 company presidents to fifty dollar hookers. Believe me there's not much to choose between them."

"I can have you removed, sir." He was reaching for his walkie-talkie, when a voice boomed over the PA system.

"John Prince. Mr. John Prince. You are required in Court Room One, John Prince."

I turned my head heavenward and said, "Thank you, God." With that, I went inside. *Deus ex Machina*, indeed!

"Good of you to join us, Mr. Prince. You are late." It was a statement of the distinctly obvious from Judge Senuk. He was propped up on his bench, a witness was in the box and Harry was on his feet.

"I would have been here sooner but the fire department told me I couldn't." I plunked my briefcase onto the desk, pulled out my pad and pen and sat down. "I hope I haven't missed anything crucial."

The court clerk was, once again, the lovely Cindy. She smiled at me. Or my witticism. I'd like to think it was both.

"Mr. Befus was just telling us about buying liquor from your client." The Crown was new to me. He already had smarmy down and was dressed like he was on his way to a job interview.

My confusion must have been obvious. Senuk intervened. "This is Mr. Daniel Baker for the Crown. He may be a little ahead of himself. Mr. Befus has told us that he had called a telephone number in search of a bottle and had been told to come to a certain residence here in town. Is that about right, Mr. Baker?"

"Yes. I am much obliged to Your Honour." He said it like that, too. Capital letters. He didn't waste much time and turned to the witness. "Now, Mr. Befus, you've told us that you went to the accused's residence on April the fourth."

"Mr. Baker, I think it is only fair to Mr. Prince and to his client not to lead at a time like this. Don't you?"

"I am so sorry, Your Honour. I do apologize." A flick of the judicial finger signalled him to continue. But more carefully this time. "Ah, Mr. Befus, how did you know where to go?"

"He told me where to go, I guess."

"Where was that?"

"I can't remember the address."

"Are you sure?"

"Yeah. It's been a couple of months now. You know. It's hard to remember these things."

"Well, what colour was the house?"

"It wasn't a house."

"What was it, then?"

"A trailer, like."

"A trailer like what?"

"A house, I guess."

"So?"

"So what?"

"What colour was this trailer that was like a house?"

"Green, I guess."

"You guess it was green."

"Yeah, it looked green."

"So, it was a green trailer."

"I can't be real sure. It was kinda dark, like."

"Did this house, this house trailer, did it have a number on it?"

"I dunno."

"What do you mean you don't know?"

"Like I can't be real sure."

Danny Boy was getting a bit flustered. He shook his head back and forth. "If you don't know what the number was, how did you know to go to this house, I mean trailer?"

"'Cause he told me, that's how."

"Who told you?"

"That guy. On the phone."

"And who was that?"

"I dunno. I never seen him. It was on the phone, like."

"All right!" It was a touch louder than it might have been. "When you went to this house, trailer, whatever it was, did you see him there?"

"I dunno. Coulda been another guy, I guess. I never asked." Bernie Befus was concerned. "I wouldn' wanta say it was this guy when it mighta been like some other guy, you know."

Baker was now slashing his way through his papers, looking for some way out. Finally, he sighed heavily. "Let's go to the trailer, then."

"Ya mean the house?"

"Yes. The house. The trailer. The green house or trailer or whatever you think it was."

"Ya don' hafta get all upset about it, ya know."

"Fine. Let me ask you this. Did you see who gave you the bottle of whisky?"

"Nobody give me no bottle of whisky."

"What do you mean? When the police stopped you in your car and asked you where you got the bottle of whisky, you told them that you got it from this man over here." He was flushed and spoke like a machine gun, all the while stabbing his finger at me.

Before I could object, Bernie spoke, just shaking his head. "Nobody give me nothin', Mr. Baker. Like I told you, he *sold* it to me. He didn't *give* me nothin'."

"So, how much did you pay him for this whisky?"

"I'm not real sure. A hun'ert bucks, I think."

"You think!?"

"I can't be real sure. I was drinkin' an' all. You know."

I was a bit surprised because old Danny Boy sat down at that point.

There hadn't been a clear identification of my client by the witness but the Crown had pretty much pointed him out. I decided to take another tack.

"Mr. Befus, is it?"

"Yeah." Apparently honest so far.

"You say you got stopped by the police."

"Sure did."

"When was that?"

"Which time?" The courtroom erupted. Local knowledge trumps hot shot from Yamnuska Centre.

"You mean there have been other times?"

"Oh yeah. We're kinda on a first name basis. You know, 'How ya doin', Bernie?', 'Real good, Ron'." He laughed at the memory.

"And all of these stops would be for what?"

"Objection, Your Honour. The defence lawyer is trying to ask for my client's record by a side wind."

For the uninitiated, "side wind" is a legal term. No self-respecting weatherman would ever use it. I haven't encountered it in sailing, physics or anatomy, for that matter. It means, basically, being sneaky. Accusing a lawyer of being sneaky is a bit like claiming that dogs bark or snakes are scaly. Not bad analogies, actually.

"Mr. Baker, the witness is not your client. You are a Crown prosecutor and Mr. Befus is your witness."

"I apologize, Your Honour. But . . ."

"Aside from that, Mr. Prince is entitled to ask these questions."

"But, he's incriminating my . . . I mean, Mr. Befus."

"Maybe. We'll all see. Won't we?" He turned to me and I was back on the road.

"So, Mr. Befus, what were all these stops for?"

Bernie got an "aw shucks" look, smiled and said, "I dunno. Liquor mostly, I guess."

"Okay, so is it fair to say that the police stop you all the time and search your car for liquor?"

"Yeah. Pretty much."

"And you let them?"

"Well, not if I can get away. You know, like if I can get back home with the booze, I drink it."

"And if you don't?"

He shrugged. "They get the booze."

"Do you know what they do with it?"

"Yeah, they pour it out."

"Where?"

"Mostly on the side of the road." His eyes hardened. "It's a wicked waste, man."

"I can imagine." I smiled at him. "So, did they do that this time?"

"Yeah, an' I'm out a hun'ert bucks, too."

I smiled again, in spite of the bit of evidence that trickled out. "I don't have anything more to ask you. Thanks a lot."

"Hey, any time, man!"

The Crown called Constable Bea ("for Beatrice," she assured us) Spendler on the stand to put an empty bottle of Golden Apple in as an exhibit. It even had stickers all over it. I was left to cross-examine her.

"Now, Constable Spendler, did you take a sample from this bottle?"

"No, sir. I did not." It was mechanical. Monotone.

"No little nip?"

"What are you suggesting, sir?" More monotone. I was beginning to wonder what happened to the A model.

"Did you have . . . I don't know . . . a little taste, maybe?"

"No, sir. That would against policy, sir."

"And you don't go against policy, do you?"

"That is correct, sir."

"Now, when you poured out this bottle, was that part of this policy?"

"It is, sir."

"Really?"

"Yes. Policy 256-32R requires us to dispose of any liquor seized on the spot in the presence of the offender."

"Doesn't that assume that the person is guilty?"

"If he has the liquor, he is, sir."

"If you poured out the contents of the bottle, you have no way of saying what it is."

"Is that a question, sir?"

"Let's just pretend it is, yes."

"I have a way of knowing."

"And what's that?"

"The label of the bottle says that is whisky which is forty per cent alcohol by volume." She seemed almost assured, as if, somehow, a tiny bit of humanity had crept in. Hubris is like that. Even in the best of machines.

"Do I take it from that that you believe whatever it says on the label?"

"Yes, sir. Why would they lie?"

"Yes, indeed. Why would they? So, whatever is on the label must be the truth?"

"Yes, sir. There are laws."

"So you have never read anything on the label of a product that was untrue or seemed inaccurate to you."

"No, sir. As I said, there *are* laws."

"Indeed. So, you believe it when the package says 'New!', 'Improved!', 'Giant Economy Size!'?"

"I don't understand, sir."

"How about 'For the prevention of disease'?"

"Sir?"

"I have no further questions."

* * *

At the end of the Crown's evidence, I stood up and made application to the court for dismissal of the charges. I said that there was no evidence that what was found in Mr. Befus's possession was alcohol or, for that matter, that my client had sold it to him.

Dan Baker got up and went on for about twenty minutes. He told us that it was obvious what must have been in the bottle. It was whisky. The label said "whisky" so whisky it must be. (I didn't have the heart to tell him that Golden Apple was not and never could be whisky. Paint remover, perhaps; soul destroyer, to be sure; whisky, never. I am a connoisseur and, if anything, the makers of Golden Apple should be in jail for fraud!)

His Honour had heard more than enough. "It may well be the policy of the local police to destroy evidence before it can be brought before the court. But it is not the role of this court to guess what concoction may have been foisted on Mr. Befus by the accused or anyone else. I am left in a reasonable doubt as to what was provided to Mr. Befus, although I must say that, given his admitted proclivities, it is more likely than not that the substance in question was alcohol.

"Beyond that, however, there is no evidence that the person who purveyed the bottle entitled '*Golden Apple* whisky' to him was the accused aside from the leading and quite improper evidence asked in a leading question by the Crown prosecutor.

"I am afraid that I am left with no choice but to grant the defence's application. The charges are dismissed."

With that, he was up and gone.

Harry turned to me. "What happened? When am I tellin' the court what happened?"

"Never."

"Whaddya mean?"

"I mean that the Crown couldn't prove the charge and you have been acquitted."

"That's not right, Mr. Prince. I've gotta have the chance to tell the court what happened."

"What happened, Harry, is that you were selling booze to an alcoholic."

"Yeah, but I got a right to tell the court what them guys are doing to me."

"So, you want me to bring the judge back so the Crown can get you to admit you're a bootlegger? Is that it?"

"Don't you know nothin' about law, Mr. Prince? I gotta have a chance to defend myself against them guys. And your job is to help me do it."

"Let me let you in on a secret, Harry. No, it's not. I don't prove people innocent. I don't help you commit judicial suicide and I don't get paid to help you make a fool of yourself. You are quite capable of doing that on your own and I can save the taxpayers of this province the expense of it all. I hope that's okay with you."

"You're an arrogant prick, Mr. Prince."

"Good of you to notice." I turned to Cindy. "A drink, my dear."

"Only if you don't buy it from Harry." Unfortunately, he was out of earshot.

SMILE

Inviting me to a wedding is a bit like having Genghis Khan over for a Tupperware party: quite a bit is lost in translation. But Bobby Cherry is, if nothing else, an inclusive sort of guy. Besides, his blushing bride/gorgeous groom was my former candidate in the recent hustings. (There's something oddly suggestive about that word although I'm told it comes from the Norse for "house thing." Maybe, it was all too appropriate.)

As a preacher's kid, I'd seen all manner of weddings from the coolly proper to some that suggested no one could really wait. I've seen brides so thin and winsome that I couldn't imagine they'd survive the wedding night and some, so bristling that I feared for the survival of the groom. (Maybe, that's why someone else is referred to as the best man.). One memorable ceremony ended with the respective families, both well charged with liquor, looking as if they were going to make the wedding a twofer with a funeral. The church *was* handy.

Marriage, the encyclopedia tells us "is an institution in which interpersonal relationships (usually intimate and sexual) are sanctioned with governmental, social, or religious recognition." Then, along came the gay-bisexual-lesbian-transgendered to raise the romantic stakes that much higher. If they thought that getting married would make them more mainstream, they got the wrong river.

Of late, even with the plethora of romantic movies, books and magazine articles, marriage seems to be dying off. It is much more convenient to come and go without having to formalize things unduly. That's how things used to be in the gay community. Maybe, we can leave all the reproducing to them, other than the occasional "mistake." They can adopt them. Everyone will be a lot happier.

My proclivities are pretty anti-matrimony, even though I committed it once. It was all the idea of my former in-laws who wouldn't have the good names of Fred and Mona Ulder sullied by the all-too-public thrashings of their daughter with a young articling clerk named Jack Prince. Fred was one of the managing partners in my former firm in Toronto, Whitmann, Richards, Illingsworth and Tisch. Finding me in the tender embraces of his only child, the supposedly winsome Wendy, in the firm's formal library during Christmas festivities was a bit more than his (or Mona's) social standing could take. A formal wedding, with the publication of banns, and a lush string orchestra in the poshest of Anglican cathedrals, erased many stains. Our divorce some years later completed the process.

I never did do divorce work: happy clients forget to pay; miserable ones are worse.

So, I wasn't really intending to watch Bobby and Myron Horschewicz bind themselves to a life of misery, torture and mutual loathing, however much fun it seemed. But word had gone around the office that a unanimous presence of legal aid lawyers was expected. I can't say if this came from the sternly affianced Megan, she of the blond hair, severe glasses and blazing engagement ring, who mediated on all things social, or our high priestess and messenger from the political gods, Carrie Anne Bloodworth. I can't imagine why *she* wanted to show up at the vaguely eccentric coupling of a political opponent other than to suggest that she was in touch with "evolving social norms." It wasn't quite mandated. There *was* the suggestion that our absences might result in our being tied to the back bumper of the wedding party's car, along with a number of tin cans.

Rollo isn't much of a church attender at the best of times so he didn't make too much fuss about being left behind. I wondered if Carrie Anne would notice, her nose forever prominent in the social, political and other winds.

The damage was to be committed in the local United Church. As I may have said, I'm more than a little familiar with the institution. The name of the Reverend Hugh Richard Herbert Prince is rarely used in the better circles of that church in the wilds of Ontario but there was a time that it was either a curse or a punchline there, sometimes simultaneously. I am more than familiar with church's politics, organization, liturgy and peculiarities. Let's just say that it was often referred to in our home as "The Church of the Eternal Happy Hour." And not just by me.

There aren't a lot of United Churches named after saints. Maybe, they realize that sainthood, while a goal, is unrealistic. Lately, they've tended to name them after parks, rivers, streets and rich benefactors. Older ones are named after religious affectations, like Grace and Trinity. This way they can avoid the excesses of "St. Peter and St. Paul in Bondage," "St. Justinian the Conqueror" or "Our Lady of the Freckles and Really Bad Skin".

Yamnuska Centre United had settled for the least offensive, if most obvious. It was a squat building from a time when bricks had been cheap or farmers, well paid. The end of the building abutting the street had a stained glass window that memorialized some long dead politician whose family had been left with more cash than good taste. On it, Christ stood, his hand on the head of a blond-haired child, as if there'd been a bit too much wine at the Passover Seder and Our Lord and Saviour was in need of a bit of a crutch. His eyes were a cross between the truly confused and the utterly mad. If He had taken one step forward, He would have crushed the lamb at His feet and possibly twisted the blond kid's head off.

The narthex (the part at the back where, being good Christians, everyone gets together and decides whom they're not going to sit next to) was pretty jammed with the somewhat dazed. I had the impression that not many of these people had ever been in a church. Or not much, recently. The affianced Megan was there, sparklie in one hand, fiancé in the other. She was especially confused. Church geography is just one more thing to pick up in marriage preparation class.

I looked for anyone else I knew. There's only so much nudging and cooing that I can take in even the shortest of weddings. I felt a hand on my elbow. Kathy Markle.

"I thought you Catholics went directly to hell if you ever darkened the precincts of a place like this."

"Jack, this is the wedding of the season and I will risk the wrath of Father Ron not to miss it. Now, behave!" This was matched with a squeeze, rather south of my elbow.

"Where's Brian?"

"Brian is at home. He's on the phone making homophobic jokes with some cattle rancher he knows in Montana."

"So, may I do you the honour of escorting you to the nuptials?"

"I thought you'd never ask."

We made it to the door where a rather younger—and scantily bearded—version of Bobby Cherry stood in a purple suit. His voice croaked. "Are you friends of the Cherry or Horshowicz family?"

I smiled. He looked like he needed it. "A bit of both, I'm afraid. But don't get us too close. You never know what's going to happen."

He almost giggled. Kathy was more formal. "Behave, Jack. We're in a church!"

"Don't worry. I've been in one before. Not much danger of bolts from the blue."

The kid found us a place, more or less central, somewhat to the back. Maybe, he was worried about possible accidental discharges, too. We settled into our pew and I began riffling through the hymn book. You never can tell what you'll find there. A flash of diaphanous organdy whisked by with a red-suited usher in hot pursuit.

"Ma'am. Ma'am." The speaker had hair to match his finery and a face to match it all. It was hard to tell if it was exertion, embarrassment or natural colouring. Behind him, puffing to catch up was a vision of silver: hair, suit and, no doubt, tongue.

Carrie Anne Bloodworth had made her entrance and I, for one, was impressed. Her outfit did much to emphasize the overlarge beak and gave me to wonder if it didn't have some more sordid uses. Kathy jabbed me in the ribs. "Inspector Serge Duceppe. Detachment Commander."

"Police?"

"You got it."

"What's she doing with him? I thought she had her eye on some staff sergeant named Merv."

"I guess she got a promotion."

"I've never heard it called that before. Does that mean that Bobby and Myron are about to become even more important?"

"Shhhh! Jack. This is a wedding."

"Is there a Mrs. Duceppe?"

"Yes, but she calls herself something else. She's French, you understand."

I didn't. "Where's she?"

"Home, I expect."

Someone behind us who hadn't heard that eavesdropping is considered rude, smacked me on the back. "She kept her maiden name."

I expected he was referring to the absent wife and decided it wouldn't improve my standing to add, "If not her maidenhead." I only nodded and smiled obliquely, which is probably the only accepted manner of smiling at such times and places.

Since gossip and listening in were now out of the closet, along with much else, I strained to hear the older woman in front of me scolding her husband (or whatever). "They prefer to be called gay, dear. No, I don't think Myron should carry a bunch of pansies."

"It *would* make a good bouquet."

Some people just can't be stopped.

Another voice. "I said that I thought an organ solo was a bit much. What's *your* problem?"

As if on cue, the music swelled into "The Impossible Dream". I started humming. I couldn't quite bring myself to sing. With the crescendo came a vision: Bobby righting "unrightable wrongs." The whole idea of "love pure and chaste from afar" was challenged by where we all were and why we were all here. Still, the whole idea of "one man, scorned and covered with scars" put me in mind of those magazine covers from my youth: a snarling, sneering lout, muscles gleaming, one hand clinging to a lithe and terrified blonde, the other firing off a submachine gun wildly at whatever ravening hordes --- commies, Nazis, militant vegans. Somehow, Bobby Cherry never struck me as the Tommy gun type. Besides, Myron isn't a blond. When we got to that "last ounce of courage", I'm sure I cracked the final note.

Some young thing drenched in gothic black was hauling on her swain, steering him into our row so we would all be a bit closer than was probably wise in the springtime heat. Her mouth was set but her words, clear enough: "Freddy, you aren't here to make a scene. No more jokes about who's giving away the bride. There isn't one. Why do you have to be so . . . prehistoric?"

The organist swung into "Someday Soon." That might have left the cowboy element somewhat mollified. At least, it wasn't "Cowboys Are Frequently, Secretly Fond of Each

Other." Less appropriate, but we weren't there to create a scene, Freddy or no Freddy.

Inspector Duceppe was nuzzling something into Carrie Anne's ear. I was going to call out "Get a room!" but recalled a bit of scripture: "In my Father's house are many rooms." Christianity always has a way of screwing up a good one-liner. Carrie Anne turned to him and commented loudly enough, "No, I think crossed swords might be taken the wrong way." That ought to give a new meaning to red Serge.

We were saved any further comments by a new music cue, "I'm a Backdoor Man." I hadn't figured Bobby for a blues guy. This caused a coming together of figures from all over the church. To our left, down the aisle marched what I took to be Bobby's sibling, flushed in his violet tux. A second brother, this time in deep blue was a shade behind him. They were met at the front by retainers from clan Horschewicz, one in red and the second in orange. From the wings of the sanctuary, Bobby, clad in sea-foam green, and Myron, in canary yellow, found their way to a space cleared for them in front of the communion table. All turned and faced the congregation as the parents made their way to a pew at the front, Mrs. Cherry howling into the wad of a handkerchief. If I'd had the nerve, I would have joined her.

And lo—this being a church such language is appropriate—lo, a minister emerged decked out in the whitest of robes with a multi-coloured scarf echoing the rainbow before us. Most of the congregation gasped, if that's the right word, and the organ was suddenly silent.

He was tall, his face only somewhat obscured by a Van Dyke beard, more commonly seen on the Prince of Darkness. I suppose Martin Luther might have been paraphrased to note that "the devil shouldn't have all the coolest facial hair."

"Brothers and sisters in Christ." I half waited to see if he might add something to illustrate the many who might find themselves somewhere in between, but he didn't. "We come together in God's house to celebrate the love and commitment of Robert and Myron and to join them into holy matrimony." I flashed on Bobby in the STD clinic but stifled a snicker.

"Marriage is an estate beloved of God. It is He who created our first parents, Adam and Eve . . ." He stopped, looked down at his text and blushed. He turned the page. "His Son, our Lord and Saviour, Jesus Christ, performed his first miracle at the wedding in Cana, turning water into wine, even as He turned the sinful into the blest.

"Marriage takes many forms and has many meanings. To some, it is a legal contract. To others, a remedy for lust. St. Paul famously said that it is better to marry than to burn with passion. Truly, this is so." He looked down at his book. He was confused. Mrs. Cherry had stopped her sniveling long enough to clear her throat. Bobby was looking at his shoes. Maybe, he was drunk. I was at my wedding. Myron simply beamed. I thought he might be pregnant. Who knows these days?

The good reverend flipped over a couple more pages of his book, then slammed it shut, placing it precariously on the baptismal font. He straightened himself and turned to Bobby and Myron, inviting them to join hands and face each other.

"Robert and Myron have written their own vows which they will recite to each other in the company of this congregation and the Holy Spirit."

Bobby squeezed Myron's hands and began. "From the time that I first laid eyes on you, my love, I knew we were meant to be one in the eyes of God. I pledge to you that my love has never grown less but grows more and more each time I hold you. I promise that I will always love you and that I will never lie down angry with you but will always be tender in our joy and supportive in our sadness that we might be together as one, always."

Well, that certainly drew a few gasps. I'm not a very visual person. I remain thankful.

Myron bowed his head slightly to his left and smiled at Bobby. "Bobby, you are my own true love. You are the sun of my day and the star of my night. You guide me to our love with your firmness and sensitivity. Before I met you, I was an empty vessel. My life was like a desperate desert. I thirsted in my loneliness for you and for your love. But that is all behind me now.

"I pledge and promise to you, my beloved Bobby, that I shall be faithful and true to you. I will look for support and caring from you and from no other. I will love you and be yours so long as we both shall live and I shall dwell with you in the warmth of that love, both now and forever."

By now, Mrs. Cherry was as red as her name suggested. Myron's father seized her and clutched her to his chest, the familiarity of earned kinship, I guess. Bobby's father merely sat there, his fringe of white hair now set off with a rising crimson.

The minister intervened and added the words required by the province to make this a legal and binding contract. No doubt, a collective sigh of satisfaction was released. I turned to Kathy and she was wiping a tear away. I assumed it was one of happiness. "Isn't it so beautiful?"

"Like poetry." She turned and I smiled.

Parents and siblings were all invited to the front and interspliced into a circle so that all might be blessed and the circle of life continued. Or not, I suppose.

"The families of Robert and Myron invite all assembled here to join them in the Memorial Hall just to your left as you leave the sanctuary for refreshments and celebration. Myron and Robert and their families will join us in half an hour after pictures are taken in the park. I would remind you that the use of confetti or similar substances is forbidden. It's simply too hard on our janitor" God's blessing and, I hoped, mercy were invoked and we stood for the wedding party to stomp its way out to a machine gunning of flashes. I, for one, thought kindly of that old custodian, so weakened by age and infirmity that tiny bits of paper broke his spirit.

* * *

Kathy and I left in search of a drink and Nanaimo bars. The hall was more or less empty, the smokers having retreated to the safety of clean air, and their friends, to stand on the curb. The room was decorated in paper streamers with "Robert and Myron" emblazoned on a blushing heart above a head table.

"Well, Ms Markle, I don't think that anyone will be serving us any time soon."

"Should we go outside?"

"Unless you want a tour of the Cathedral of Yamnuska Centre, the Apostate."

"What's an apostate?"

"A cruel name given to anyone who dares defy the will of Mother Church."

"It sounds vaguely sinful."

"Oh, you wish."

She giggled. I put my arm around her and we went on a tour. I am fairly familiar with the layout of most United Churches. After all, I spent or misspent much of my young life getting into places I had no business being. So, we slipped out of the Memorial Hall, capital *M*, capital *H*, and wandered in the general direction of the sanctuary. No one stopped us as we reached the front.

"Are we allowed to do this? I mean isn't this like the holy of holies or something?"

"You mean where we whip up the concentrated grape juice and whole wheat bread cubes?" She looked at me as if I were speaking Greek. "Of course, but then it's all grape juice and Wonder Bread. No harm; no foul."

"It was a beautiful service, wasn't it, Jack?"

"I guess." She smiled. I knew that smile. I liked it, too. So, I took her in my arms and held her.

"Are we supposed to do this? I mean here."
"Probably not."
But she reached her arms around my neck and kissed me. "Well, maybe we shouldn't."
"How's your little project with Brian?"
"You sure know how to cool the mood, Jack." She sat on a nearby, overstuffed chair, sighing. "Not well, if you have to know. I never thought fucking could be such a burden."
"Making love. You're in a church, you know."
"Yeah, yeah. With Brian, it's pretty much fucking. I've known guys that hammer nails with more sensitivity. And they take longer, too." She shook her head slowly and sighed.

I knelt beside her and put my hand behind her head. "I'm sorry. I didn't mean to make things any worse."

She smiled. Sadly, I thought. "It's okay. Let's get on with the nickel tour, all right?"

"This way, then, ma'am." She hooked her arm into mine and we wandered in the labyrinth behind the sanctuary. It didn't take long and the doors were all firmly closed. "And this, lady and gentleman, is the choir robing and music room. Note the stained and out of tune upright piano, a Kawai, if I'm not mistaken."

She squeezed my arm, then moved her hand down my back. I took her into my arms and kissed her. If Brian had been doing his duty, he clearly was not doing it very well. The more I touched her, the more she responded to me. We were on the floor in no time and, with the inappropriate rearranging of various bits of clothing, I was back in the saddle again. It was probably just as well that Bobby and Myron didn't have *that* song on their Top Ten List.

We lay there in each other's arms, she lying on my chest, smiling. I swept a lock of hair from her forehead and kissed her again. She kissed me. "Are you looking to do this again?"

"I shouldn't have done it the first time, Jack."
"Why?"

"Well, there's the minor matter of being married to someone else."

"So?"

"Isn't there a commandment about adultery or something?"

"Commandment is so strong. Maybe, a divine suggestion. I'm sure God knows how to wink. At least, I hope He does."

She pushed my face and laughed at this. "And there's the fact that we're in a church, for God's sake."

"Well, there was a wedding and I always figure that someone should get pregnant just before or just after a wedding."

"Oh, you do, do you?"

"Sure. Anything else?"

"Well, it doesn't feel right, you know, doing it in a choir room, right behind a church."

"Hell, fifty thousand choir masters can't be wrong."

"You're awful!"

"You think so? At least half of them were heterosexual encounters, too."

* * *

I didn't really know what to expect at the reception. It took a while for us to straighten things up so that it didn't look like we'd been up to exactly what we'd been up to. Fortunately, choir rooms have mirrors and we found a brush for our respective hairdos. Still, when you walk into that room, even if it's not arm in arm, you have a sense that everyone is looking at you, suspicious. You can almost see the winks and hear the back of the hand comments.

The Memorial Hall, big *M*, big *H*, was, by now, pretty much packed. Men had loosened their ties and poured entirely too generous amounts of rye into glasses, and only barely filled them with Coke or ginger ale. They talked about hockey and farming and the government, mostly just nodding at various slighting comments. Wives and girlfriends were seated about on chairs. Goodness only knows what they were talking about, other than the fashion statement that the rainbow wedding party had made.

Kathy drifted off to find a bathroom and I considered the liquor supply. Rye isn't my drink. If you want a lousy taste in your mouth and wake up the next day with a worse one *and* a hangover, rye is your drink. Besides, with the amount of Coke you end up taking in to get decently drunk, diabetes is a definite danger. I checked the bar out for a decent vodka, or even gin, but wound up with a commercial beer, which is better than rye, only because you can't get drunk enough to do serious damage.

Supper was called and Kathy and I sat together as if we were mere colleagues, which, of course, we were. But she smiled a lot. I was happy to see it.

The next table, significantly closer to the guests of honour, contained none other than Inspector Duceppe and Ms Nasal Sex, herself, Carrie Anne Bloodworth. Next to her, looking frightfully tolerant, was Myron's erstwhile political opponent, Jolly Jeff Wooster, constantly allowing the assembled throng to caress his hand, so recently added to the tiller of power in our province. It had all the pageantry of a papal audience. At one point, more people were so busy fondling Jeff Wooster that war could have broken out without comment or notice by most of us. And Carrie Anne seemed particularly entranced. Inspector Duceppe had that dark look of a man at a horse race, whose sure thing seems to be pulling up lame in the back stretch.

All this was interrupted by the tinkling of a knife against a water glass and the announcement of the wedding party. We stood. We clapped. All things considered, maybe we shouldn't have.

Once ensconced, the good reverend stood and intoned a blessing on Bobby, Myron and us all. Great gouts of overcooked beef was ladled out by women, well prepared for the task by years of serving harvest parties. Nothing would do but that some fool felt obliged to clank another knife against a water glass, compelling the blushing wedding couple to smooch. Frankly, after about three of such interruptions, I figure the only thing left would have been for Myron and Bobby to have cleared the head table and started the honeymoon early.

Once supper and the smoochfests ended, tables were withdrawn and dancing broke out. The wedding couple danced. The parents danced. The people danced. I asked Kathy, but she just smiled.

"I have to go. Brian is probably waiting."

"I can imagine."

"No you can't, Jack. And that's probably just as well." She looked down and smiled. "I had a lovely time, Jack. It was great." Then, she laughed. "The wedding was kind of fun, too."

DRAMATIZE YOUR IDEAS

I used to wake up to "morning television." Now, I don't. There's something about a perky blonde thing, coiffed in a mountain of perfection, burbling on about famine in Africa or typhoons in south Asia like she was going on about the shocking increase in mascara prices or that awful guy in the bar last night. Not that there's much difference to me. If I don't have to look at some naked skeleton, I don't think that much about Africa or Asia. Besides, I probably *was* that guy in the bar. It's just that anyone that chipper who greets me when I wake up had better be up to no good. And the last words out of her mouth—if she insists in talking at all — should show real gratitude. Begging doesn't count. Sighing's good.

But things weren't improved too much by the dulcet tones from my clock radio as I struggled to wake up.

> "Our lead story at seven o'clock: in a stunning turn of events, Minister of Justice and Attorney General, Ted Buchinsky has resigned from cabinet to be replaced by local MLA, Jeff Wooster. In his surprise announcement, the premier announced that Ted Buchinsky, elected only ten months ago has resigned due to ill health. His replacement will be local MLA Jeffrey Wooster, a political rookie and local

businessman. At the time of his swearing in, Wooster had this to say:

> "I may not be a lawyer but I bring to this position the common sense and clear thinking that has allowed me to find success in business, the values of family and faith that have stood this province proud throughout our history and the financial integrity to put our justice system on a course of efficiency and effectiveness that will be the envy of every province in this country."

A chorus of local worthies jibber-jabbered about how they felt that this was a real "feather in the hat" for Yamnuska Centre. I don't know anyone who really uses that expression anymore. The only hats anyone seems to wear around here are tractor caps and they usually look pretty silly with bird plumage dangling from them. I was reassured that somewhere in this little city, someone was keeping that special hat while a local bird was denuded, all for the sake of local pride. It did me good just thinking about it.

> "In related news, the new Attorney General didn't waste any time making it clear that he wanted to see changes in his department:

> "Things are gonna change. I think that all of us are getting pretty tired of spending millions of our tax dollars on vicious criminals. We've all heard about the country club prisons, the cable TV, the best food money can buy. Well, things are gonna change. I'm here to tell you that my department isn't gonna put up with this. We're gonna end all this luxury for a bunch of people who can't even be bothered finding real work, you know, those thugs and scum that think

jobs are for suckers, who live off the hard work and energy of our good people. So, things are gonna change."

Obviously, all my clients had been misinformed. They thought that going to jail was a bad thing. Years without freedom. Tedium. Surrounded by dangerous people who would as happily cut their throats as say "good morning." Here, it was like winning some sort of all-expense paid trip to Wonderland. Who knew? Jolly Jeff Wooster, for one, apparently.

> "Minister Wooster went on to say that the present 'Cadillac legal aid system' only serves to subsidize criminals and protect terrorists at the public's expense and would have to be reconsidered in light of present financial circumstances."

Since I had a quota of terrorists to protect, I snapped off the radio and went for a shower, where I considered the possibilities of inviting the perky blond from TV to my place for a little in depth coverage.

* * *

"Jack... I mean, Mr. Prince. Mr. Proper Witch is on the line."

I'd spent the early minutes of my morning considering whether a career change to criminal was appropriate. Criminals have all the benefits. They stay awake all night and sleep all day. No one keeps track of their hours and they don't pay taxes. If they don't like their boss, they just kill him. Or her. And, according to Jolly Jeff, they get Cadillac legal representation when they do get caught. Then, it's off to the Hotel Wonderful for two years less a day of the *Folies Bergère* and four-star cooking. What's not to like? They should give prison sentences out as prizes on game shows.

"Thanks, Gail. Cadillac Legal Services! My name is Jack and I'll be your concierge to all the extravagances a man could ever want."

"I musta got the wrong number. I'm lookin' for that Jack Prince fella." It was Harry. I guess he hadn't heard about the splendours of incarceration.

"You have tracked me to my lair, Harry. What can I do for you?"

"Prince? Jack Prince?"

"The very one."

"What's wrong with you? You on drugs or somethin'?"

"Not that I am aware of. What can I do for you today, Harry?"

"Oh, it is you! I thought you were someone else for a minute there."

"Just let me check." I put the phone down and had a sip of mint tea. "Nope, same old Jack Prince, I'm afraid. Now, what can I do for you?"

"I'm in jail."

"Then, you should be glad."

"I'm not glad at all. You sure you aren't on drugs, you know, one o' them happy pills?"

"My only drug is sunshine, Harry, and my happiness is to be but one small part of the Cadillac legal aid system of this province."

"Well, what's all this about me bein' glad I'm in jail. I am in jail and I ain't glad, not one bit."

"Oh well, I suppose word hasn't gotten that far north yet."

"Word? Word o' what?"

"Jail. I'm told it's now luxurious."

"What'er you talkin' about, Mr. Prince. Jail ain't changed and it's not luxurious or whatever you called it, either."

"Well, there you go. One day on the job and Jolly Jeff Wooster is transforming the entire system. Pretty soon it will all be swill and breaking rocks in the hot sun. Know any good work songs, Harry? A little *Hunh! Ahhh! Hunh! Ahhh!*"

"You been drinkin', Mr. Prince. Maybe, I should call back in a couple o' hours when you're, you know . . . sober."

"Couldn't be more sober, Harry. Just what did you do this time?"

"I didn't do nothin', just like always."

"So, does this 'nothin', just like always' have a name?"

"I don't get you."

"Harry, when they arrest you, they usually tell you what your "nothin', just like always" is. You know, like murder . . . or alarming the Queen."

"I still don't get you."

"What are you charged with?"

"Oh, that."

"Yeah, that. It usually helps to know what you're charged with so we can figure out little things like whether you should actually be there."

"They called it defamatory libel."

"What?"

"D-e-f-a-m-a-t-o-r-y l-i-b-e-l."

"They charged you with that?"

"Is it serious? Can I go away for a long time?"

"I don't even know *if* it's a crime. They still burn witches up there, Harry?"

"Hunh?"

"Oh good, this is where I go '*Ahhh!*'"

"I don't get you."

"Just a little jailhouse humour, Harry. Don't think anything of it."

"So, is it serious? I mean is it a crime?"

"I don't know. What do they say you did?"

"I got them signs on my van, you know."

"I seem to recall that."

"They say them sign's against the law. How can they be against the law when that other judge, the one on my appeal, said I had a constitutional right to have them signs? You tell me that, eh? How can they say that I can't have them signs when a judge says I can?"

"What do the signs say, Harry?"

"Nothin' too bad. You know, 'Them Cops Lied' and 'Moskilsippi: Kangaroo Court?' and 'RCMP, Crown, Railroad Justice in Moskilsippi?'—stuff like that."

I flipped open my *Criminal Code* and there it was: section 300, defamatory libel. Punishable by up to two years in the Chateau Crowbar, according to the next section.

"So, what's the problem? They aren't trying to keep you in custody for this pending trial, are they?"

"Whaddaya mean?"

"Aren't they just going to release you?"

"They said they would but they want to take my signs an' they say I can't put no more up on my van."

"So, let them have their signs and just wait. Once the trial is over, you can put all the signs you want on your van."

"They can't do this to me, Mr. Prince."

"They can unless you want to sit in there until you have a bail hearing."

"I ain't gonna lose my right to put signs on my vehicles to protest what I believe is unjust in this here town. I was on that probation order, right. You remember that, don't you? You were the one who took it to court and that judge said, 'Harry, you can keep your signs'. He said, 'You cannot take away Mr. Popowicz's rights away for freedom of speech.' Now, what they did today, it not only violates that section of the thing, is that, when I was in front of the police station, them RCMPs come out and I tried to go back in my van. He says, 'Harry. Wait. I'm not going to arrest you. I just wanna talk to you.' As soon as he got where I was standing, he just grabbed me by the arm and he says, 'Oh, anyway, you're under arrest.' So, I went, I went peaceably. Like, I don't resist arrest. No way! I can't afford to in this here town."

"So, you won't sign the undertaking that the police gave you?"

"I'm not givin' up my rights to no snivelly cop. This ain't Russia."

"Not the last time I checked but things change pretty fast."

"Whaddaya mean?"

"Nothing. Harry, if you want to get out today, you have to sign their undertaking. Otherwise, you'll have to go to court and see if you can convince the judge not to put that restriction on you."

"I ain't gonna do it. No way!"

"That's fine. Tell them you want to go to court."

"They'll do it?"

"Sure. Why not? It's what they do."

"Okay, but them guys ain't takin' my signs and that's the end of it. No way! I'll stay in here 'til Hell freezes over."

"Not likely with all this global warming. By the way, try the crème brulé. I'm told it's to die for."

"Hunh?"

I resisted the temptation to say 'Ahhh!' and hung up.

* * *

"Mr. Prince, I can't believe that you spoke to Mr. Popowicz like he said you did."

"Does that make you an agnostic or a true non-believer?"

Carrie Anne ignored me as she bored home. "He says that you were rude and simply refused to help him. Surely, that can't be true. Is it?"

I ignored the syntax. It would only confuse her. "You said it; it can't be true."

"Mr. Prince, that's not good enough. I thought you had at least some professionalism."

"Oh, I've got lots." I just left out where and what it might be. It was best not to antagonize Carrie Anne at times like these. It wouldn't do to raise the "Rage of the Bloodworths." Anytime, actually.

"He said that you don't care about him and that you want to see him dead."

"One thing you can say about old Harry, he certainly catches the flavour of things."

"What's that supposed to mean?"

"One good thing about Harry dead: the only ones who'll be disappointed will be the buzzards and worms."

"That's just what I mean, Mr. Prince. You have no sense of decorum or propriety. Wanting a client dead . . . Your sentiments are disgusting and unworthy of a member of the bar and an employee of this office. And I think they indicate some very serious problems on your part."

"No doubt about it. I've got problems and Harry's getting to be number one."

"Then, deal with him, Mr. Prince, and don't force me to come in here and give you a dressing down. And I suggest you direct *some* of that professionalism you say you have in Mr. Popowicz's direction before he goes to Legal Aid Central and lays a specific complaint." She gave me that haughty look, the one where you have to lean back so she doesn't swipe you with that beak. "Otherwise, I can tell you that they take complaints like this very seriously and I wouldn't want to see you caught up in the middle of the complaints process." It had all the menace of the threat of a visit from the Spanish Inquisition and I was quite sure that Carrie Anne probably made sure that the hot pokers had reached just that special temperature. Anything more would be . . . *inappropriate.*

"What do you want me to do about it? Harry's gotten himself in trouble, again, and he won't listen to good advice."

"Your attitude, Mr. Prince, has been a constant source of concern to me. I suggest you adjust it or there will be serious repercussions. Do I make myself clear?"

"Absolutely transparent." I smiled.

She turned crimson and headed for the door. "I expect you to deal with Mr. Popowicz in a professional manner by five o'clock."

I briefly considered the possibilities: proctology? Prostitution? Pathology? All worth considering in Harry's case. I gave her my most endearing smile and closed the door behind her.

* * *

I made it to Moskolsippi by mid-afternoon.

The court house was now freshly stickered with more dire warnings about things to avoid doing, having or thinking and some of the consequences for doing, having or thinking them. I briefly looked for gun emplacements, Dobermans and foul-smelling guards with rubber gloves. Seeing none, I advanced on the airport scanner.

"Not necessary, Mr. Prince. You are a member of the bar and are subject to a 10(d) exception."

"10(d)?"

"It's in the act. I'm sure you've read it."

"Nightly. I keep it with my porno stash, between *Not Quite Legal Nymphets* and *One Ton Trollops*. Those big girls're hungry for lovin', you know."

He was a young kid. He just stood there, his eyes flicking from me to my briefcase, then back again. His mouth opened, then closed. It put me in mind of a fish. I went to put the briefcase on the scanner.

"Ahh, that's ... um ... quite all right, Mr., uh ... Prince." He thrust it back at me. Once I'd taken it, he rubbed his hands, unconsciously, on his pant legs.

I made it to the court, just in time to see Harry standing before the judge, his white mane spirting out behind him, holding what appeared to be a copy of the Criminal Code and thrusting a finger in the general direction of the Judge. Harry looked the very figure of an Old Testament prophet. I wasn't sure if I should go in or not. With Old Testament prophets you always have to be worrying about burning bushes, frog-filled rain storms and rivers running with blood. Fortunately, I don't have a first-born son to worry about.

My mind was made up by a voice from behind me. It was Ada.

"Mr. Prince, could I have a little talk with you?"

"Harry's in there. I think he needs me right about now."

"This is about Harry, Mr. Prince. He's not well, you know. If he was well, he wouldn't be doin' this stuff. It's like he's gone all crazy like, you know."

"Ada, I really have to get in there..."

"This won't take long, Mr. Prince." That's a sentence that belongs in the same section of the "Liars' Hall of Fame" as "This won't hurt much" and "Things couldn't be any worse."

"All right, but I've got to get in there to deal with Harry."

"Harry'll keep, Mr. Prince."

I feared she was probably right and followed her into a witness room next to the courtroom. She took a good thirty seconds to lower herself from her walker into a chair, groaning and sighing as she did so.

"So, what can I do for you, Ada?"

"You gotta get Harry to stop, Mr. Prince. I ain't too good and he's not too good either."

"What's the matter?"

"I'm dyin', Mr. Prince."

Well, that's a real conversation starter. What are you supposed to say? "Sorry to hear that but it sure *is* a nice day." How about, "Will it be quick or can I step out for a coffee?" And there's the ever sensitive, "And how do you feel about that?"

I settled for the pseudo-sensitive. "I hope you're comfortable." If I had wanted to be a grief counselor, I would have learned all that supportive guff. I'm a lawyer. Supportive guff is merely grist for the cross-examination mill.

"Don't you worry none about me, Mr. Prince. I'll be just fine. It's Harry I'm worried about."

"Why is that?"

"He just can't do it, Mr. Prince. Can't do it."

"Can't do what?"

"Much of anything, if you ask me. I get him up in the morning and put him to bed at night. He just fusses and fumes about this stuff with the town all the time lately and I can't help him. It's like he's a dog with a bone is what he is. A dog with a bone."

"Yes, well, he can be pretty stubborn all right, Ada."

"Stubborn. He's stubborner 'an two mules in love, if you ask me."

I hadn't and was now glad I hadn't. "So, what am I supposed to do? Harry only seems to be happy when he's fighting with somebody."

"Well, you're the one with the fancy education, Mr. Prince. Surely, you can find somethin' to get Harry to stop bein' so bullheaded."

"I don't know what that would be, Ada. Harry's the way Harry is. He's not likely to change as far as I can see. The only thing that makes him stop making trouble is being in jail. And that only lasts so long. Sooner or later, he's out."

Ada snuffled at this. "That's all you can do? You can't talk to him or something? Lord knows I tried, Mr. Prince. Tried and tried. Nothin' works."

"I know you have, Ada. I know you've been a true friend and that's something Harry doesn't seem to have too many of."

She sniffled again. "Now, I ain't one to complain, Mr. Prince, but there's got to be somethin'. I don't have too much time left to me and this . . ." She banged her walker with her twisted hand and started crying harder. "It's just this, Mr. Prince. When I'm gone, who's gonna take care o' Harry, eh? He can't take care of himself and he'll just get crazier and crazier."

"I don't know, Ada. But you should start taking care of yourself." All right, so I do know a few, all-purpose phrases for the pseudo-sensitive. You can't be a preacher's kid and not pick up some of the jargon.

"Pffff! I'll be just fine when my time comes... as long as I know my Harry's gonna be all right."

"Ada, I've got to get in there. I'm supposed to be getting Harry out of jail right now."

She waved her little claw hand at me. "You get in there, Mr. Prince. Send my Harry home for supper, okay?"

* * *

As you may have noticed, representing Harry Popowicz was hardly the answer to a maiden's—or anyone's—prayer. When I got into the courtroom, Harry and His Honour were in mid-colloquy.

"Mr. Popowicz, you have a charge of criminal libel and a charge of failing to obey a probation order. Do you have a lawyer acting for you on those matters?"

"Your Honour, this is not what I'm here for today. I'm here for a show cause hearing."

"I beg your pardon."

"I was remanded, I was remanded on Friday."

"So you were. And that is why you are here."

"For a show cause hearing. Your Honour, I've got to be able to explain what happened in order and why I'm here today."

"Do you want a show cause hearing today?"

"Your Honour, I was..."

"Could you just answer my question, Mr. Popowicz? Do you want a show cause hearing today, yes or no?"

"Yes. The JP ordered it for today."

"Now, do you have a lawyer acting for you?"

"I contacted my lawyer today and he instructed me... well, I was told that he turned very ill and he isn't able to assist me because he's very sick. That's what his boss told me. She said, 'Harry, Mr. Prince is a very sick man.' That's what she said. She said, 'Harry, Jack Prince is a very sick man.' When I contacted her, Legal Aid, I mean, she said, 'Harry, Mr. Popowicz, you got no other lawyer that will take your cases because you've made all the other lawyers who've acted for you quit so, for now, I suggest'—she suggested that I come for the show cause hearing today and present my circumstances myself for the show cause hearing."

"That's quite surprising because I see Mr. Prince here in the back of the courtroom."

I smiled. "Rumours of my demise have been greatly exaggerated, I'm afraid."

Senuk's face did not betray any sense of humour. "So you say, Mr. Prince. So you say. I am wondering if you are acting for Mr. Popowicz on these matters before the court."

"Such is my fate, I fear, Your Honour."

Senuk sighed what I thought was a fairly judicial sigh and welcomed me up beside my client, whom I noticed was shackled on his feet.

"Your Honour, are these shackles really necessary? Mr. Popowicz is an innocent man — in the eyes of the law at least. He should not be bound up like a hog on the way to market."

"A very colourful metaphor, Mr. Prince."

"Actually, I believe it is a simile . . . like." I still couldn't get him to crack a smile. I snatched a look over at Cindy who was, by now, buried in a stack of papers. *She* seemed to be enjoying things.

"Quite, Mr. Prince. Just for your information, court security now requires all prisoners to be secured whenever they are in the presence of the court. We can't be too careful."

"Careful is one thing, Your Honour. Abuse is quite another. It is my view that chaining up prisoners is unnecessary and an insult to them."

"Mr. Prince, we frequently deal with very dangerous persons who are brought before this court."

"Then, they are the ones you might consider trussing up like chickens. Otherwise, people should appear before this court as they are—innocent until proven guilty, beyond a reasonable doubt." I am not really sure where this all came from but you never can tell when Carrie Anne will be ordering a transcript—just to check up on me.

"Mr. Prince, your colourful language is all very well. Whatever discomfort leg shackling may cause a prisoner is, in my view, quite minor compared with the overall danger that many prisoners pose to this court, as I am sure you are well aware. I, for one, am confident and comfortable with the new regime. As for any *tiny* impact that seeing a person in leg shackles may have on my sense of fairness, I believe that I can overlook it in coming to a fair and just resolution. Now, if we can get on with things."

Harry took this as his cue. "I would like to be able to explain why I'm here, why I'm here today, Your Honour."

"I know why you're here, Mr. Popowicz. You are here on a remand warrant issued by the Justice of the Peace. Now, you have a lawyer to represent you. Why don't you let him do so?"

"Excuse me, Your Honour. I have to be able to say the situation because I have to have due course, due process, so I don't end up in jail on remand and I have a right to explain the situation."

"Mr. Popowicz, Mr. Prince has come here today at tremendous expense to the people of this province who pay his salary. There isn't much point to his being here if you are going to represent yourself. Do you understand?"

"No, Your Honour, I don't. I was arrested in front of the RCMP station by one Corporal Morris and one Sergeant McAffee. Corporal Morris, I had a sign walking up and down the sidewalk and he come out the front door and he said, 'Mr. Popowicz,' and I started to go back to my vehicle across the street."

"Mr. Popowicz, this is not the time to get into the merits of whether you should be or should not be in custody."

"No, Your Honour, I'm geting to the point where—"

"No, you are not getting to the point. You are wandering, you are not even near the point. Now, do you want your bail or show cause hearing or not? Do you want it today, tomorrow, or the day after that?"

"When I was in the—"

"When do you want your bail hearing?"

"Sir, I already had gone in front of the RCMP. They wanted me to sign an undertaking, an undertaking in which I refused in the RCMP station because they had conditions on it. Then, I went in front of the JP with the document. She made changes to it because the document said, 'Mr. Popowicz is not allowed to carry signs, post signs anywhere, any place, at any time, any signs on my vehicle.' So she changed it to not carry signs that pertain to any police officers."

"Mr. Popowicz, you are not getting the point. You are here because a Justice of the Peace remanded you for a show cause hearing. I am not a reviewing court. This is not a place to institute *habeas corpus* to determine the lawfulness or unlawfulness of your arrest. I asked you if you had a lawyer. Mr. Prince says he is your lawyer. Do you want him as your lawyer? You have yet to answer that question. I have asked you, do you want a bail hearing this week? You have yet to answer that question. Instead, you are rambling about matters that I cannot yet deal with. Do you want a bail hearing, yes or no?"

"Yes, sir, I would like a bail hearing."

"When do you want it?"

"I was remanded, only three days I can be remanded and I need a show cause hearing today, Your Honour."

"You are not listening to me." He was puffy now, red. "Mr. Prince, perhaps you can be of some assistance."

"I hope so. We at Legal Aid are proud to be here today to provide a Cadillac legal aid system only serves to subsidize criminals and protect terrorists at the public's expense."

"Have you been drinking, Mr. Prince?"

"Not recently," I lied.

"I mean the same water that Mr. Popowicz seems to be using."

Harry took this opportunity to tug on my sleeve and start rambling into my ear. "Tell him about how them guys, them cops, have been treatin' me bad. Tell him or I will."

I turned to him and in voice that was quite distinct answered, "Harry, you don't buy a dog and then bark yourself."

"Who you callin' a dog? You can't be callin' me a dog. I'm no dog. Your Honour, my lawyer just called me a dog."

"I definitely have not been drinking his water. Perhaps, someone left the toilet seat up."

Cindy could not control herself. Her face now scarlet, she erupted into a fit of coughing.

Senuk threw down his pen.

"We will be adjourned for fifteen minutes until counsel and the court staff can each recover." He stomped from the bench.

Harry turned to me. "You can't call me a dog, Mr. Prince, even if you are my lawyer. I know that. You can't pretend that you can, neither. I'll report you to that boss of yours and then I'll report you to the lawyers association."

"Harry, why don't you just drag your chain back to your cell and give them a call. Quite frankly, if you get out, you better just watch yourself."

* * *

I thought I did quite a decent job of putting forward a panoply of good reasons why Harry should join the rest of us on this side of the bars, hauling only the invisible ball and chain that holds us all back from the very angels we might be. I may even have used that phrase.

The Crown didn't want Harry out. At least in jail, he was restricted to a list of people he could harangue by telephone for the ten minutes per day allotted him when not instructing counsel. She put up a wooden performance that consisted mostly of quoting various sections and case citations in a bored monotone. It was brief. She sat.

Judge Senuk sat there, pursing his lips and considering. He looked like a small child about to present his parents with an "accident" in his diapers. He finally spoke. "I'm going to reserve on this overnight."

"Your Honour, Mr. Popowicz has been locked in a very small room at the police detachment for three days, now. It is a room no bigger than the average bathroom, with no outside light and no communication with any person beyond a guard who comes by every fifteen minutes and checks to see that he hasn't done himself in. In my submission, it is unfair, cruel and, if I may say so, injudicious for him to remain there a second longer than he should."

"Mr. Prince, there is nothing cruel about Mr. Popowicz's accommodation. If he didn't like them, he could have gone along with what the police asked of him. He chose not to. I guess you could say he has made his bed; now, I don't want to hear him complain about having to sleep in it—if only for one short night. We are adjourned until 9:30 tomorrow morning."

* * *

I met Cindy at the courthouse door and walked down the street with her for all the free world to see. We passed the RCMP detachment building and I noticed Harry's truck in a lot at the back.

"What's that doing there? Don't tell me they're using it themselves, now."

"No, silly. It's been seized as evidence."

I looked at it again. It was still festooned with various screeds against the good burghers of Moskilsippi and those sworn to protect them. The writing was neat. I thought again of how Harry had missed his true calling.

I looked at the lot. "Shouldn't it be more, I don't know, secure? I mean, there isn't even a fence around it."

"Sure there is. Don't you see it?"

There was a single strand of wire along three sides of the lot. The fourth yawned open. "But there isn't even a gate."

"This is Moskolsippi. Who's going to bother stuff at the police station?"

"I guess."

"I've got two questions of my own."

"Oh?"

"Yeah. Where do you want to drink?"

"Wherever. What's the other?"

"You buying?"

* * *

I barely made it to court on time. Cindy, for her part, was already there and looked as perky as ever. We sat in the courtroom for ten minutes without a judge. I looked at her and smiled. She smiled back and shrugged her shoulders. "I haven't seen him yet this morning. He's usually quite early."

The Crown felt obliged to intervene. "Maybe, you should go look for him," she brayed.

Cindy got up and made her way to the door. She tugged at it but it wouldn't budge. So, she disappeared out the clerk's door and was gone. Ten, then twenty minutes passed. I chugged water from the court-provided pitcher. I hoped it was today's supply. It was fairly warm. I looked for a box of aspirin in the Legal Aid briefcase but found only Midol, left, no doubt, by one of my colleagues. They would do. I took a couple and tossed the bottle back in. Maybe, if I cramp up again next month, they'd still be there.

The judge's door snapped open and we were almost to our feet when Cindy emerged and said, "Just a couple of minutes." Back she went and fifteen minutes passed.

At last, she burst through and announced Senuk's return. He looked, somehow, sallow. His face was flushed and there was a trace of water dripping from his hair, now tacky and brushed carelessly across his scalp. His tabs were askew and a couple of the buttons on his vest seemed not to have found their holes. He looked as if he had spent a night deep in labour, refining a difficult, even precedent-setting, decision with the precise calculations of his finely tuned, judicial mind. The balancing of the rights of the accused and the needs of an ever-fearful state for protection against the predations of criminals is almost microscopic in its precision and its strictures played across his forehead in lines of concern and a determination for that exactitude that we all expect of those rare creatures so blessed by nature and training that they can sit in judgment of their fellows, in fairness and justice.

Either that, or he had been drinking even more than I had.

He raised his rheumy eyes to counsel and said, "I am releasing Mr. Popowicz on an undertaking to keep the peace and report to court on the day of trial. There will be no other terms or conditions. He has already been in custody far too long."

With that, His Honour rose and departed whence he had come. I turned to Harry. His breakfast of frozen waffles and coffee still stained the creases of his lips. If he were elated by his release, it was not obvious. "See what you gotta do to get fair justice around here. You just gotta do it yourself." He rose, dragged his chains across the floor to a cop who bent and, obligingly, freed him.

"You're welcome, Harry. All part of your Cadillac legal aid system that only serves to subsidize criminals and protect terrorists at the public's expense."

"Laugh on, funny man. You just laugh on."

"Harry, laugh and the world laughs with you. Cry and they'll probably just lock you up overnight—if you're lucky."

* * *

I was sighing and thinking about my return trip to Yamnuska Centre, when Cindy came out.

"I'm on my way for coffee and I bumped into you."

"Oh?"

"Yes, there's a new, non-fraternization policy for clerks and lawyers."

"What's that supposed to mean?"

"Clerks are forbidden to maintain friendships with members of the bar."

"Sleeping with you doesn't count?"

"So long as we're not friendly about it, I guess."

"But no non-patronization policy for judges?"

"Whatever that means."

"Precisely my point I think. What was all that about this morning?"

"With Judge Senuk?"

"Uh-huh."

"I'm not sure I can say."

"Even if I blackmail you for fraternizing with a lawyer."

She smiled. "You forced it out of me, you understand?"

"In an unfriendly way, of course."

"Of course." She smiled. "You remember what you said about Mr. Popowicz's cell being no bigger than a bathroom."

"Of course."

"Well, Judge Senuk went to the bathroom in his chambers last night but he left his security fob on his desk. He couldn't get out."

"How long before anyone realized he was there?"

"This morning."

"You?"

She nodded.

"What about his wife? Didn't she realize he didn't come home?"

"That's hard to say. Maybe, she wasn't paying any attention and just went to bed."

"Small wonder, I suppose."

"In a phrase."

"She can't be that bright: small things entertain small minds. I'll bet it'd be pretty hard to figure out if he was having sex with you or not."

"I think you got it with 'small wonder'."

"Well, if I see her today and she has a smile on her face, I guess we'll know."

About that time, a grey Volvo station wagon with a small, white-haired man barely peeking over the dashboard pulled out of the courthouse parking lot."

"You'd better scrunch down so he doesn't see you."

"Uncle Wilmer doesn't really care."

"Uncle Wilmer?"

She just smiled. "On my mother's side."

THE BEST OF ANY ARGUMENT: AVOIDING IT

"And I expect you to act professionally, Mr. Prince."

To this day, I have no idea where Carrie Anne had come up with all this "professionalism" nonsense. Had she been to one of those management seminars where everyone gets emotionally naked and reveals their innermost hidden secrets so they can break down the walls of authority and build collegiality? Was she secretly sipping legal *aperitifs* with Judge Morceau and his band of judicial jaw-slappers? Had she been dipping into the *Code of Professional Conduct*, all the better to rid herself of HRH Prince's wayward son by means fair or foul, like a report to the law society? Who knew? Quite frankly, who cared? But lately, every third word from her creamy-brown lips seemed to reprise some form of the word.

"I am the soul of professionalism, Ms Bloodworth. Utter the name Prince and the adjective, 'professional,' is assumed, I assure you." I had been on my way to my office, mail in hand, but hadn't managed to put the door between us.

The chocolate lips pursed and the eyes rolled heavenward. "Your recent behaviour in court has been reported to me by a source, Mr. Prince. I would hardly call it professional."

"That's just as well. The only professional sources in court are police witnesses and they are known to be practised liars."

"I beg your pardon."

"No need. We all know that nobody lies like a cop." I paused. "Or is it lays? I'm always getting confused about that. Anyway, you, of all people, should know what I mean."

"What's *that* supposed to mean, Mr. Prince?"

"Why Ms Bloodworth! As the head of this unit of Legal Aid, I'm sure you are well aware of the concept of 'testilying,' so favoured by the local constabulary." I hooked the doorknob with my palm and dragged the door open.

"Testilying?"

"Yes, I knew you are well aware of the fact that many of our constables, sworn to uphold the laws of this land and province, frequently add a creative touch here and an imagined, aggravating tidbit there, all to finesse the finer details of their evidence. As our director, I'm sure many of my colleagues have already brought this to your attention."

"Actually not."

I shrugged. "Perhaps, they've been much luckier than I." I was almost in the door.

"What's all that got to do with professionalism, Mr. Prince?"

"Just my point. I was so sure that, in some quiet moment, you could bring it up with your friend, Inspector Duceppe. I'm sure he must be quite concerned about it."

"What's Serge got to do with it?"

"Nothing, I hope. But then, I'm sure he'd want to be made fully aware of it so we can put a stop to this frightful business, immediately."

I was swinging the door behind me but she held it open. "I don't appreciate being given the brush-off, Mr. Prince."

"You don't mean . . ."

"Yes, I do. You think I don't know what's going on with your shabby, little practice and your disreputable personal life. I'm quite well aware of what's going on and it smacks of unprofessionalism at its worst. And don't try to deflect it with your puerile and jejune references to what you *think* is going on in other people's lives."

"Isn't that a tautology?" So I did go to the first three weeks of a course in logic until I realized that the prof was married and not particularly interested in my version of extra-curricular mark grubbing. You pick up things when you're . . . well . . . trying to pick things up.

"I'm not interested in your stupid deflections, Mr. Prince. Your dealings with Mr. Popowicz have been characterized throughout by objectionable conduct."

"That's just Harry. Think nothing of it."

"I was referring to *you*, Mr. Prince. And now, I hear that you referred to him as a dog. I couldn't believe it."

"Good."

"Good?"

"Sure, if *you* couldn't believe it, then it must be simply unbelievable."

"Do you deny it, Mr. Prince? Did you or did you not call Mr. Popowicz a dog?"

"I did not."

"I don't believe you."

"Then, why did you bother asking?"

"There will be a letter on your desk by close of business, today. Consider it a written reprimand."

"Consider this door . . . closed."

* * *

It didn't stay closed long. The day was hot and the office, relatively quiet.

"Mr. Prince, it's that Hairy Properwitch, again. Can you take the call?"

"Why don't you suggest that he take a long walk in the cool rain, Gail? I'm looking at the photos in my latest kiddie porn case and I don't want to lose track."

"But Mr. Prince, it's not raining and he's called three times today. He just won't leave me alone."

"I can sympathize, Gail, but the sexual harassment guidelines have prevented me from expressing it, myself."

"What's that supposed to mean?"

"Ask Dave."

"Who's Dave?"

"Isn't that the name of your fiancé?"

"It's Danny. I already told you that three times."

"Then, you have to stop calling out his name. 'Oh, Dave! Dave!'"

"Jack!" She flushed. I could hear it. "I'm putting Hairy through, Mr. Prince."

"Must you?"

Harry would not be denied, so I took the call.

"I'm gettin' sick o' all this stuff from them police types, Corporal This and Sergeant That. You know what I think? Them guys are in on it, too. Yeah, they're all part of this whole conspiracy to get me outta town. Stoppin' me and friskin' me and takin' my van away from me. They're all tryin' to take away my rights. I got rights. I got the right to have my van and put all the signs I want on it and they can't do nothin' about it. No way!"

"All right, Harry, what did they do now?"

"Ya know they got my van?"

"The one with all your signs on it?"

"Yeah. I ain't got another one. Maybe, if I did, they'd leave me in peace. Too busy pickin' on me and not arrestin' them drug dealers an' stuff an' all them guys on the reserve that's always gettin' into trouble."

"So, what am I supposed to do, Harry, write a poison pen letter to the police complaining that they aren't arresting enough drug dealers? Maybe I could sign it 'Concerned Friend of Harry Popowicz'."

"Laugh on, law boy! You just think this is just one big joke, a big, big joke, and you're the head comedian. I know you got your head so far up—"

"Harry, why don't you just go someplace and curl up and die?"

"You sayin' I ain't worth livin'? Is 'at what you're sayin'? I don't deserve to live? You'd like that, wouldn't you?"

Professionalism. It was the watchword of the day. I must be professional about this in my every word, thought and deed. There was no purpose of my descending to his level and acting childish. Nothing to be gained. I, at least, am a member of a learned profession and duty-bound to demonstrate professionalism at all times in my every dealing.

"Sure, Harry. Why not?"

"I've got half a mind to—"

"You exaggerate, Harry. I don't think you've got that much. Don't waste it."

"I'll be callin' that Carrie Anne lady. She don't think too highly of you callin' me down."

"I expect you've got her on speed dial, by now, Harry, but if you need the number . . ."

"Oh, laugh on, pretty boy. You're just gonna laugh yourself to death."

"Too bad you won't be around to see it, Harry." And I hung up.

Professionalism: a standard of knowledge, behaviour and practice accepted by practitioners of endeavours involving learning and a code of conduct, such as law and medicine. That about summed it up.

Maybe, it was more like dentistry: pulling teeth without anaesthetic. My teeth, in this case.

* * *

You can always count on bureaucratic prose to contain the leaden attraction of road kill. Actually, a few flies buzzing about might give it life. Roadkill feeds birds like ravens and magpies. And it even cleans up nicely after a good rain. All in all, maybe roadkill *is* more alluring. Far more.

Carrie Anne's reprimand didn't take long to arrive. It came by way of Gail shortly after lunch. I noticed that Ms Stockard had lent a deft typing hand to it. It wasn't just the CAB/Ds in the corner, either. Her leering smirk was more than enough.

"Dear Mr. Prince," it began. "Dear" was more a matter of formality than any suggestion of personal intimacy, I am sure. If she could have gotten away with something along the lines of "Look, you cretinous, chauvinist troglodyte," she would have. Well, maybe not. They *are* three- syllable words. Much too short. Not in her vocabulary, either.

> "Dear Mr. Prince:
>
> I have frequently been required to reprimand you verbally about your manner and attitude towards both staff and clientele. Your attitude demonstrates a complete lack of professionalism and sensitivity. Despite my many requests that you change your attitude and actions, you have stubbornly refused to do so.
>
> Most recently, I have been in communication with Harry Popowicz, one of your regular clients. His reports to me are disturbing. In particular, he has alleged the following:
>
> - It may be that you are having personal difficulties. If so, I suggest that you might, as during a recent trial you referred to him as a 'dog.' Our clients are human beings, Mr. Prince. Disparaging comments about them does not assist, particularly as many of them already have issues with self-worth.
> - You have indicated to Mr. Popowicz that you would like to see him dead. I trust that this was not an indication of your personal

views but more a form of frustration on your part. This comment is unfortunate and quite uncalled for.
- You have referred to Mr. Popowicz within earshot of staff members as 'Pop-off' and similar taunting references to his last name. Not only is this insulting and demeaning to a client, it is a clear violation of the Human Rights Code that we endeavour to support and foster in this office. Such references are offensive and must not continue.
- Your overall attitude towards authority figures is reprehensible. It betrays a lack of due respect for your superiors and other participants in the legal system. Your attitude must change if you are to continue as an employee in this enterprise.

You may wish to consult with one of the professionals at Kindred Personal Services Corp., the government's support service for employees with personal and addictions issues. Their telephone number is available from Ms Stockard.

Please treat this as your first and last written reprimand. The next step in any discipline may be a suspension or a more serious sanction. Please govern yourself accordingly.

Yours truly,

Carrie Anne Bloodworth

Chief Operating Officer,

Yamnuska Centre Legal Services"

I was in the process of figuring out whether to fold this into a paper airplane, shred it with great ceremony or use it to paper-train Rollo, when Gail waltzed in.

"It's that Pooper man again, Jack."

"I'm shocked, Ms Deare, truly shocked."

"Why? He calls you all the time, doesn't he?"

"But Ms Deare, your reference to him is insulting and demeaning to a client and a clear violation of the Human Rights Code that we support and foster in this office. Such references are offensive and must not continue."

"Have you been drinking again, Jack?"

"Only the elixir of political correctness as promulgated by our learned leader and final arbiter, Ms Carrie Anne Bloodworth."

"Oh her," Gail huffed.

"Ms Deare, that doesn't sound like a hearty endorsement of our beloved, hard-charging, ever-vigilant chief operating officer. What's the matter?"

Gail looked behind her and closed the door. Despite this, she almost whispered to me. "She sent me a letter."

"A letter?"

"Not a very nice letter."

"Ahhh!"

"She said I was ineffectual and bordering on an insubordinate clause or something."

"And what are *your* sins?"

Gail paused, looking confused, then checked over her shoulder. "Well, Dan and I sometimes—"

"Not that. What did she say you did wrong?"

"Just about everything. I was late twice and I talk to the other girls too much in the office and I talk on the phone to my fiancé. And I don't support her directions about you."

"A-ha!"

"But I'm not supposed to tell you about those."

"You haven't."

"And I'm not going to."

"What if I guess?"

"Even then. And I couldn't tell you, anyway."

"Not even if I bribed you?"

"No."

"Or blackmailed you?"

"Nah. Besides, you don't know anything about me."

"Then, I'll just make stuff up about you."

"You wouldn't dare!"

"What if I bet you that I couldn't guess it and I did?"

That confused her. "Whaddaya mean?"

"I'll guess what she told you and if I guess right, I'll give you ten bucks."

This really confused her. She thought hard about it. "Wait, wait, wait! Let's see if I get you. You'll guess something and if it's right, you'll give me ten bucks."

"That's right."

"What if you guess wrong? What do I have to give you?"

"That's too tempting, Gail."

"What is?"

"Tell you what, you don't have to give me anything. How's that?"

"Mr. Prince, there's a catch to this. I know. You're a tricky guy. But you can't fool me. Un-uh!"

"Un-uh, no you won't or un-uh, I won't fool you?"

"Huh?"

"Okay, first guess. Carrie Anne has been reading my mail."

"No fair. You've seen her reading your mail. That doesn't count."

"So, I don't have to give you ten bucks for that?"

"Why not?"

"Okay, ten bucks."

I was just fishing it out when she said, "Can I get ten bucks more?"

"What do you think this is, allowance time with daddy?" She giggled and looked at me. "So, there's more, is there?"

"Maybe."

"Let's see. She's been listening in on my phone calls?"

"I'm not going to say anymore but you owe me twenty bucks."

"What else?"

"No, I'm not going to get into any more trouble for you, Jack."

"She's got somebody reporting to her about what I do when I'm out of the office."

"Well, that's not quite right. Can I have the ten dollars anyway?"

"No. Not unless I get it perfect." I looked at her. She was smirking and trying to look away. "Not someone. More than one someone."

"Okay, I'm quitting at thirty."

"How about in the office? Has she got someone or more than one someone here spying on me?"

"Jack! I'm gonna be in real trouble."

"Okay, for the full fifty—are the secretaries in on it?"

She looked at me. Shocked. "But Jack, I never tell her anything. Well, not anything real bad."

I fished two twenties and a ten out of my pocket. "You'd make a perfect double agent, Gail."

Her eyes widened. "You mean like James Bond? And I could have a license to kill?"

"Why not? I'm sure Carrie Anne would love to give it to you on a one-time-only basis."

"Really?"

"Your secret's safe with me, Gail. Tell Dan from me that he's a lucky guy."

"Oh, I never tell Dan anything."

"I can tell. I'm sure it's better that way."

* * *

The Popper had hung up. It was fairly late and I hoped I'd escaped for the day. It wasn't to be. A new call came in at five minutes to five, just as good secretaries everywhere are packing up all their electronic gadgets, adjusting their game faces and donning whatever they need to meet the evening. My intercom buzzed.

"Mr. Harry Popowicz to speak with you on line one, Mr. Prince." It was Ms Stockard, almost winded from another day of stealth, low cunning and betrayal.

"Why thank you, Ms Stockyard. I'll take it in here." It was my plummiest voice. Anymore syrupy and I'd have caused an epidemic of diabetes.

I took two reasonably deep breaths and answered. "Why Mr. Popowicz, what a pleasant surprise!"

"I called you and you didn't bother calling me back. What kinda lawyer are you anyway?"

"That's what we call a moot point in my profession, Mr. Popowicz."

"I don't wanna listen to any o' your blabber about mutes and points and stuff like that. I'm upset."

"Oh, I am so sorry to hear that. Just what's the matter?"

"I'll tell you what's wrong, Mr. Prince, I'll tell you what it is. They're tryin' to believe take away my rights again, which has been proved in the Queen's Court that I have rights, even here in Moskilsippi. Sure there's conditions I have to follow, but I won't sit idly by and let them come up and say 'You can't put them things on your sign,' 'cause politicians all the time're accusing people for lyin'—one even accused the president of the United States of bein' a moron. Now, I got freedom of expression which means I can say what I want, especially when it comes to the word, liar, 'cause I looked it up in the dictionary. It means lie, but it also means somethin' that's not true, to gain somethin'. In my case, which is going to be appealed, I got document proof that that's exactly what happened."

The words were English. Some of them actually formed sentences. But I don't think I've ever heard them put together in quite that way. Harry had done some homework, obviously. It's just I didn't know whose homework it was.

And he didn't even let the dog eat it. Maybe, I should lend him Rollo, the SALTEA dog.

"Help me with this, Harry. What *are* you talking about?"

"Them cops. They took all my signs on my van and my van too. So, when I made some new signs, they took them too. Now, I'm tellin' them cops, if they want to do something about that they can take me to civil court and sue me for defamation but they can't stop me from protestin'. As far as you go, Jack Prince, I'm on a probation order right now and keep the peace and be of good behaviour is already on that one and I'm having a lot of trouble here voicin' my opinion under the law. When I do something legal, I don't' believe that should be in violation of a probation order and it shouldn't be no crime, neither."

"Let me see if I've got this, Harry. I know they took your van because it had all those signs on it."

"Yeah, an' they're sayin' it's evidence. How can it be evidence when I didn't do nothing wrong and, if I did, they can take me to civil court and sue me for defamation? They can't stop me protestin' all the corruption and inside deals that go on around here, can they? You tell me that, Jack Prince. You tell me that."

"Harry, did you get more signs?"

"You're damn right I got more signs, real good ones, too. And I'm gonna show them signs all over this corrupt town if I have to ride a bicycle to do it, you can be sure of that, for sure."

"Be sure to wear a helmet." It seemed a good closing line.

"Why would I do that? Are you trying to tell me somethin', Mr. Prince? You been talking to them guys and didn't tell me?"

"No, Harry, I wouldn't want anything to happen to you."

There was a silence on the other line. I thought he might have fainted. Silence on a telephone line with Harry Popowicz is about as likely as a female pope. Finally, "Whaddaya mean by that? Is that a threat?"

"No, Harry, it is not a threat. It is a simple observation. You could get hurt. You could even get killed."

"How do you know that, Mr. Prince? You tell me that. Somebody been talkin' to you? Somebody tryin' a kill me?"

"Kill you, Harry? Why would anyone want to do that?"

"You tell me."

"You're the one with the enemies, Harry. I'm sure if some of them got their way . . . you'd be dead." He hung up and I said into the now buzzing phone, "And if I had my way . . ."

AROUSE AN EAGER WANT

I stumbled onto it quite by accident. I was cruising the internet in search of something to keep me from thinking about Carrie Anne and the Popper *and* Judge Senuk *and* all the rest. I should have been working but I did charge the time against Perry the Perv's file, in case Carrie Anne needed to have the full seven and a half hours accounted for. And Perry's problems wouldn't really cause me much grief.

Perry? Well that was another matter. Perry had formed an unwholesome affection—you might call it an obsession—for women's sneakers. In the best of all possible worlds, this wouldn't have been any problem. He could have found himself a job cleaning up the women's locker room and he sniffed away to his heart's content. Unfortunately, Perry hadn't found such a job and, given his unbroken string of seventeen charges for possession of stolen property, to wit: women's shoes (subclass, sneakers), there wasn't much hope that he would. There is something about a compulsive shoe sniffer that puts people off, including those who hire folks to clean up the ladies' change room. It's not as if he did much to them. The shoes were all perfectly re-usable—after a careful washing. And Perry liked virgin shoes—not for him some sneaker that he'd had time with, like some all too familiar girlfriend or wife. No, Perry liked his playthings freshly used. It wasn't as if he discriminated as to which foot it came off, either. Perry wasn't a *complete* pervert.

So, when the police, armed with a warrant from the local judicial vending machine, crashed his door in and discovered thirty two single sneakers, assorted sizes and feet, from Adidas through Saucony, Perry was pretty much busted. For the eighteenth time. In a world of low hanging fruit, Perry pretty much picked himself. There wasn't much to be done. I suppose someone of greater ambition might have suggested psychiatric treatment but Perry had long ago exhausted the local psychological fixers. He was going to jail for about eighteen months, where he'd have to get his jollies sleeping with his nose to the feet of his roommate. It would probably cost him a few decks of cigarettes but sex is a thing that is paid for—one way or another.

And jail was pretty much inevitable. In Judge Morceau's mind, today a sneaker fetishist; tomorrow, who knows? He might graduate to high leather boots and we all know where that leads.

So, I was cruising along the Infobahn, as at least one bureaucrat insisted on referring to it, on Perry's nickel, as it were. I came upon an article that told me that some European government or other was passing legislation to grant equality status to gorillas and other primates. Basically, they felt that, since they could use simple machines, communicate with picture boards and earn scale in the movies, apes should be accorded something approaching equality with their near cousins, human beings.

Why not? We've accorded equality to everyone else, including Perry the Perv and the Popper. They have the right to take abuse from Judge Morceau or Senuk and the equal opportunity to sleep on the top bunk at the local hoosegow. Lately, they had an equal chance to be represented by Jack Prince, Barrister and Solicitor, Terror of Crowns and *Locus Classicus* of Yamnuska Centre Legal Aid.

I sort of figure it's time that all these apes and their ilk pulled their weight financially, anyway, and gave Harry and Perry a bit of a break on the off-the-wall stuff.

The door cracked open. It was Gail. She checked behind herself and slipped in.

"Aren't you supposed to be getting ready for court, Jack?" She'd obviously peeked into my research project. "I mean Ms Bloodworth doesn't want any of us looking at anything on the net."

"Well, Carrie Anne thinks we'll find pictures of her there so we can blackmail her."

"Really?"

"Sure. Didn't you know, Gail? In her youth, Carrie Anne paid for her tuition at Bible school by pole dancing. Can you believe it?"

"Not! She doesn't look Polish to me."

"There you go, then. She's fooled us all, then."

"You don't think I should say anything, do you?"

"No, we'll keep it as our little secret." I nodded conspiratorially. "What brings you to my lair, Ms Deare?"

"Pardon?"

"It's your name, Gail."

"Oh, yeah. Right."

"So?"

"Oh, I'm supposed to remind you that you have to go to court for Mr. Properwitch tomorrow. Is that okay?"

"Which, the going or you're telling me?"

"I don't get you, Jack."

"Just as well. I don't think the fiancé would approve."

"Huh?"

"Thanks for telling me, Gail."

* * *

The trip to Moskilsippi was becoming so familiar that the car knew the way without much help from me. I suppose, if all else failed, Rollo could take the wheel and make most of the curves. Given his predilection for things narcotic, he might just run into that young cop and find himself charged with impaired driving. I mean Rollo gives urine samples out on every pole and fencepost, almost daily. The cop wouldn't even need to make the demand.

Harry's defence to the defamation charge was what the law refers to as "mistake of fact." As I recall from first year criminal law, if a person honestly believes in a certain course of action which is not illegal and proceeds on that basis, he lacks the necessary intent or *mens rea*. He is, therefore, not guilty. Don't worry about *mens rea*. I'm told it means a guilty mind. Which is not to be confused with a dirty one. Thankfully, or I'd be doing life. My theory was that, whatever the truth of what Harry posted on his various placards, signs and other confused writings, he, at least, believed it. Best of all, everyone thought he believed it. It was a no lose proposition. It might even work, too. It isn't too often I actually have a well thought-out defence. At worst, it would make things last until late in the day.

I figured I could stretch things out until about 4:30, which would justify my staying overnight (with any luck) in the arms of dear Cindy. We had a 1:30 start time and I was confident that any Crown worth his or her salt would waste a couple of hours drawing the evidence out of the mouth of five or six cops, all saying more or less the same thing. I figured it would take a good fifteen minutes to clear security, anyway. By now, Senuk had probably approved body cavity searches and random drug screenings just to get into the building.

I parked in front and more than the usual number of spectators had gathered. They were dressed up in more than the usual frippery for court. The only people I know who wear suits to court are lawyers, who have to, and undercover cops who prefer them to wearing the uniform and thirty pounds of hardware about their belts. Someday, one of them is going to faint and have to be righted by a crane.

I made my way through the throng to discover that Judge Senuk was now doing weddings on the side. They probably paid better. The bride, all of about a hundred pounds of her, including a soon-to-be-born child, was smiling like a model in a condom commercial. The groom had that trapped, "What do I do?" look. I wanted to suggest he take my car and leave it abandoned on the road where I could find it in time to return it to the government garage the next day. I've been married. Machines that kill or mangle your body are infinitely preferable.

It was almost time for me to amaze and dazzle with my fancy legal footwork. I looked for the airport scanner and the usual guards and retainers. They weren't there. I was astonished but thought it had been moved to the courtroom door. It was not. And no guard, either. In fact, even the signs had been taken down. We could have been in a strip mall.

I made it in the door in time to miss Ada, who was calling my name from somewhere behind me. Harry was already there, hefting the Bible as if about to use it in some religious form of shot put. With flowing white hair and purposeful mien, he could have joined Team Old Testament Prophets.

We were called to order and stood for His Honour, an electronic security card now dangling from a band around his neck. He looked at me and actually smiled.

Something was definitely amiss.

I looked at Cindy. She smiled back. It made me wonder.

"Is the Crown prepared to begin the matter involving Mr. Popowicz?"

It was my old sparring partner of things Popowiczian, Ms Couture. She seemed a bit haggard. "I was wondering if I could have a few words with my learned friend, Mr. Prince."

Until she added my name, I was about to look around. I smiled. I'm nothing, if not adaptable.

"Of course, Ms Couture. Take as much time as you'd like." With this, he smiled again and rose lightly from the bench. He didn't use the electronic security card, just opened the door. "Let the clerk know when you need me."

I've read some science fiction, when I couldn't find erotic thrillers to fill my rainy Saturday afternoons. I was thinking, drugs? Body doubles? Or maybe, a full on replacement. The thought of the real Judge W.C. Senuk somewhere in the control of a supposedly superior race of space travelers gave me pause. In a contest of mind control, my money was on Senuk. Up until they resorted to the dreaded anal probe, that is. I smiled at the thought. It might do him good.

I was jolted from my reveries by Ms Couture. "Mr. Prince, could I have a word with you." I walked towards her. "Outside."

I wasn't sure just why I would want to consult with her "outside" as she put it, but I went. She didn't look too fearsome. We found a room and locked the door against invasion. She sat at the table. I leaned against the wall.

"Just what are you intending to use as your defence in this case?"

"Ah, well that might just be telling."

"I have researched the law on this charge."

"In the original Latin?"

"What's that supposed to mean?"

"Oh, I don't know. I rather thought this sort of thing had gone out with the stocks and dunking old biddies to see if they were witches."

"Oh, it's been charged a number of times. On conviction, I think we would be asking for substantial jail."

"Do you have the facilities?"

"What do you mean?"

"Aren't you going to have to find a dank dungeon or heavy stones to press him? You know, *peine forte et dure* and all that stuff."

"You really *are* a strange man, Mr. Prince."

"It's Jack and I know. You should see where I live."

"I think I can do without."

"Ah, but I can't. I need it day and night, day and night."

"I'm not that interested in your sex life."

"Well, actually, neither am I and I think I'm the one who should be."

"I have a reason for calling this meeting."

"Other than to discover my defence, cunning and crafty as it is?"

"And to share in whatever bizarre fantasies run through your brain. Yes."

"Ah well, and sharing *is* a generous activity."

"I can imagine. I am prepared to take a plea to anything you want to make this thing go away."

"What sort of plea?"

"I don't know. Cause a disturbance. Mischief."

"Oh, you mean a *guilty* plea."

"That's usually what we mean when we speak of taking a plea."

"Oh, well, I don't think so."

"Don't you think you should take this to your client?"

"Why? What's he got to do with it?"

She threw up her arms at this and made an interjection that sounded something like "Plewgh!"

"Well, if you put it like that, I guess I'll just have to take it to him for his careful consideration."

"Fine. I'll wait for word from you."

She left and I summoned Harry who came, pushing Ada in a wheelchair. He answered my question before I could even form it. "Walker's busted, wrecked." Ada gave a look that suggested it hadn't been an accident.

I told them what the Crown had offered. Harry, for once, was quiet.

"I think you should take it, dear." Ada could probably use the time to get another walker.

"Well, you tell me this, will you, Mr. Prince? And I want it clear from you so I don't have to ask a lot of questions. You tell me this—what are they asking for?"

"A guilty plea to something other than a serious offence that would put you in jail for a while."

"Well, you tell me this, then, and I don't need a lot of your lawyer talk, neither. What do they want me to do? I mean, I been to their jail a whole bunch of times. They just keep puttin' me in jail and I don't like it much, you understand?"

"I guess that's why they make jail unpleasant. So, you don't want to go back."

"Well, I don't know. Just what do they want me to do? I'll tell you what they want me to do. They want to put me in there with a bunch o' drunk Indians an' hope they kill me, that's what they want, isn't it?"

"I don't think they've gone that far, yet, Harry."

"Oh you don't, eh? Well, let me tell you this, Mr. Prince, an' I know what them guys're like, you know. They'll just keep puttin' me in jail for longer and longer times until one day they'll just put me in there forever. That's what they'll do."

"Oh, Harry, don't be like that." It was Ada and she was almost crying as she leaned forward in her wheelchair. "Harry, why do you have to fight with them all the time? It's not worth it. I mean, I don't have too much time left and all you want to do is fight with them. Why, Harry? Why?" Trust Ada to sum it up so well.

"But it ain't right, Ada. You know that. I gotta fight with them 'cause they just won't leave me alone. You know that, don't you?"

"Harry, who's goin' to take care of you when I'm not here? You can't fight them alone, you know."

"But I gotta keep fightin', Ada. It's what I hafta do." He had a pained look, as if explaining this for the fourth time to a particularly dim child.

Ada turned her chair to the door. "All right, Harry. You do what you hafta. Just do what you hafta."

"I take it that means no?"

* * *

I informed learned counsel for the Crown of my client's decision to put them to the legal test. She said nothing, just pursed her lips and returned to the courtroom. Cindy called for the Judge and we were back at it.

Ms Couture rose. "I—I mean the Crown is ... troubled by this case as it is obviously a clear case of a recalcitrant accused taking things to extremes. We are particularly troubled that it is this accused who has been before you so many times before."

Ordinarily, I would have objected to this diatribe. I mean, the Crown can call its evidence, see what it is and, then, make whatever comment it wishes. That's the way it's done. There was no jury to impress and I figured Judge Senuk was either impressed or not, long before he heard a word of evidence. But I was running out the clock so I would have an excuse to stay the night.

She continued. "As I am sure you are well aware, the accused, Mr. Popowicz, has spent much of the last year testing the patience of this court and the local authorities."

His Honour chose this point to interject. "I am aware that Mr. Prince is not making any objections to your statement, Ms Couture. But I am equally aware that what you are saying is more in the nature of a closing statement. Will you be calling evidence or not?"

Just like the old poop to put the law between Jack Prince and his less worthy desires.

Couture continued. "I am laying out ... I mean, laying this out for Your Honour so you can be aware of the position of the Crown."

"I am more than aware of the position of the Crown. It is frequently for sending Mr. Popowicz to jail for more and more time. Am I wrong?"

"No, Your Honour. You are quite right."

Ah, a bit of random candour from our friends at the Crown's office. This was a red letter day. I was hoping for further revelations. Besides, the clock was moving . . . but so slowly.

"Then, are we going to have Mr. Popowicz's trial? I have other things to do." I flashed to the wedding party. Maybe, he had another couple penciled in at 4:30. I made mental note to send him a CD of "Wedding Favourites." Maybe, he could consider franchising. My old firm could do a bang up job of setting the whole thing up.

"Ah, yes, Your Honour. The Crown does not feel that it should proceed on this matter at this time."

"Are you withdrawing the charge, then?"

"No, uh, we don't feel that that would be the best course of action."

"Then, call some evidence. Get on with it! I don't want to tell the Crown how to do its business but we have things we can all be doing. Call your first witness, Ms Couture."

"The Crown . . . does not . . . have any witnesses, Your Honour. We believed that Mr. Prince would accept our very generous offer that we made to him in the hallway."

"I don't want to hear about any offers, Ms Couture." I summoned a vision of His Honour sticking his fingers in his ears and singing, with closed eyes, "Lullalullalulla." Instead, he turned to me. "Well, Mr. Prince. What do you have to say?"

"Your Honour, I have come to court today, with my client in hand, ready to defend him against the scurrilous allegations hurled against him by an unfeeling Crown." That's not what I said. I wish I had. Purging is good. Instead, I simply replied, "I'm waiting for the Crown to call some evidence."

"Well, Ms Couture, the ball's in your court." I hoped that the Crown looked upon it as a tennis metaphor.

She sighed and threw down her pen. "Fine, Your Honour. The Crown directs a stay of proceedings in this matter."

A stay is a freezing of the charges for a year. After that year, it's as if nothing ever happened. I explained this to Harry outside the courtroom, taking as much time as I could.

He shook his head. "That's no good. I want you to appeal it."

"What?"

"I didn't get no chance to tell the court about all the things that they been doin' to me. It's not right, Mr. Prince, not right."

"Harry", I said, shaking my head, "You can't appeal a stay of proceedings. It's over. Go home. Take care of Ada. It's over."

"I want you to file an appeal, Mr. Prince. Appeal, right now. I don't want to hear nothin' else—no stays or whatever. I want an appeal. I got my rights, right in that Charter of Rights thing." He was almost singing it as he turned and started wheeling Ada away.

"Harry, why don't you just go find a nice cool ditch and die in it? I don't know why you feel you've got to be the centre of attention. Someone should just finish you off."

He turned and for the first time I actually saw him angry. "You'd like that, wouldn't you, Mr. Prince? You an' all them cops an' everyone would just like me to go away an' die, wouldn't you?"

"You don't seem to have any other, useful purpose in life, Harry. Except for Ada, I don't think anyone cares what happens to you. *I* certainly don't."

"I keep you in business, Mr. Prince. You only got a job because of me. You think I don't know. Ms Bloodworth told me all about you and your job. You just better hope I stay alive a good, long time. That's right, Mr. Prince, a good, long time."

"No job is worth it, Harry. So, go find a hole to curl up in before someone digs one for you."

Our raised voices had attracted a crowd. Even the groom from earlier had returned. He couldn't restrain himself so he asked me. "What were you two yelling about?"

"Life insurance. I recommend it."

* * *

I decided that Carrie Anne didn't need to know how long the trial took. I waited until 5:00 for Cindy, who was able to leave work within seconds of quitting time.

"I heard you and Mr. Popowicz had a bit of an argument."

"Just a discussion about tactics."

"Oh?"

"I have some. He doesn't."

"You don't like him much, do you?"

"Nope."

We walked a bit farther and I put my arm around her.

"Not here. People will see."

"Well, how about a drink, then?"

"I can't."

"Why not?"

"I told you. I'm not allowed to be friends with any lawyers. Another memo just came down."

"How about sex? You don't have to be friends with me to do that, do you?"

She smiled. "You think so?"

"Sure. Husbands and wives do it all the time and ninety percent of them can't stand each other. So?"

"So, if you want to get together, we can't do it where anyone can see us."

"Is that a yes?"

She gave me directions and we parted . . . just, not as friends.

* * *

There was time to kill before our meeting so, once I had found a motel room, I went to the bar.

The biggest difficulty with this bar was that it was dark. I found a place to sit which wasn't part of the libido lottery playing out among those so inclined. I ordered a scotch which, of course, they didn't have. From what the waitress told me, they had little that was vaguely potable, at all. So, I ordered something that I figured had to have been distilled and, was, therefore, unlikely to carry any fatal bacteria.

I was on my second and considering the time and my level of intoxication. She was what is euphemistically referred to as "full-figured." Had she been a car, she would have been advertised as "mid-sized," in deference to her ability to take curves. Somehow, in the murk, she had found her way, unerringly, to me. Her name was Sally, although she pronounced it, "Shally." Had I been a police officer, I would have had reasonable and probable grounds to require a breathalyzer. This being a bar, it seemed superfluous, even a bit rude.

She parked herself by my side and demanded my name, which I gave her. I tried looking into the half-distance, as if in search of my better half. Being a gentleman—for the first ten minutes or so of any encounter—I tried not to look down her dress directly, although it was clear her allurements were already well displayed.

"You gonna to buy me . . . a drink?" I was glad that she could focus enough to get a whole sentence out, however slurred.

"Sure. Why not? What are you having?"

"How about 'Sex on the Beach'?"

"A bit cool this time of year, don't you think?"

"Har, har, har! You're a funny guy, you know, Jack. Real funny!"

"Glad to be so entertaining. But what would you like . . . to drink, that is?"

"I tol' ya. Sex on that Beach."

"So, it is." I summoned an appropriate figure from the mists and requested that potion. When it came, it had a price tag that suggesting either gold inlays in the ice or the going price for the particular act. I paid. She hoovered, demanding another.

She finished a third and proceeded to lick the inside of my ear. I hoped I had washed it this morning and made a note not to leave her alone with Rollo.

I tried to stand up. "Where ya goin', Jack? You're not gonna leave me here aaaall alone, are ya?"

"Uh, I've got a busy day tomorrow and I need to get my beauty rest."

"You don' need no beauty rest, Jack. You're already real beautiful. I like you." She moved the arm that wasn't draped across my back down to my crotch and proceeded to rub. "Don't you like me, Jack? Hunh?" She flipped her hair out of her eyes and it flopped right back. "Donchu?"

"Yes, Sally, you're simply wonderful but I really must be going."

She stood with me. "I'm goin' with you, Jack. We're gonna pardy, okay?"

"Do you think that's wise, Sally? I'm sure you came with someone and he's probably looking for you this very minute."

"Ah, that fucker! He's passed out in the john with that slut, Shirley McMurchie. I seen 'im an' I told 'im, 'You gonna boink a skank like Shirley McMurchie, I'm gonna fin' my own.' That's what I said to him. You think that's right, Jack? Eh? You think he should be boinkin' Shirley McMurchie? Do ya, Jack?"

"I don't know Ms McMurchie. What's she like?"

"She's a tramp," she slurred. "A skank. That's what she is."

We'd made it to the door and I started down the street, trying to outdistance Sally. What she lacked in speed, she more than made up for in volume. "Wait for me, will ya, Jack! Wait up!"

I tried ignoring her but finally gave in.

"Sally, I'm going to take you home, now. All right?"

"Sure." She giggled. "You take me home."
"Where do you live?"
"I don' live nowhere."
"Everyone has a home somewhere."
"No' me. I live with Donny an' all he wants ta do is boink Shirley McMurchie. Boink! Boink! Boink!" She started to cry. "So, I don' have a home no more. I live with Donny Boy an' all he wants ta do is boink that shkank, Shirley McMurchie. I don' have no home no more."

The tears came fast. "Sally, I need to know where to take you. So, tell me where you live."

"I wanna live with you so you can boink me an' boink me, just like Donny an' Shirley McMurchie." She grabbed me and slobbered all over my face what I thought was intended as a kiss. I would need a shower.

In the end, I took her to my room and set her on the bed. I went to the bathroom to clean up. I returned to find her passed out, completely naked, splayed on the sheets. I put some covers over her and told Rollo to take care of her. I hoped the noise of starting the car wouldn't wake her.

Just doing my bit for interspecies equality.

* * *

"Remind me again why we're meeting in the middle of a sheep pasture."

"So my father won't find out."

"You mean he doesn't know you've got sheep. Maybe, when he called you Mary he should have noticed the little lamb that was following you around."

"They're his sheep, silly. Of course, he knows he's got them."

"But do they know?"

"Who? The sheep?"

"Yeah."

"What do they care? They just eat all day, poop out those little round things and every so often a bunch of them go to market and the other ones don't even seem to notice."

"I bet you didn't know about the movement to grant them equality rights with people."

"Sheep?"

"Among others. It's a growing movement in Europe." Cindy made this little hissing sound. "You laugh now."

"I'm not laughing. I just made a sound like I can't believe it."

"Well, believe it. And when they get their rights, you just wait. They'll be hiring guys like me to enforce them."

"You're kidding."

"I hope not. I have to be careful to make sure I don't get you pregnant."

"Well, I better not. I drove three hours to get these pills. They better work."

"How many did you take today?"

"Just one. Why?"

"That's not good then."

"What isn't?"

"We've already done it three times. What if it only the first one works?"

"Well, if it doesn't it's too late now. So, let's see if you're up to taking another chance."

* * *

Four *was* my limit. Any more and I'd have to take multi-vitamins. I'm against doping in sports.

We lay in the back seat of the government car just being contented. We'd probably steamed up the windows but I didn't care. Cindy was a thoughtful lover. She'd even brought some wine. With that, we didn't need to worry about staying warm. Besides, we had body heat. Quite a bit of it.

She kissed my chest and nuzzled me.

"Why did we have to sneak out here with the sheep and the lambs? We could've done this in my room at the motel."

She giggled and sat up on one elbow. "I've lived in this town practically my whole life. Everyone knows me."

"I'm pretty good at smuggling people in and out of hotel rooms, you know."

"I can imagine. You just don't know what a small town is like, do you Jack?"

"I've lived in a few."

"Well, in Moskolsippi everyone knows what everyone is doing all the time. If you go to the bathroom more than five times a day, someone will calling Doc Smythe to see what's wrong with you."

"I'm sure people have sex in Moskolsippi. I mean I've seen a few children about. You don't just smuggle them in from nearby villages, I hope."

"They're almost all legitimate. Kids marry here at eighteen, nineteen and have their kids while they're young. My parents were only seventeen and eighteen."

"A religious thing?"

"Pretty much."

"And you're an atheist?"

"Maybe, just an agnostic."

"So, I've sullied your chastity, I guess."

"Don't worry about it. You're not the first."

"I think I figured that out about time number three."

We lay back and enjoyed the moment. Cindy was suddenly up and upset.

"What time is it, Jack?"

"I don't know. Maybe four, four thirty."

"I've got to go." She reached around for her clothing, finding most of it.

"What's the hurry?"

"My dad. He gets up about five thirty to pee. I've got to get in before then. Otherwise, he'll hear me."

"So? You're an adult, Cindy. Surely, he knows that."

"You don't know my dad."

"The jealous type?"

"Don't joke about it, Jack. I'm serious. First, he'll take a strip off me and then he'll come looking for you—with a gun." She groped around.

"What are you looking for?"

"My panties."

"I don't see them. Do you need them?"

"Probably not."

"Well, if I find them, I'll mail them to you. Here or at the office?"

She didn't say so I got up with her and opened the door. The flock had moved our way. Mostly, they just lay on the grass, some chewing their cuds like some secretaries I could mention. It all put me in mind of all those Bible stories about the shepherd and his sheep.

Cindy straightened herself up and combed her hair with her fingers. I helped her, then leaned in for a parting kiss. It was sweet. I can't say why but I opened my eyes and saw a large ram, sort of a stringy fellow, wall-eyed and angry looking.

"What the hell is that?" It seemed a reasonable question, she being a sheep lady and all.

"What?"

"That." By now, the sheep was trundling towards us, his head down. He seemed to have a serious intent to leave us damaged in some way. I pulled Cindy behind the car, which he used for target practice. I heard the left fender crumple. There would be an interesting explanation when I returned the government car: a stationary collision with an angry sheep.

Cindy turned. "That's Psycho Sammy. We better run for the fence." We did.

"Psycho Sammy?" I was puffing for breath and scraping the occasional bit of sheep pasture off me.

"Yeah. He's my father's ram. He's sired over three hundred lambs."

"Well, I don't know much about sheep but his technique seems to be something out of the Marquis de Sade."

"Who?"

"A French guy."

"You knew him?"

"Not intimately."

"Probably from Quebec, right?"

"No. France. He was into painful sex." She looked at me. "No, not just careless guys; whips and stuff."

Cindy just looked at me. "You mean you go in for that kind of stuff?"

"Not willingly."

"So, how do you know about it?"

"Just like you know about sheep. It's something just I picked up somewhere, I guess."

"You mean, like VD?"

"No." I checked her out to make sure she was okay. There were a few wisps of hay in her hair but she looked fine. So, I kissed her again. I'm like that.

"I've got to go. We'll do this again sometime?"

"Wild horses couldn't keep me away." I said nothing about psychotic sheep.

She was gone in a second and I was left with the problem of getting back to my car without finding myself on his horns. Sammy was sneaking a peek every so often, before turning his attention to his flock. He seemed to be more interested in them than in me so I crept in the general direction of the car. He saw this and whirled . . . as much as a two hundred pound ram can whirl. I have to say that I panicked about that point and ran headlong into the flock who shambled to their feet at this point and began milling about. Sammy was left on the horns of a dilemma, as it were: his girls or the guy trying to cut in. It gave me barely enough time to make it to the car and start it up.

Sammy was not to be dissuaded. He wasn't psychotic for nothing. He charged the car once again. Frankly, psychosis is rarely synonymous with smart. I caught him on the bumper and he was tossed aside. I stopped and checked on him.

I was certainly glad they hadn't amended the constitution to protect animals just yet. In one collision, Sammy had lost his rights to life, liberty ... *and* security of the person. I didn't wait to check further. I drove out the gate and back to Moskolsippi.

* * *

One of the skills I perfected as a teenager was re-entering the house, at all hours of the night, undetected. This is necessary if you are given to all-night rambles and your parents are creatures of domestic habit. Well, my mother was, at least.

I managed to open the door of my room and signal to Rollo not to leap up and greet me. Being the faithful canine companion that he is, he raised his head, rolled his eyes and yawned.

He was relishing his night in the sack with Sally. She lay there on her back, peacefully snoring, the sheet pulled down to her waist.

I pulled my clothes off and slipped in beside her. Rollo was not impressed and let me know it. Sally snorted, said something in her sleep and rolled over onto her side. I was left uncovered and Rollo took the opportunity to lick me once, rather impertinently, I thought. I hauled on the sheet to cover myself and tried to claim what was left of a night's sleep. This was just enough to waken my companion.

She rose, blearily, tossed aside the hair that covered her eyes and said, "Who the hell are you?"

"Jack Prince. Don't you remember?"

"I didn't ... you know ... with you? Did I?"

I smiled. "Well, we're here, aren't we? I hope it was good for you, Sally."

"Oh God, God, God! Oh my God! Oh, jeez!"

"What's wrong?"

"God! If Don finds out, we're finished. You won't tell him, will you, Jack?"

"Who's Don?"

"He's my boyfriend."

"The one with Shirley McMurchie?"

"You know Shirley McMurchie?"

"Only by reputation."

"Well she's got one, I can tell you." At this, the hangover hit her and she left me. I heard water running in the bathroom and she came out. She had a wet face cloth that she held over her face. Given her clothing situation, that didn't seem the most strategic location. She lay on the bed facing me, tossing the face cloth onto the floor behind her.

"So, we did it last night?"

"I don't know about you but I did it four or five times."

She groaned. "Oh, God! God! God!"

"What's wrong?"

"I've only ever done it with Don. I love him, you know. I was saving myself for him."

"I don't follow. You've done it with Donny but you're saving it for him?"

"It's a chastity thing. We're promised to each other and I said I'd never do it with anyone but him and now I've done this."

"What about Don or Donny or whatever? He promised you, too, didn't he?"

"Yeah." She started to cry. "That's different."

"Really? How?"

"He's . . . you know . . . a guy." She sobbed. "And now, you and I . . ."

"Do you feel like we did something last night?"

"No. I guess I was too drunk. I must of passed out."

"Well, if you don't feel like you did anything last night, why do you have to say that you did?"

"Donny'll know. Guys know this stuff."

I kissed her on the forehead. "No, they don't."

"They don't?"
"Nope."
"So, it'll be just like nothing happened?"
"Pretty much."

This seemed to satisfy her. She lay back and seemed to drift off. Then, she got up on her elbow. "Hey, what's your name, again?"

The temptation to lie was almost overwhelming but I didn't, for a change. "Jack."

"Jack, I don't know how to ask this but I've got to know."
"What's that, Sally?"
"Can we do it . . . you know . . . one more time so I can see what it's like—with someone else?"

* * *

Command performances are rarely the best and I was thankful to finish and get some sleep.

She woke me about 7:30 and we showered together. She wanted to and I needed someone to wash my back.

I invited her for breakfast but she begged off. "I gotta find Donny. We got to get back to Springdale."

"Springdale?"

"Forty klicks down the road. We can't party there. People all know us. I wouldn't want my old man to know what I been doing."

The logic of this escaped me and I escorted her to the door. She stopped.

"Something happen to your car?"
"Where?"
"The left fender. Looks like you hit something."
"Not that I remember. Must have been kids."

I dropped her off downtown and went looking for a car wash.

ADMIT YOU'RE WRONG

I was late getting back. To be honest about it, I was about a day late getting back. No one seemed to notice. Carrie Anne's door was closed. That meant either that she wasn't in or she was in hatching whatever diabolical plots intrigued her at the moment.

Gail got up immediately and came to me.

"Jack . . . I mean, Mr. Prince. How are you?"

I looked at her. She seemed distressed. "Don't tell me, Gail. Carrie Anne has just been snatched away by the Forces of Darkness."

She stood there confused. "No, she's at Legal Aid Central for a meeting. Isn't she?"

"Ah, close enough." I swung my suitcase into my office. Rollo dodged aside and found his favourite resting spot. It wasn't hard. He'd more or less worn a hole in the floor and the drool had peeled the wax off in an almost perfect circle.

"I heard. It was just horrible."

"What was? Harry's getting off. All the skillful work of a day or so. Nothing for anyone like me, I'm afraid."

"Oh, that just makes it sadder and sadderer."

"No, Gail, my dear. It was a victory, total humiliation of the Crown and all its forces. Not just a technical skirmish but a major rout. The day was ours!"

"Not Harry's, Mr. Prince."

"Of course it was Harry's. Who else shared in my total humiliation of Her Majesty and All Her Unhappy Minions, but the estimable Harry?"

"Not Harry, Mr. Prince. He didn't win nothing."

"Perhaps, I've missed something Gail. Just what has dear old Harry lost this time? His welfare cheque? The keys to his liquor cabinet? Ada?"

"Harry's dead, Mr. Prince. You would probably say the Popper has popped off but Mrs. Stockard said that was bleak humour and there's no place for it in this office."

"Harry's dead?"

"As a doodoo bird."

"That's fairly dead, as I recall. Well, if not dead, certainly dying. What happened, Gail? His ego get over inflated until he exploded? Popped as you so gracelessly put it?"

"Oh no, Mr. Prince. He was run down on the highway." She leaned in to me. "The police think it was flour play."

"Foul play?"

"Yeah, that."

"When did all this happen?" I was desperately hoping for a time just after I actually left Moskolsippi. I didn't need Carrie Anne figuring out that I'd cost her a night in Bidy Bye Inn. I could have saved her the money for all the time I'd spent there.

"They say it was either late last night or early this morning. They're giving him one of those autosoapy things. You know."

"An autopsy?"

"Yeah, that."

"Well, I sure hope they don't have too good a look at his brain."

"Why's that, Jack?"

"They'll probably need a microscope."

"Oh, really? Is it that rare?"

"Yeah, Gail. That."

* * *

Things were always a lot quieter when Carrie Anne was out on one of her missions to the godhead—Legal Aid Central. Even Stockyard took it down a few notches and mostly sulked in her corner. I mean Igor isn't much of a threat when Dr. Frankenstein is off knouting the serfs or whatever he does in his spare time. So, I heard them come in.

The police, I mean. Gail showed them in and I invited them to sit.

"Mr. Prince, I'm Sergeant Dowd and this is Corporal Guthrie. We're from Major Crimes." He made it sound like it had to be capitalized.

"Have a chair, gentlemen. Or should I say have a chair *each*?" Dowd looked at me in a somewhat strange manner. Guthrie made a note on his little pad. I, for one, sat down.

Dowd fixed me with a glare. He reminded me of too many of my former employers at Whitmann, Richards, Illingsworth and Tisch when they were about to lower the boom on some poor associate for not bringing in enough coin. I was mostly exempt after I scored the boss' daughter for however long, but I knew the look.

"We've heard of your little jokes, Mr. Prince."

"Ah, the notable Prince charm. Quite." Guthrie made another note. I wanted to help him out by spelling "charm" but I left it at that.

"I would have thought a man of your situation would be far more thoughtful, Counsellor. A man has died." He spoke the words like a misguided undertaker. They were flat, almost metallic. Besides, anyone who refers to a lawyer as "counsellor" has already made up his mind.

"Yes, the unfortunate Mr. Popowicz."

"I understand he was a client of yours, sir?" It was a question. But then, as the song says, "A question ain't really a question, if you know the answer too."

I shot a glance at Guthrie. He sat there, pen poised. I guess they'd already worked out what they were going to ask. It saved the need of bringing along a court reporter. They cost a fortune. I nodded.

"Is that a yes, Mr. Prince?"

"Except among certain tribes in central Africa, as I understand it. There, it's apparently an indecent invitation among the menfolk for a short tramp in the tall grass or anywhere discreet, I suppose." Guthrie got this look on his face. Confusion doesn't really cover it. He looked to Dowd who just shook his head, trying to make it look part of his act.

"Do you really think a joke is appropriate at a time like this, Mr. Prince?"

"No?" I tried to make it sound as much a question as I could.

"I thought not." He looked down at the notes he was carrying. We were straying a bit too far from the script for his tastes.

"So, when did you see Mr. Popowicz last?"

"At the courthouse. He'd just won his case and we wished each other a fond goodbye."

"Uh-huh." He checked his script again. "We heard you threatened him?"

"Not that I recall."

"So, maybe you did and you can't recall it?" He was going faster now, the gears and transistors whirring. Guthrie was having trouble keeping up. Maybe a court reporter would have been worth the expense.

"No, I'm pretty sure I'd remember threatening a client. We don't do it all the time."

"Mr. Prince, I have witnesses from the court house in Moskolsippi who are prepared to testify, *under oath*, that you told Mr. Popowicz, and I quote, 'You could get hurt. You could even get killed' or words to that effect. Did you or did you not utter such a threat against Mr. Popowicz?"

"I may well have said it but it wasn't a threat."

"More of a *promise*, then, sir?"

"More of a casual observation, sergeant." I turned to Guthrie. "That's casual, with a *c*."

"Was 'You're the one with the enemies, Harry. I'm sure if some of them got their way, you'd be dead' another one of your . . . *casual observations*, Counsellor?" There was now some venom in his questions.

"Pretty much."

"Is this the way you deal with all your clients, Mr. Prince? Doesn't sound too professional to me."

"Very few of my clients are like Mr. Popowicz, Sergeant. Is there anything else? I have things to do today."

"Just this. John Appleby Prince, you're under arrest for the murder of Henry Latham Popowicz. You have the right to retain and instruct counsel without delay. If you cannot afford a lawyer, Legal Aid duty counsel is available to you twenty four hours a day. You need not say anything. You have nothing to hope from any promise of favour and nothing fear from any threats. Anything you do say may be taken down and used as evidence against you. Do you understand these rights as I have read them to you?"

"I'd look pretty stupid if I said 'no,' wouldn't I?" I looked over at Rollo. He was studying something on the floor.

Sergeant Dowd stepped back. "Corporal, if that dog moves, shoot it!"

Rollo yawned. I was glad Guthrie didn't take everything literally.

They patted me down and handcuffed me tightly behind my back. Together, they hauled me out through the office. Everyone was standing there watching a mini version of my 'perp walk.'

"Nothing to see here, folks. Just go back to what you were doing."

"Call Scottie, Gail. He'll know what to do." It was all I could get out before I was shoved in the immediate direction of the front door.

Carrie Anne walked into the office at that point. "Put the phone down, Ms Deare. I'll take care of Mr. Prince's lawyer."

I guess she'd greased her broomstick to get back from LAC so quickly.

* * *

What they don't tell you in books or on TV is what it's really like to be arrested. When you hear the words, you are frozen. You feel an adrenalin rush like no other: pure fear. Your blood turns to sludge and your mind clicks off like a circuit breaker. If I had broken into a confession of everything that I had ever done, legal or not, it wouldn't have surprised me a bit. If I'd broken into a tuneless version of "Swanee," in black face and on one knee, it wouldn't have surprised me, either. Mostly, I'm glad that my mouth didn't work at that point. The way things were going, I was sure there'd be an extra charge of political incorrectness fluttering about the courts, along with first degree murder. I could imagine the information: "John Appleby Prince did, with malice aforethought and without colour of right, break into a racist parody, contrary to the provisions of the *Political Correctness Act* and all measures of good taste and musical acuity."

I was hauled off to the detachment, relieved of my shoe laces, belt, tie and self-respect. A swarthy member of the RCMP leaned me against a wall and gave me a mauling that probably amounted to a fairly complete sexual assault. Put it this way: if I did that to most women I have known, biblically and otherwise, I would have been in bed—or traction—in a trice. Then, one hand holding up my pants, the other in the firm grasp of my accoster, I was escorted to a cell.

Television portrays jail cells for people just arrested as bull pens, full of the detritus of the world—tattooed, hairy, bulked-up and homicidal—all looking at the new fish like avid sharks. My cell was not the least like that. In many ways, it was worse. Aside from the white concrete walls, it was furnished entirely in stainless steel. The toilet, thoughtfully positioned *facing* the cell camera, promised evenings of chill blains for my legs and bottom. The bed consisted of a plastic mat and a wool blanket perched on a stainless steel platform. There was enough room to pace. The only light came from a bulb, well protected by a plastic shield, some ten or eleven feet up in a corner.

The morning was quiet and I passed the time reviewing the latest gossip from several fine works of tabloid art. I am still pleased to know that there's a boy in Saginaw, Michigan, who is now treated well after years of taunting, all because he has the body of a shark. His teenage years in front of him, I can only imagine the first time he takes a girl to lover's lane. With his luck, she'll have crabs.

About noon, a slot in the beige door opened and I was served a hamburger and tea, all compliments of a local Chinese restaurant. That took all of about three minutes to devour. I was left to my own devices and to choose between rereading "The Shark Boy of Saginaw" or sleeping. I figured my dreams were better written.

Of course, that meant that the investigators took it as a signal to drag me out, clutching my pants, down a hallway to what they called the interview room. It was a rectangle with a table against one wall and a grey, metal chair beside it. A second chair, this time on wheels stood in the centre of the room. I was directed to sit on the grey chair while Sgt. Dowd perched on the rolling one. He had a file that he placed on the table and tapped several times with a pen. The file had my name on it with some sort of cross-reference to the late, now lamented, Harry Popowicz.

"Do you recall the rights and warnings I gave you when I arrested you?"

I nodded.

"You can't nod. This is being recorded and they can't hear a nod."

"I thought it might just rattle."

"What?"

"Old joke. I thought you might know it."

He cleared his throat. Either he was a smoker or he had slipped a few cogs. "Right." He tapped the file a few more times, flipped it open, then closed it again. "You do acknowledge that you have received your rights and warnings?"

"Mm-hmm."

"Words. I need you to say the words."

"Which ones?"

"Yes or no."

"Okay. Yes."

"That's better. Now, have you had a chance to call a lawyer, yet?"

"No."

"Do you want to call a lawyer?"

"Sure."

"We can make arrangements for one if you'd like."

"I would."

"Fine." With that, he got up and left. Three minutes later, he came back in and led me out to a room roughly the size of two coffins. "You know the number?"

"Nope."

"So, who do you want to call?"

"William James Wallace MacLean with Legal Aid in Sunareka."

He stiffened. I didn't know if I'd uttered the charm to get me out of this place. "We don't pay for long distance calls."

"Well, I don't have my calling card on me and they won't let me use my home number."

"That's your problem, Mr. Prince. We'll get anyone you like—locally, that is. Whaddaya wanna do?"

I thought about troubling the office. That didn't seem like a very good prospect. None of the lawyers there were much use in my fix. Carrie Anne probably put me in here. That didn't leave much. I'd be better off with my shoe laces tied to the lever on the toilet in my cell.

"I guess I'll deal with it later."

"You don't have to, Jack. You can call any local lawyer."

We trudged back to the interview room where we were joined by Cpl. Guthrie, pad in hand. He'd brought his own chair. I was glad. Otherwise, I'd have been forced to stand.

We went through the usual waivers of rights all over again, then Dowd sighed. "Well, Jack, what do you have to say?"

"Nothing."

"Come on, Jack. We know you and the deceased didn't get along too well. We got lots of witnesses. I'm sure anything you did was only because of your frustration. I mean, we all know that Mr. Popowicz was a very difficult client. We've had our dealings with him, as you know, and you've had your problems, too. We know that. So, tell us what happened here."

"Nothing."

"Jack, we've got a body in our morgue and something happened to it. Why don't you tell us?"

"What?"

"What you did with him."

"Nothing."

"You did nothing to him or you have nothing to say?"

"Both, I guess."

"Now, Jack, we've had our little differences over the years. I can appreciate that cops and lawyers don't always get along too well. But let me tell you, I've got an awful lot of respect for you. Cpl. Guthrie here, he's got a lot of respect for you, too. We all do. Just because we're on the opposite sides of things doesn't mean that we can't reason with each other. So, how about it?"

I shook my head.

"Now, Jack, that respect I been telling you about, it's about being a man and doing the right thing. And we both know what the right thing is here, don't we?"

I nodded.

"Great! Now we're getting somewhere. The right thing is for you to tell us what happened here so we can all put it behind us. How about it, Jack?"

He made it sound like I should confess to killing Harry and then we'd all go off and have a beer somewhere—just us guys. I shook my head.

"Jack, I'd hate to think that you aren't man enough to admit your mistakes. Are you a man, Jack?"

I tried to look puzzled. What did he think I was? A centaur? Shark Boy?

"Come on, Jack. I know you know Ida, Harry's girlfriend or wife. Doesn't Ida deserve some closure, Jack?"

"Ida?"

"Yeah, Ida. Harry's old lady."

"Ada."

"Oh, right. Ada. I musta got that wrong." He made as if to correct his file notes. I noticed Guthrie didn't. "So, Jack. I can call you Jack, can't I?"

Since he hadn't ever asked and since he knew my middle name, I didn't really care either way. I shrugged.

"Jack, don't you think that Ada needs some closure? Now, you've started to open up to me and I can tell you're not a bad guy, right? So, you wouldn't want this to drag out too long, would you?"

I sat there. So far, we'd blown a morning and a bit of the afternoon.

"Jack, don't you think that Ada needs to know that Harry's killer has owned up to things so she can rest easy? She doesn't need a long trial and testimony and all that stuff, does she? I understand she's not too well, herself. You wouldn't want her to pass without knowing who killed the man she loved, would you?"

I never thought of a trial as that much of an inconvenience. From my point of view, the guy showed up in my office or at court. He pleaded not guilty. Some months later, I'd show up and we'd have ourselves a little trial. If it was

Morceau, it was mercifully short, if unpleasant. If it was Senuk, not so short and about as unpleasant. So, I looked at Sgt. Dowd and shook my head.

At that point, "Mutt" Guthrie stood up and threw his notes on the desk.

"Look you piece of shit shyster! We got you!" He threw open the file and tossed some photos on the desk. They showed Harry, not at his best. He was lying on what appeared to be a roadway with his left arm and leg askew and the back of his head bashed open. "You did this, you fucking coward! You ran over a helpless old man and you didn't even have the guts to stop. So stop wasting our time!" This last was shouted not three inches from my face. I'd have to have the nurse check my hearing when I got to my next stop on the penal highway.

"Gordon, Gordon. Sit down. Calm yourself." It was the ever reasonable Sgt. Dowd. "I'm sure that Jack wants to tell us what he can, don't you, Jack? So, what is it, Jack?"

"I'm confused."

"Good. That's a good start. Why don't you go on? What are you confused about? What happened between you and Mr. Popowicz? You can tell us."

"No, that's not what I'm confused about?"

He was soothing. "So what is it, Jack? Tell me. Maybe I can help."

"I'm sure you can."

"So, go on. What's all this that's confusing you?"

"You remember telling me 'you need not say anything'?"

"Of course, Jack. We respect your rights. We wouldn't be very good as police officers if we ignored rights, now would we?"

"True."

"So, what's the problem?"

"Well, I don't want to talk to you at all. I have absolutely nothing to say. If I've learned anything over the years, it's that clients give away the store when they start talking to cops."

"Only the guilty ones, Jack. You know that."

"Oh, okay. Then, I've got nothing to say. I'd like to go back to my cell now. Shark Boy is waiting."

I didn't see him even move. Guthrie was in my face with a stream of screamed profanity that could have peeled paint. I wouldn't need dermabrasion until I was well past forty at this rate. He pounded the table and tossed the pictures at me.

I looked up at Sgt. Dowd. He just shrugged.

The tirade went on for about ten minutes. Guthrie was pretty good. I didn't see him take a single breath in that time and his face was only starting to show it. In no particular order, he questioned my paternity, sexuality, morality, opacity, capacity, both mental and physical, veracity, and loquacity, or lack of same. He finished with, "Sgt. Dowd, with your permission, I'd like to take this dirtbag down to the morgue and let him see what he's done to that sweet old man."

Dowd continued his paterfamilias trick. "I don't think so, Corporal. I don't think the pathologist is quite finished, yet. Why don't we give Jack a few minutes to collect himself and think about things?"

They left.

* * *

I'd like to say I'd held out.

They tag teamed me for the next nine hours or so. They didn't bother with coffee breaks, just kept whacking away. I know from one of my cases that people who transport cattle are required to give them rest and water breaks every eight hours. (My client said that his watch was broken so he couldn't. No one believed him. It was probably because he wasn't a cop.) Those guys who want to give animals Charter rights had better be careful. If police interrogations are anything to go by, cattle would be *losing* rights.

About eight thirty, I said, "Okay, you want to know if I killed Harry, no I didn't."

Guthrie was up on his feet. "Look, we've been over this, must be fifty times."

"I lost count at sixty nine."

"What?"

"Never mind. I didn't kill Harry Popowicz."

"Prince, we got the car you drove that night. You may not realize this but we got your car. Guys over at your vehicle agency found the bent fender that you didn't report. And we found blood on it, okay. You may think you washed it all off, but you didn't. No one's that good. So don't go on saying you didn't kill Harry Popowicz. Don't insult my intelligence, okay!"

"Well, I didn't kill Harry Popowicz."

"Gawd!" was all Guthrie could say.

Dowd leaned back, hands behind his head. "So, you didn't kill him, Jack. I believe you."

Guthrie made a sound like "Bluourgh!" and shook his head.

"Now, Corporal Guthrie, maybe Jack didn't kill Harry. Maybe, it was all an . . . accident. Is that it, Jack?"

"It wasn't an accident."

"So, it was on purpose then? Is that what you're saying, Jack? Is it?" Guthrie had a low excitement threshold.

"No."

"So, what is it, Jack?" Dowd still managed to look cool and unflustered all these hours later.

"I didn't kill him."

"Maybe, you hit him and you didn't think you killed him. Is that it?"

Before I could respond, his cell phone rang. He answered it. The conversation went on for several minutes but his contribution was minimal.

He hung up and turned to me. "You know someone named Sally Ryder, Jack?"

I wasn't sure at that point but the name didn't seem too familiar. "Not that I know of."

"She says she knows you. Says you took her to your motel room that night. She's sure of it. She recognized your dog."

"Oh."

"She says that after she went to sleep, you left for a few hours. She wasn't sure when you came in but it was quite early in the morning. Lots of time for you to go out and find your client and sever—what do you guys call it? Yeah . . . *the solicitor and client relationship*. Unlike most shysters, you did it with a car. You met the old man, you argued with him and you ran him down in the driveway of his own apartment block. Sounds like a good case of murder to me."

"You want to hear what really happened or not?"

Guthrie was smiling. He had dental work like a shark's. "Don't need to now, shyster. We already know."

* * *

I've spent time in some really quite awful hotels—well, motels, mostly—in my life. There was one in Bobcaygeon that never really rented rooms by the week or night, more by the hour or minutes. If you weren't hot and sticky before you got there, the beds pretty much made sure you were when you left. That sort of thing can really spoil the moment. Another, somewhere in the "Golden Horseshoe" (where the nail goes in) promised "We accommodate every taste" and—if the bug bites were anything to go by—delivered.

My cell at the police station could have been advertised: "Air Conditioned! Room Service! Entertainment Nightly!"

I sat on the plastic mat and considered my state, mostly feeling sorry for myself, when the first blast of wintry air wafted in through the venting system. There was the thud of a door opening and closing somewhere outside and the mournful song of some souse being booked into the drunk tank. It seemed a bit early for this but maybe they had a "no waiting" policy in Yamnuska Centre. At this rate, he'd be sober enough, soon enough to make room for someone else and make it back for last call.

I flipped through a movie magazine again to discover, shock of shocks, that some supposedly famous couple or other was getting divorced after both of them had "come out" to each other. Well, score two for Bobby's team. Not that that should matter to him now that he was a happily married man. Frankly, it was a peek into a sex life that I could have lived without. Maybe, I was becoming a prude. Well, my timing was impeccable.

Another thud. This time it was accompanied by shrieks and a barrage of cursing. If swearing actually worked, I expected to find someone turned into pillar of salt—or worse—once I emerged. I lay down and considered the ads promising me baldness cures and penis extensions. A lot of good either was going to do me.

Further thuds indicated that we were more or less filling up. There wasn't much hope I'd find myself a buddy to talk to, given where I was and why. I tossed the magazine aside and considered the ceiling. It had neither cobwebs nor water stains. If this was to be a step up from the motels of my past, it would need a willing woman or two—and things weren't that promising.

There was a slot in my door that opened and a disembodied voice inquired whether I wanted some coffee. I would have preferred tea but I took what was offered. Section 12 of the Canadian Charter of Rights and Freedoms purports to protect us from "cruel or unusual treatment or punishment." I was sure I had a breach. And I hadn't been in custody that long.

The night wagged on and, between dips into the variegated sex lives of Rex and Sarah and naps, I found myself being offered the blue plate special with a warning that I wouldn't get anything more until breakfast. I felt like yelling "Is that a promise?" but settled in. Well, it wasn't a blue plate at all, more a tin one. I heard once that the TV dinner was invented by a man named Birdseye. Perhaps that is apocryphal. If I'd been told that I was actually eating the eye of a sparrow, I wouldn't have been particularly surprised. Of course, it was all to be washed down by the caffeine-laden strychnine that passed for coffee. Since the choice was that or sipping, Rollo-like, from the toilet, I hazarded a second cup and hoped that it might work its ultimate magic while I was deeply asleep.

It did. But it consisted of six trips to the bathroom. I wondered about the guard monitoring the "eye in the sky" and wished I'd heard about the penis extensions sooner.

Sleep was like a leaky tap: it came in spurts and dribbles. And we had the irregular entertainments of various folk who had found themselves on the wrong side of the law. Once ensconced, several considered the "Joshua at the Walls of Jericho" method of remedying their incarceration. One particularly ardent soul kept up a caterwaul until his voice gave out. I was thankful for the inventions of concrete and rebar. Otherwise, I had visions of being crushed when the walls came a-tumblin' down. I considered lecturing him on the silent prayer resorted to by Paul and Silas when they were delivered from prison by an earthquake but, maybe, he hadn't made it to the New Testament quite yet. (There are certain consolations in an early biblical education. Belief isn't always one of them.)

The morning, when it came, was largely quiet. Most of my comrades had slipped into either sleep or a stupor, for which I was glad. All it meant was that, when I awoke, I felt like a largish vulture had spent the night perched in my mouth, burping. I caught a glimpse of myself in the *eau de toilette*. My hair was sticking up like stubble; my beard made me look like the criminal I was charged with being, maybe even worse; and my eyes were red. Worst of all, I itched.

I knocked at the door. It took a while until a guard appeared.

"Yeah. Whaddaya want?"

"I was wondering if I could have a shower and maybe brush my teeth."

As the poem goes, answer came there none.

"Hey, how about a shower?"

"Can't do it."

"Why not?"

"Got no members to supervise."

"I have to be in court at nine-thirty."

"Yeah. You and five other guys."

"I'd like to wash, at least."

"That's why you got a sink."

He was right. I did. Like the sparrows of last night's dinner, it wasn't quite big enough for me.

* * *

Either the guard couldn't count or there had been a last minute rush. There were actually eight of us for court. I was handcuffed and shackled, unlike my fellows who were merely handcuffed together, right hand to the left of the person in front of him, left to the one behind. As a result, I got pride of place next to the driver's compartment.

When we got to the courthouse, I was the last out. There was a fair mob of reporters, all leaning in with cameras and microphones, shouting questions and holding up the early editions of their papers. One read, "Death for Client. Life for Lawyer?" Another, obviously more attuned to Harry's predisposition, read "Pest Removal?" and was accompanied by a cropped picture from my wedding. My favourite was from a national tabloid: "Making a Killing with Legal Aid?" A reporter I recognized from his contributions to the national network—where he'd made a life for himself standing in front of wheat fields and washed-out bridges—leaned in. "Neil Fury. CBC News. How does it feel to be on the other side of things?" I was standing there, unwashed, unshaven, smelling like a goat in heat, my feet and hands chained together, holding up my pants like I'd just been caught in an act of self-abuse on national television. I looked at him. "Just another day at the office, I guess."

The questions flowed like a torrent at that point. I didn't have a chance to answer any of them as I was hauled off, two inches above the ground, as cameras whirred and microphones caught breathless bulletins. Just as I got to the door of the courthouse, the mob whirled and charged off to interview the Crown prosecutors assembled at the main door, scripts in place for the media scrum.

Unlike the others, I had a cell to myself. It was the young offenders' cell, or so I inferred by the fact that the toilet and sink were both a bit shorter than I, at least, was used to. I mused at the irony of being charged with a major crime but having only minor facilities. Then, it was off to court.

* * *

Dishonour Morceau was in his element. He wasn't used to having the national press to preen for. In Yamnuska Centre Provincial Court a big case consisted of having the local reporter there from the *Yamnuska Centre Clarion* with her six megapixel digital camera and an interviewing style in which she brayed her name like a dyspeptic donkey before requiring you to explain three years of law school in a bite-sized morsel. She was there. In awe. It was as if she had gone reporter to reporter, calling their names, preening and saying how she just *loved* their story on the water troubles in Medicine Hat and couldn't they just do lunch. They were all pumping her for "local colour" and I had the feeling that she would be the one they interviewed on the national radio shows. I could hardly wait.

"John Appleby Prince. A charge of murder." Morceau looked at me with what I thought was either admiration or surprise. Maybe both. "Do you have a lawyer, Mr. Prince?" He was almost smiling. "Do you . . . need one?" I thought I caught a chuckle.

"Actually, I don't right now."

"Will you be getting one?" Now, the grin was almost feral.

"Sure. Why not?"

"You mean, you won't be . . . representing yourself?"

"Not at this time, thanks." I smiled at him. That should put him off.

"Do you waive the reading of the charge, then?"

"Sure. I'm waiting for the book, anyway."

"Which book is that, Mr. Prince?" he asked, as if to say, "Are you already selling this sordid story to some publisher somewhere?"

"The one that my learned friend, Mr. Cherry, is trying to throw at me."

"This is no time for levity, Mr. Prince. This a serious charge. Your lamentable habits of making fun of the court system—and just about everything else, if I might say so—have no place in this matter. Do I make myself clear?"

"As a bell, Your Honour," not adding that I hoped the press had picked up on what a ding dong he really was.

"I should hope so. Crown, are you seeking an adjournment?"

Bobby Cherry was looking for a week so a week it was.

With that, I was shuffled off to the cells below and, from there, to the Yamnuska Centre Correctional Centre, there to sit like new cheese, until I had improved enough to be released on an unsuspecting public or was ripe enough for trial.

BE HEARTY IN YOUR APPROBATION...

I had been to the YCCC, or "The Cube," as some mathematically-inclined soul had styled it years ago. I doubt that many of its sad assortment of never-wases and never-would-bes connected the name to the lower echelons of junior high math. When I had been there before, it was in through the front door, a quick tussle over a plastic name tag with whoever was manning "control" and on to an antiseptic room with a phone and a broken computer. There I plied my less than honourable profession, taking confession, without benefit of clergy, from the poor creatures who populated my practice. Now, I entered—or should I say the police van did since I was but one of its unwilling cargo—through a door I had never seen before. We were summarily dumped to be inspected by our hosts. None of them looked too happy about it either. I even recognized a few who in days past referred to me as Mr. Prince, with only a hint of malice. Now, it dripped from every comment—and the "Mister" part had somehow been forgotten.

We were relieved of our outside clothes, checked for vermin, showered, and molested in ways the police hadn't thought of. If they had, even they might have thought it indecent. There is simply nothing left of your privacy when a flashlight has been maneuvered so expertly about. At last, I was given sweat pants and shirt, photographed and introduced to my new friends in Delta pod.

The Cube is a modern facility. It is divided into living units called pods, full of shuffling souls, all decked out in the same green sweat clothes. Some lolled about, many played cards at various tables; some smoked in the breezeway between the yard and our unit. I thought I saw a couple actually reading. I hoped that speed-reading wasn't on the local curriculum. Someone might suffer a jaw injury.

I was steered to cell Delta 4A. I half expected some steroid-abuser with a lantern jaw and prehensile tail but was met by a mole of a man who insisted that I call him Bernie. So, I did. Bernie, it seemed, knew far more about me than I thought possible.

"You the lawyer fella?"

I looked about. "Uh-huh."

"The one that killed his client, like?"

"No, he's in the next pod over."

Bernie wasn't to be denied. "You guilty?"

I decided that a short lesson in constitutional law was in order. "No. I am innocent until or unless a jury of my peers finds otherwise."

"But ya did him, like, right?"

"Who?" I asked conspiratorially.

"The client fella, like. You know." He leaned in to me as I sat on the lower bunk.

"You are referring to the late Henry Latham Popowicz, I presume?"

"Who? Oh, yeah, that guy." He had sat beside me as I unrolled my towel and the few personal items they allowed me.

"And you want to know if I killed him."

"Yeah. Like, we all need to know if you're a standup kind a guy, like."

"And killing somebody makes me one?"

"Well, yeah, like."

"Like, no, Bernie. For what it's worth, I guess I'm not a standup kind of guy . . . like."

"Whaddaya mean, like?"

I leaned in to him, almost whispering in his ear. "I didn't kill him, Bernie. Lawyers don't kill their clients. We consider it unethical. It's almost as bad as stealing from them."

"Hunh?"

"Don't worry, Bernie, I'll teach you all the four syllable words you like but I think we should start with shorter ones first." With that, I lay on my bed and closed my eyes.

"This ain't no good."

"No?"

"You ain't too friendly for a lawyer."

"You know many lawyers, Bernie?"

"Just my own, like."

"And who is that solid soul?"

"Some chick from Legal Aid named Megan MacCarthy. She's a real looker."

"I'll take your word for it."

"She's a lot friendlier than you are."

"I'll bet. She give blow jobs in the interview room or something?"

"Naw! Nothin' like that."

"Well, neither do I." I plumped up the pillow.

"But, like, she's a lot nicer than you."

"Wait 'til you get to know me. Maybe, I'll let you take a thorn out of my paw sometime." With that, I rolled over and pretended to go to sleep.

* * *

I wasn't close to asleep before I'd drawn a real crowd. Maybe, Bernie was selling peeks of the killer lawyer for half a deck of cigarettes a piece. I looked up five minutes later to see quite a flock of my fellow toilers in time. One of them decided he needed to prove he was the boss of this mob.

"You paid your rent for that bunk?" He had spiked hair that made him look like a porcupine suffering a shortage of quills.

"As a matter of fact, I tipped the concierge on the way in. I was expecting a proper down comforter. Why don't you be a good lad and see where it's gotten itself to?"

"You making fun o' me, buddy?" He adopted what he thought might be a fighting stance.

"No, I thought you were doing quite a good job on your own, son."

"Who you callin' son, whitey?"

I rubbed my eyes with one hand. I had a headache coming on and I really didn't need to get into a battle of wits with someone who was so obviously unarmed. "What did you go and do that for?"

"What's that, whitey?"

"Go and abuse my human rights with an apparent racial slur. You know I'm just going to have to report you."

"Go ahead, whitey. Around here, snitches get stitches." Well, that was original. "You go talk to the man." He preened and strutted a bit.

"Man? No, no, no, no, no. I do believe you're mistaken. The last time I checked it's a she."

"Who's a she?" At least, he'd dropped the epithet.

"The human rights commissioner. I'm sure it's that white-haired babe. Not much to look at but she packs a mean punch. You keep your racist ways up and she's bound to make a finding against you and you know what that means."

"No, what's it mean, whitey?"

I winced. "There'll be a judgement and maybe an order that you apologize to me and we both know how embarrassing that would be for a man in your position. So, let's cool it with the 'whitey' business. Even in jail, I think we should remain civil even if we find each other's points of view somewhat at odds.

"I could punch you out right now, you white bastard. You know that?"

"Yeah, but you won't."

"Why not?"

"'Cause I probably know your lawyer and you wouldn't want her mad at you. She might not take your case at the Human Rights Board."

He was confused. "How you know it's a broad?"

"Educated guess." I rolled over and went to sleep.

* * *

My first visitor came that night.

I was busy teaching my thirty one new best friends how to play Texas Hold 'Em. I'm not the world's best teacher. On the other hand, I didn't think I was that bad, either. As it was, I was up a couple of cartons of cigarettes when the correctional officer came over.

"I hope you boys aren't gambling."

I smiled. "Trust me, they aren't," I said, without adding the obvious that it was pretty much a sure thing.

"Well, Tex, you got a visitor." He noted my raised eyebrow. "It's all right. I'll take you."

I turned to my students. "Now, remember guys, you don't want to get stuck with the 'Old Maid.'"

"It's your lawyer."

"Really?" I was wondering how Scottie got word of my plight when I turned into the doorway of my old familiar office, broken computer still stacked against the wall. "Scotty, how the hell—"

"Hello, Jack. How are things?" It was Chuck Ewanchuk.

I stood there, nodding slowly. "They've been better, Chuck. And you?"

"You don't know how excited I am. You're my first murder. What do you think of that, Jack?"

"I was thinking exactly the same thing, actually."

He didn't get it. Nor would he. Chuck, at the best of times, can test the patience of a saint. And I have never aspired to any particular sanctity.

"Well, Jack, where should we start?"

"You might try opening up your briefcase and taking out a legal pad?"

"Why?"

"I don't know. Maybe, you could make notes of our little meeting."

"Oh, yeah. I could do that. I was thinking about this as sort of a getting acquainted meeting. You know."

"You bring flowers?"

"No."

"Chocolates?"

"No."

"Wine?"

"What are all these questions about, Jack?"

"Chuck, I bring at least one of those to any getting acquainted meetings I have. And then, I really try to get lucky. Now, just in case you're thinking you might, put those thoughts and any trailing appendages away and take out your legal pad. We've got work to do."

"I should tell you, Jack, that I can't stay. I've got someone waiting for me and I've only got a couple of minutes."

"Chuck, I think it's safe to say that we are acquainted and I am more than familiar with the legal aspects of my case."

"Like I said, Jack, I have a date tonight."

"Well, take my advice, then, Chuck. Use a condom."

"I don't think we'll go that far. What would I do with a condom?"

"Swallow it in case of oral sex."

"But I might choke."

"Better you than her."

* * *

When I got back to the pod, the national news was on. The regular reader was off, again, and some tender thing with sculpted blond hair was on.

> "And now to the small prairie city of Yamnuska Centre"—a tiny map blossomed over her right shoulder with an arrow pointing us out for all the country to see—"where the remarkable story of a local lawyer, accused of killing his own client, is unfolding today. Neil Fury has our story. Neil?"
>
> "Wanda"—I was amazed; both managed to recognize each other—"I'm standing just outside of the small, prairie city of Yamnuska Centre, where today John Prince stands charged of murdering his client, Henry Popowicz, of nearby Moskolsippi."

Frankly, it didn't look too much like the Yamnuska Centre I knew. Once again, Neil had found a field of grain to stand in front of while he delivered his prairie-themed exclusive to the great unwashed masses of the East. I have come to the conclusion that if you asked anyone in Montreal or Halifax what we do in the West, they could universally point to the "amber waves of grain," although at this time of year they were mostly still pretty green. There are probably children in central Ontario who believe that we have nothing out here but grain fields and passing trucks. And mostly, they'd be right.

> "Prince was charged after the battered body of Henry Popowicz was discovered in the parking lot of his rent-subsidized condo complex. Police believe that Popowizc, who was known as a local eccentric and a person frequently

> in trouble with the law, was struck down in the early morning hours by a car driven by his lawyer. They speculate that Prince and Popowicz had suffered a recent falling out and that Prince had run over the sixty-two-year-old, former transportation company owner with his government-issued car."

The picture changed to a local street where Carrie Anne's beloved Inspector Serge Duceppe, well-coiffed for his fifteen minutes, stood.

> "It is our belief that the accused John Appleby Prince" —the same cropped picture of my wedding appeared—"and the deceased had quarreled over a legal matter and that Mr. Prince caused the death of the decedent through the use of his government-issued motor vehicle."

There were some shouted questions the voice of a female reporter fought her way through.

> "Can you tell us, Inspector, whether you believe that there was more to the relationship between the lawyer and the deceased?"

Duceppe's face lit up with astonished gratitude at this, as if to say, "Of course."

> "I would not like to speculate as to that thing. Our investigation is continuing into many aspects of this."

Neil Fury was back.

> "Obviously, Wanda, the police are playing their cards very close to their vests. We really can't say where there investigation is taking them and what further revelations will unfold in the days to come. Tonight, though, John Prince sits disgraced and accused of murder in a local jail, while Henry Popowizc, his former client, reportedly a much troubled man, lies dead in the local morgue. Wanda?"
>
> "Thanks, Neil. A fascinating story, one we'll continue to follow in the days and weeks to come. Now, to the conflict in central Asia..."

My fellow inmates looked at me with a mixture of fascination and respect. It wasn't often that you got to spend your remand time with a nationally-known murderer. I wouldn't have to argue with Bernie over the bottom bunk.

* * *

The next day brought none other than Carrie Anne Bloodworth. I'm not sure who told her where to find the Cube. I am pretty sure it was her first time. And like a lot of first times it was to be over all too soon. She was standing in the visitor's room, flicking looks out the window and biting her nails.

When I arrived, she asked the guard to stay.

"These are for you." She handed me two envelopes and put on her coat.

She was almost out the door when I rapped the fan of letters into my left hand and asked her, "You're not going to stay and chat about the office?"

"I really have nothing to say beyond what's in those." She rubbed her left hand on the side of her leg.

"What? Nothing about sending Chuck out here to represent me? I thought I had choice of counsel on serious charges like these and you sent Chuck?"

"As you well know, Mr. Ewanchuk is a fine lawyer, one with a far better reputation than you have."

"Well, we could argue about that all day."

"You needn't bother. I haven't heard a single complaint about Mr. Ewanchuk from anyone."

"That's 'cause they're too dumb to know any better."

"I get my information from a variety of sources, Jack. You may be very interested to know that Mr. Ewanchuk has established himself as one of the finest young criminal minds in the legal aid system."

"After you, no doubt."

"I can't say that I'm a specialist in the area but I trust the information that's come to me. We had an office case conference and I am satisfied that he is the best equipped to represent you on these charges. Now, if there's nothing else . . ."

"Choice of counsel?"

"If you ever read your office memorandums, you'd know that that policy is under review and until it is, Mr. Ewanchuk is your lawyer. I trust that's clear. Anything else?"

"Yeah. What's this about an office case conference? You mean you discussed my case with everyone in the office?"

"Of course, Jack. In serious matters like this, it's always good to get a number of points of view and a free exchange of ideas."

"Does two count as an exchange?"

"What?"

"So, you've been through my file and gone over what Chuck passes off as notes?"

"Of course, Jack. We work as a team at Yamnuska Centre Legal Aid." If smarmy were money, I had just met the world's richest woman.

"So, whatever I say to Chuck will get back to you."

She smiled. "It always has, Jack."

"You're enjoying this, aren't you?"

She turned and walked into the room. Her face was up against mine. "You have no idea how much, Jack Prince."

I took advantage of our closeness; the guard couldn't hear. "And you have no idea how much better it is . . . the second time."

* * *

The first letter I opened was from the law society. It read:

> "Dear Mr. Prince:
>
> We have been informed that you have been charged with the first degree murder of your client, Mr. Henry Lathem Popowicz. If true, your actions with respect to your late client are not in keeping with the highest standards of the legal profession nor of any acceptable standard of professionalism.
>
> While the Law Society recognizes that you are presumed to be innocent until proved guilty, it is our responsibility to protect the people of this province from any misconduct at the hands of their legal representatives. We believe that the allegations against you impact on a number of areas forbidden in the conscientious and ethical practice of law. As you are no doubt aware, *The Code of Professional Conduct* states:
>
> (1) The lawyer must discharge with integrity all duties owed to clients, the court or tribunal or other members of the profession and public [Chapter I];
>
> (2) The lawyer owes a duty to the client to observe all relevant laws and rules respecting the preservation and safekeeping of the client's property entrusted to the lawyer.

> Where there are no such laws or rules, or the lawyer is in doubt, the lawyer should take the same care of such property as a careful and prudent owner would when dealing with property of like description [Chapter VIII];
>
> (3) The lawyer should encourage public respect for and try to improve the administration of justice [Chapter XIII];
>
> (4) The lawyer should assist in maintaining the integrity of the profession and should participate in its activities [Chapter XV];
>
> (5) The lawyer should observe the rules of professional conduct set out in the Code in the spirit as well as in the letter [Chapter XIX].
>
> Given your present circumstances, we believe that you will agree that, for the good of the profession and in keeping with the principles enunciated above, your continuing to practise law would not be in the best interests of the profession.
>
> The Benchers have, therefore, concluded that, until such time as your present difficulties are resolved, you should stand suspended. Please conduct yourself accordingly.
>
> Should you have any questions, please contact the undersigned at your convenience.
>
> Yours truly,
>
> Gerald D. Protheroe
>
> Secretary Treasurer"

I was not surprised that there was no rule in the entire Code of Professional Conduct that forbids killing a client. Bleeding them dry financially and leaving them in the lurch when the money in trust runs out are okay. Killing them, not so much.

The second letter was from LAC and was cc'ed to Carrie Anne. It told me I was suspended with pay "pending a full review of this matter by the entire board." At least, it didn't thank me for my services to date. That was a shame. After all, whoever killed Harry had probably saved them tens of thousands.

* * *

My next visitor was Cindy. She had come to Yamnuska Centre for a dentist's appointment and her mouth was still frozen. We sat in the main visitor area.

"You can' hell 'em 'othing, Yack. My nad'll hill me if he e'er foun' ou'."

"Oh, and I love you very much, too, Cindy."

"I'd not fair, Yack! You can' hell 'em 'othing. B'lease! I godda rebudation, Yack. You can' hell 'em 'othing!"

"So, your reputation is more important than whether I go to jail for twenty-five years?"

"Thad's nod fair, Yack."

I leaned into her. "Cindy, I won't say anything if I don't have to but you can say I wasn't there. That's the important thing. We don't have to say what we were doing, only that we were together, all right?"

"No, no, no, no. I can'd do id, Yack. I can'd."

"And if I subpoena you?"

"Whad's dadt?"

"A court order to testify."

"I'll lie."

"Was the sex *that* bad?"

* * *

The papers kept coming in. Towards the end of the week, there was a bit of a lull but, on the weekend, there was a man on the street interview. The topic: "A lawyer has just been charged with murdering his client. What do you have to say about it?"

Velda Schultz: "Lawyers are well known to be greedy bastards. They'll do whatever they can to get their hands on stuff. If you ask me, it doesn't surprise me in the least."

Ed Hirsch: "It don't surprise me none. Things are getting to be so's you can't trust no one."

Rev. David Thirsk: "The Bible says we reap what we sow. I can't imagine how anyone can defend people like that. They can't have any sort of conscience, if you ask me."

Don Latchley: "It's all kind of confusing. I'm not sure what to think. I mean what did this Prince guy get for killing the other guy? I bet if they knew that we wouldn't need much of a trial."

Alice L'Hirondelle: "It don't make no sense to me. I don't know nothing 'bout it. We don't get no lawyers on the reserve so I don't know much."

* * *

I was getting so that I could live without visitors. They were like kids at Halloween. They show up and you're actually glad to see children dressed up and having innocent fun. Then, the little ones all scream at you like you were molesting them and the older ones gripe about what you're giving out and why can't they have more. Finally, the teenagers show up to vandalize your house. In the end, you want to strangle the three year old bunny before he becomes the thirteen year old mobster. Of course, you can't; there are laws against it. No wonder people resort to razor blades in apples and rat poison in the Chicklets. Crazy? I don't think so. Just slightly ahead of their times.

So, when I got word that Kathy Markle had found her way to the cubby hole with the broken computer, I just about declined in favour of watching the rerun of a really dopey game show.

She smiled when I arrived.

"You here to gloat like Carrie Anne or do you bring greetings from the good people at the Crown's office?" I slumped into the guest chair.

"We are in a fine mood, aren't we?"

"Well, let's see. I'm in this fascist guest house charged with murder and if I'm convicted, it's what a minimum twenty-five years to parole? At which time I'll almost be old enough to collect a minimal pension. I'm suspended from my job, which doesn't really matter because I won't have it when I get convicted. I'm suspended from the law society because my actions aren't—how did they put it? Yeah, not in the best traditions of the bar. For all I know, Rollo has taken up with some family who will feed him chocolate. Oh, yeah, I'm being defended by someone who couldn't spell criminal if you spotted him a *k* and both *i*'s."

"If you're interested, word around our office is that killing Harry Popowicz should get you the Social Services Meritorious Service Medal Second Class."

"Only second class?"

"Sorry. They keep the first class ones for the killers of defence lawyers and judges."

"Well, I could always go for the trifecta and off Morceau and Carrie Anne. Anything else?"

"Don't even talk like that, Jack. The walls have ears, you know."

"So I hear. Why are you here?"

"Two reasons, actually."

"Good news, bad news?"

"Both."

"Which do I want to hear first?"

"Either one." She smiled and sighed.

"So, is it twenty questions, now? Animal, vegetable or mineral?"

"It had better be animal. If it's vegetable, it's all your fault. No one in my family's that far gone—unless you count Aunt Gertie."

"Who's Aunt Gertie?"

"My great, great aunt. She's what? A hundred and six or something."

"What's she got to do with me?"

"Nothing. Although, knowing you, I wouldn't put it past you. You ever go to Vancouver?"

"Not recently."

"That's probably a relief."

"I'm not following."

"Just as well. It's probably the hormones. You know what a hormone is, Jack?"

"Sure. The sound one makes after you pay her a hundred bucks. Works every time. She'll moan all night."

"That's disgusting. How can you be the father of a child of mine?"

"Whoa! Let's just rewind this tape a bit. The 'father of your child'?"

"Yeah! Isn't it great?"

"You mean you and I are . . . going to have a baby?"

"Pretty much."

"What about Brian?"

"Oh, he doesn't know."

"I'm glad. I probably wouldn't make it to trial if he did."

"You're probably right."

"But you and Brian have been going at it for something like a year, right?"

"So."

"Why can't it be his?"

"Because it isn't."

"How do you know this?"

"Well, unless I'm like a female polar bear and store up sperm in a little sac, it's yours."

"You mean you haven't . . . I mean you and Brian haven't . . ."

"Nope."

"Great! Now, I won't make it to my prelim. He'll gun me down on the courthouse steps."

"Oh, don't be silly."

"You just said I probably wouldn't make it to my trial if he knew. Why would he wait that long?"

"He'll never know. He doesn't keep track of stuff like that. He's just bursting with pride that he's finally made a little Brian he can take to rodeos and whorehouses."

"What if it's a Briana?"

"He probably won't take her to the whorehouses."

"Probably?"

She smiled.

I shook my head. I was going to be a father. I've spent almost twenty years avoiding just this discussion. Well, I haven't always avoided it. There was Jennie Douglas, when I was sixteen. She thought my condom had broken and was sure she was up the stump. That was the longest three weeks of my life. I had visions of having to go to her parents and confess some of my many sins—those directly involving their daughter. I spent several days trying to dream up just what I'd say. I'd gotten to the "I know you're probably going to be disappointed in us" when word came that "better late than never" had real meaning. I think Jennie married an accountant and has four kids. Well, somebody in the family should be good with numbers.

Still, being a father—really, about to be a father—does give you a different perspective. "Are you going to leave him?"

"Who?"

"Brian. I mean he isn't going to want to bring up someone else's kid, is he?"

"Who's going to tell him, Jack?"

I thought about my pending assassination on the court house steps. "Not me."

"That's good." She sat back and patted her belly. There was nothing significant to pat. I suppose it's the idea of the thing.

"It's a cuckoo thing."

"I don't know about that, Jack."

"No, it's like a cuckoo."

"People get pregnant all the time. Get used to it."

"No, the cuckoo lays its eggs in the nests of other birds. They hatch sooner than the other birds' young and take over the nest. I've never figured out why the other birds don't notice the difference. I mean their young are chirping like they do and the cuckoos are all going, well, 'Cuckoo! Cuckoo.' You think any self-respecting sparrow or robin would just chuck them out."

"If they did, we'd have sparrow clocks."

"You know, Kathy, that sounds like something I'd say. What's got into you?"

"You should know, Jack. You put it there."

"What are you going to call it? Jacqueline?"

"Brian, probably."

"You should make like First Nations people and call it something immediately connected with its conception."

"What? Adulterea, if it's a girl and Rug Rat, for a boy?"

"No, I was thinking Christian. Cecilia, if it's a girl."

"Why Cecilia?"

"She's the patron saint of music. Or Saint Lucy, for Brian's sake."

"What's Lucy got to do with it?"

"She's the patron saint of the blind."

"You're bad, Jack."

"I try." We were sitting there enjoying things. Time went by. I looked at her and she seemed as happy as I'd known her. I wished I could say the same for myself. "What was the other thing?"

"What other thing?"

"You said you had two reasons. You're not having twins, are you?"

"Not so far." She got serious. "Jack, I know you don't have to tell me but I have to know."

"What?"

"You know."

"No, not really."

She sighed a long, sad sigh. "I need to know if you actually killed Harry Popowicz."

I sat there, just thinking.

"Look, I know I'm a Crown and I know you shouldn't talk to me about this. And I know if you say you did kill him, I'll have a real problem. But I've got to know."

"Why?"

"You'll just think it's dumb. Another one of your hundred dollar hooker jokes, I guess."

"No. Tell me."

"This is just stupid, really stupid. I mean I've slept with you and I've known you, what, two or three years, give or take."

"Give or take. Mostly, you give, I take."

"Don't you believe it, bub." She smiled but it was a sad smile. "It's just that I don't want my son to have a murderer for a father." She shook her head and started to cry.

"Look at me. Look at me, Kathy." She raised her face to mine. There were rivers of tears down her cheeks, a bit puffy now. "Do you think I killed Harry Popowicz? Do you think I could do that? Do you? Even by accident?"

She shook her head. "No, but I needed to hear it from you."

"Now, you have." I wiped away her tears. "You all right?"

"Yeah." She hauled out a tissue and blew her nose. "So, what happened? If I'm going to take care of your defence, I'll need to know what happened."

"You going to quit the Crown's office?"

"No, but I can do you a lot of good, Jack. You wait and see."

"You aren't just saying that to get my defence out of me, are you?"

"Bobby Cherry's been working on Chuck Ewanchuk for almost a week and he hasn't cracked yet. And he always tells us his defence. That's why he never wins."

"That's no surprise. Chuck hasn't got a clue."

"You mean you haven't told him yet?"

"No, not just that. Chuck really hasn't got a clue."

"How'd you ever get him for your lawyer?"

"Carrie Anne was too busy, I suppose."

"No, seriously, Jack. Why didn't you hire somebody like Scottie? He knows what he's doing."

"I didn't hire him. Carrie Anne did. I suppose it's a blessing in disguise."

"How so? He's pretty lame."

"Lame? The guy's the poster child for intellectual cripples. It was him or one of the lawyerettes."

"You could represent yourself."

"Last time I did that I managed to set records for spousal support in this province. And, as I recall, they even took all my pocket change, too."

"True."

I thought about it. There wasn't too much risk. As soon as Chuck figured out my defence, the Crown would know it too. So, I told her. I tried to think of a way not to mention anything about my encounters with Cindy but that wasn't really possible. So, I told her it involved a farmer's daughter, which was true.

"You know what's wrong with farmer's daughters, Jack?"

"Well, several things, apparently."

"They can't keep their calves together."

"It was sheep, actually. Shouldn't it be lambs?"

"It's a joke, Jack."

"Oh, you mean like hormones?"

"Yeah, something like that." She pulled out a pad. "I'm going to need her name."

"I can't tell you."

"You mean you don't know it. That's simple enough. There can't be too many farmer's daughters in Moskolsippi that you'd have much to do with it. I'll get the police on it."

"No, I can't tell you. She made me promise."

"Well, break it, Jack. That's what happens to promises."

"I can't."

"Why not, Jack? People break promises every day. And for smaller reasons than this. Hell, I break my promise to be faithful to Brian every time we get together. Your life—or most of it, anyway—is on the line here. I need her name."

"Only if there's no other way."

"Jack, your gallantry is touching. Stupid, but touching. I suppose I could find out who's missing a sheep. What was his name, again?"

"Psycho Sammy. But don't go trying to find out whose sheep he is."

"Not unless I have to. I won't have my son's father in the big house if I can avoid it."

"What are you up to?"

"You wait."

* * *

I was in a cheery mood until I got back to the pod. Three correctional officers were in my cell picking up my toothbrush and the two or three other items left to me in the world. The CO 3 came up to me. He was in charge.

"Inmate Prince!"

"Yes, Mr. Pound." You called them Mr. Whatever-Their-Surname-Was. It was meant to teach you respect. Of course, they called us by our surnames, and, no, Mr. Respect is taken, not earned.

"Come with me."

"Where are we going?"

"Ad Seg."

"Which is?"

"The Hole."

"Why am I going there?"

"In the best interests of the security and good order of the institution." He slapped a piece of paper into my hands and off we went.

In western movies, they often have shots of the cell area in the sheriff's office, usually a row of barred units. That was Ad Seg. It stood for Administration Segregation. All that was missing was a guy with a high voice and a limp, a shotgun canted across his thighs as he snoozed on a leaned back chair. Maybe, it was the new government's cutbacks.

Except for some guy with long hair, a bushy beard and wild eyes, I was alone in the unit. He didn't look like much of a conversationalist as he rocked back and forth, smoking one cigarette after another. The air was blue with his contributions. The guard's only comment to me as he slammed the door shut, "He thinks they're keeping him alive."

"The cigarettes?"

"Yeah."

"Don't read the packages to him, then."

I was there long enough to start choking from the fumes. Another CO collected me and took me to an interview room. Inspector Serge Duceppe stood there, a file in hand. I doubted Kathy had had enough time to brief him.

"Well, Inspector, good news I hope?"

"Not for you, Mr. Prince." He consulted his file.

"I didn't think you got yourself involved in investigations."

"In special cases, I like to keep my hand in."

"Oh, and you are taking a special interest in my case?"

"I have a personal interest in this particular case."

"Oh, and what can that be?"

He stiffened. "I can tell you that your case is significant to me."

"Because you don't like defence lawyers and now you have one in your sights."

"How do you say it in English? That is truer than you can ever know."

"A promotion in the works then?"

"Not exactly, Mr. Prince. But it is my turn to ask you questions." He consulted the file, then cleared his throat. "Do you know why you are not in the ordinary unit?"

"You mean the pod?"

"Pod?"

"Yes, a group of peas, whales, dolphins or prisoners."

"Ah, yes, the . . . pod. Do you know why you are not there?"

"According to CO3 Pound, for the security and good order of the institution."

I sat down. He didn't seem to want to but I didn't see why I should have to keep standing, just for him. "Did I say you could sit down?"

"No."

"Then, stand up."

"No."

"I am ordering you to stand up."

"Or you'll do what? As I recall, I'm in here charged with first degree murder. They've got me in the Hole. I don't know. Is there anything more for you to do to me? Taser me? Or that squirt pepper spray stuff?"

He appeared offended. "I do not wish to be spoken to by someone like you in that manner."

I shrugged.

He smiled. "You think you are a clever man, eh, Mr. Prince? You think you have all the answers and the defences and you can just—ffft!—walk out of here in a few days or months?"

I had to admit, Kathy had given me some hope but I was not about to pass that on to him.

So, I smiled.

"Smile, then. You are not worried? Well, Mr. Prince, if I were you I would worry. I would worry very much. Things just got... how you say in English? Very dicey." He hauled out a piece of paper and handed it to me.

"What's this?"

"I believe you lawyers say 'it talks for itself.' Read it! I would love to know how you are going to get out of this."

I read it. It seemed to be a statement from my recent cellie, Bernie. Apparently, he was looking at spending a lot of time in Her Majesty's Hostelry. He'd been a very bad boy. Just as apparently, he had used his time well, taking courses in creative writing and had become what Inspector Duceppe might refer to as a pigeon stool.

I handed the statement back and Duceppe immediately leaned over me, hands on the back of my chair. "So, Mr. Prince, what have you got to say about that?"

"Two things. Three, actually."

"Oh, what is the first of these things?"

"He's lying, of course."

"Of course. He has reasons to lie? What are these reasons?"

"How much time is he looking at?"

"Who says he is looking at time?"

"I don't know. What's he got? Thirty-eight charges?"

"You think he is the only one?"

"Of course. If you had any others, I'm sure you'd bring them. Cops love to gloat."

"Second?"

"Second, I think you have to provide me with more than just the ramblings of some crook on the make. I mean, his credibility has to be lower than mine. And I'm a lawyer. I know enough not to talk about stuff like that with anyone, except maybe my lawyer."

"Just so, Mr. Prince. You are a lawyer. Perhaps, you are not so good a lawyer, eh?"

"Oh, do you know any good ones?"

"Several." He paused and considered but said nothing. Then, "An' t'ird?"

I looked at him and shook my head. "And third, she's not coming back to you, you know."

"Who?"

"Carrie Anne. She's found someone more powerful, better for her career."

"I do not understand what you are saying."

"Sure you do. I've been around long enough to know what a man looks like when he's hurt. What'd she do? Get you to leave your wife?"

"We were . . . how do you say it . . . *étrangers* already."

"I'm sure."

"Then, how do you explain the fact that there is one more thing that I know?"

"What's that?"

"Did you not say to her, 'You have no idea how much better it is the second time'?"

"I don't know. Did I?"

He smiled. It was a wounded smile. They say just before some criminals are executed they have a moment when they are sure they will be spared. I'm not sure who tells us this. There aren't a lot of Ouija boards in the Death House. But he clutched at the straw of the possibility that she'd be back. And I didn't have the heart to tell him she wouldn't. Or that he'd never get the statement in. Or that Carrie Anne stood at the very edge of disbarment.

Of course, I'd have to avoid being disbarred myself. And not be convicted of murder. Well, both, actually.

But, for once, I was feeling confident. The key to my cell was in the hand of counsel for Her Majesty the Queen.

And she was having my baby.

...AND LAVISH IN YOUR PRAISE

It was a slow news day, I guess.

> "First, tonight, we go to Yamnuska Centre, today, where an already strange trial took an even more bizarre twist. Lawyer John Prince is charged with the first degree murder of his former client, Henry Popowicz, a deeply troubled man. Today, Prince turned court proceedings on their head when he fired his court-appointed lawyer and indicated he would represent himself. Our story tonight from correspondent, Neil Furey. Neil?"

The TV was on in the secure unit and my neighbour had stopped screaming. It was now a low, keening moan. I guess CBC wasn't his favourite channel but the channel was welded onto "Peasant Vision," as it is fondly referred to, chez Prince. The picture shifted to Neil and his favourite wheat field.

> "Well, Ian, today this story of professional jealousy and bizarre rebellion took a new

turn, when local lawyer, John Prince, fired his court-appointed lawyer and announced to a packed courtroom that he would be defending himself on the very serious charges he now faces. Prince, age thirty-three, is the legal aid lawyer who for almost a year defended Harry Popowicz on a variety of relatively minor charges from bootlegging to criminal defamation.

"Two weeks ago, the broken and bloodied body of Harry Popowicz was found in the parking lot of the housing complex he occupied with his common law spouse. Police investigation led them to Prince who had quarreled with the recently retired transportation company owner only the day before, following Popowicz's acquittal on his latest set of charges. Reliable police sources revealed to CBC News today that damage to the government automobile driven by Prince, on the day in question, led them to charge him with his former client's murder.

"In court today, a real shocker. Prince dismissed his lawyer, indicating to Judge Robert Morceau that he no longer had confidence in the man appointed to represent him. In an exchange with the court, Prince told the court of his dissatisfaction with his counsel and referred to him as a dog. Representatives of the provincial legal aid system advised CBC late today that they would *not* be appointing new counsel for Prince. Spokesperson Melanie Derschowicz told us, 'We are not in the business of appointing a string of lawyers for accused persons. Mr.

Prince will have to accept what we have given him or make his own arrangements'.

"The preliminary inquiry has been set to October 26th and, with all its twists and turns so far, an already strange proceeding will likely continue to cause legal heads to shake in disbelief. Paul Furey, CBC News, Yamnuska Centre. Ian?"

Publicity like this, you can't buy. Not that you'd want to, mind. Still, if things worked out at all well, I could be assured of a national reputation. The only problem, aside from being labeled a wingnut, was that I now had to find a way to defend myself.

All I should have cared about was that they spelled my name right. Then, again, who was reading any of this except the fourteen or so people who visit the CBC website and they were all probably blogging away to each other.

I have to say, none of this was particularly fair. Or accurate. But this is Canada and an occasional stab at the truth by the national media would be welcome and a bit of a relief. Other than that, the truth is whatever they decided. I was hardly in any position to sue.

They were right about one thing—the day hadn't been an unqualified success. I was led to a packed courtroom, this time in leg irons. Morceau was doing his favourite impression: the turkey vulture. I like him better when he does "Cigar Store Indian" or "Rock of Ages." Then, he doesn't talk. Turkey Vulture allows him free rein for all the squawking and preening he so likes.

"Prince, your lawyer here?"

At this, Chuck Ewanchuk lifted himself to his feet and announced that the honour was his. Morceau's snort at the word, honour, I thought indiscreet. I scanned the room.

Courts are a bit like weddings, Bobby Cherry's aside. The police and certain members of the press sat in a phalanx behind the Crown Prosecutor. The ordinary criminal classes gathered as one behind the defence, along with the more liberal press. Any remaining room was filled in by those latecomers who cannot be seated by the ushers. There is no more sardine packing since the fire marshal decreed a load limit for the room. I have to say, it had improved the overall odour of the place. And, given everything, I would have given up my seat.

"Mr. Ewanchuk, is it?" If Morceau wore half frames, he would have been peering over them. As it was, all the red meat in his diet had done wonders for his visual acuity.

Chuck allowed that it was.

"Mr. Ewanchuk, what are we doing today? I see that the accused"—and here the sneer in his voice was unmistakable—"has been before."

"Uh, yes, uh, sir—I mean, Your Honour, sir."

"So, what are we doing today?"

"I thought I would bring the matter up today to see where we were at."

"Mr. Ewanchuk, the police have better things to do than provide a taxi service for your client."

Ah, yes, let me count. There's rousting drunks, stopping for coffee every hour or so, gossiping with various young ladies on the streets of Yamnuska Centre, defeating the curse of speeding and providing employment for several graduates of the best special education programs in the country. They have also, in the past, provided several fine "companions" for the delectation of my former—and, perhaps, future—boss, Ms Carrie Anne Bloodworth. And they do arrest the occasional drunk driver or shoplifter, if things get a bit slow.

"Well, what do you want me to do?"

"I'm not sure, sir—I mean, Your Honour."

"Well, which is it?"

"Uh?"

"Crown. Can you help me out here? Obviously, this matter was adjourned last week to today's date. What are we doing here?"

A shambling fellow I hadn't seen before lumbered to his feet. "Your Honour," he brayed, "Your Honour, the Crown is seeking a resolution of this matter. We have been in communication with my learned friend, Mr. Ewanchuk, over the past week, seeking to dispose of this matter in a manner that, if I might say so, will be advantageous not only to the Crown but to the defendant, in all the circumstances, as it were." Like lawyers everywhere, this guy had fallen deeply in love with the sound of his own voice. That love was unrequited. But like faithful swains throughout the world, it remained undiminished and overpowering. I hoped they'd be happy together and that they could go off and find a place to make little whispers together. Just not in my backyard.

"Well, it sounds like you're making some progress, then." Morceau cracked a smile. I wasn't sure if it was because of the progress he'd heard about or the prospect of sending me off to some dank prison, where they haven't done any of the things he was having wet dreams about, for almost a century.

I thought that I had been left out of their little tea party entirely too long. So, I made my presence known. I could have clanked my chains, I suppose.

Morceau turned to me, then Chuck. "Mr. Ewanchuk, I think your client would like a word with you."

"No, he wouldn't." I was still considering chain clanking.

"Prisoner, you have been a lawyer in this court. I would have thought that I wouldn't have to remind you of our procedures, here. You have a fine young lawyer to speak for you."

"I beg to differ."

"I beg your pardon."

"I don't think you got anything right in that whole sentence."

"Prisoner Prince, you are not to speak in this courtroom. If you do, I may be forced to hold you in contempt."

"What's that going to do? The Crown over there is trying to put me in jail for the rest of my life. I'm living in the Hole. My only neighbour there lost his mind about the same time I lost my virginity. Just what are *you* going to do to me?"

Morceau considered this and decided to resort to sweetness and light. "Mr. Prince, you have a lawyer. Anything you say would be superfluous. Don't you have some saying about getting a dog and barking youself?" He smiled at this.

"That's insulting, Your Honour! Appalling!"

"What is, Mr. Prince?"

"Comparing Chuck Ewanchuk to a dog."

"You're right, of course, Mr. Prince. It was quite unintentional. Mr. Ewanchuk, I apologize for comparing you to a dog. The slight was not intended. It was just an aphorism." Chuck bowed deferentially to Morceau who now turned to me.

"I was thinking about the dogs, Your Honour."

"Mr. Prince, I've had quite enough of your impertinence."

"And I've had enough of my lawyer. I choose to relieve him of his obligations to me."

"You're . . . let me get this straight, Mr. Prince . . . you're firing him?"

It wasn't planned. I could have limped along with Chuck for another couple of weeks but I was already tired of all this. I didn't fancy sharing my entire defence with Carrie Anne so she could exchange pillow talk with whatever member of the scarlet service she might fancy any given night.

"Pretty much."

"And who will be representing you?"

"I will."

"Crown, what do you have to say about this?" He should have added, "In twenty-five words or less," not that it would have mattered much.

"Well, Your Honour, this will create some considerable institutional hurdles for our office, given the vicissitudes of the still incomplete disclosure process and the progress of our still to be resolved negotiatory processes, which are in flux, even as I speak. I am not entirely certain just what impediments this might present to a full hearing of this matter but I am confident that the damage inflicted on our discussions with Mr. Ewanchuk, which have not reached their full fruition, as I speak, but which might well have been fruitful, if I may say so, will be of a minor and not a significant aspect."

Count them: That's a lot more than twenty-five.

Morceau furrowed his brow. "I see." He may have. I doubt he fully understood.

All I had gotten out of all this was that my lawyer was trying to sell me out.

"May I speak?"

"Why not, Mr. Prince? Everything you've said so far has pretty much turned this into a circus. And I warn you: I don't want to hear anything about cruelty to elephants, either."

"How soon can the Crown get disclosure to me and how soon can we get a date for a prelim?"

After due consideration and several further excursions through the Crown prosecutor's wonderful world of words, we set the preliminary inquiry to October 26th. I clanked my chains in joy and made my way back to the Cube.

* * *

One thing you can say about being in segregation was that I had all sorts of time to think and prepare. If I'd been locked in a cell with my books at law school, I might be a lot better lawyer today. Maybe, they should try that. They're always experimenting with new educational techniques.

Lock up all the university students with their books and have a lecture or two per day sent in. They'd either learn or become psychopaths. There wouldn't be much change.

They gave me my laptop and all the CDs of evidence but made sure I couldn't access anything any more stimulating than criminal law on line. Porn might have made it a bit more fun. I was beginning to have improper thoughts about the latest young trashette who showed up regularly on the entertainment news shows that my friendly, neighbourhood psychotic, down the hall, feasted on when he wasn't trying to OD on news of my plight. He sat there, lighting a cigarette from the ashes of the last and moaning whenever news about me appeared. His moans changed only slightly when the latest young vixen of the pop world appeared. I trust the difference was one of attraction.

And then, he was gone. One day, they just came for him. He kicked up a bit of a fuss but they had Thorazine and he didn't have a chance. The quiet when he left was even more disturbing than his compendium of moans and psychotic babble. It meant I was alone.

My choices were to surrender to the Pablum of daily television or work at something. I turned to my case and, for the first time since I articled, actually prepared.

Law's a funny thing. Mostly, it makes perfect sense. It's like the man said in his book, most of it you learn by kindergarten. Then, you spend a lifetime trying to figure out a way around things. Really good lawyers can take the most obvious concept—don't punch anyone in the mouth, say—and turn it into a four-day tonsil tour of the great minds of the world and never use a word shorter than five syllables, half of them in a foreign tongue. But when you stripped it all away, both the good sense and desirability of keeping your balled up fist as far away from someone's mouth, was all that was left. But we are paid by the hour and the day and an excursus through morality, mortality, motility and malevolence pays better than the simple words, "Be nice."

After all, if people were friendly and honest, I'd be looking for work. Given my predispositions, it would be a permanent state. Crime pays. Sin has its wages. No one ever went broke leeching off the frailties of his fellow humans.

I took the path of least resistance and figured I'd be ready when the time came.

* * *

I'm not sure how Gail got the time off to come and see me. She just appeared one afternoon in the visitors' room. When I arrived, she was staring at a couple at the next table, who were either exchanging drugs or would soon be proud parents. The guards were fixated on us, so I kept my hands in sight at all times and smiled at Gail.

"How's Dan?"

"Dan?" She was looking about like a cat at the dog pound.

"Yeah. Your boyfriend?"

"Oh, yeah, Dan. Oh, he's okay, I guess." She peered over her shoulder at a couple of guys, one a prisoner, the other not, her eyes widening. "Are they really . . . . ?"

"Sure, it happens all the time here. Don't worry about it."

She looked panicked. "They don't . . . you know . . . in the shower?" This last was whispered.

I leaned over and whispered to her. "I don't know. I never shower. Can't you tell?"

"I don't believe you, Jack. You're kidding me again. I can tell that you shower every day."

"Oh, Ms Deare, you have found me out."

She just smiled. But she still kept scanning the room.

"So, why did you come to see me, Gail? I can't imagine that Carrie Anne is taking up a collection for me."

"Oh, Jack, it's terrible. The office is terrible. They talk about you all the time and they are all guessing how many years you'll get and saying that you will start having sex with men, you know, like in the big house."

"How do you know I'm not? It doesn't take long, you know."

"You wouldn't, Jack. You didn't." I just smiled. "You haven't. . . . Have you?"

"No, Rollo would never forgive me. By the way, how is the dear lad?"

"He's fine."

"You mean Carrie Anne hasn't taken him out and had him put down?"

"She tried but I stopped her."

"She what?"

"She said she was sending him to the pound because we can't have a mad dog in the office but I said 'he's just a little pissed off since you left'. And she said it didn't matter because we can't have all the likelihood . . ."

"Liability?"

"Yeah, like that. But I said, 'Rollo won't hurt anyone. I should know.' But she was going to send him away anyway and she told Mrs. Stockard to call the police to get him and shoot him. But I wouldn't let them."

"So, what happened?"

"Well, when they came to get him, I locked the door to your office and I told them that I didn't know where the key was. And when they went away to get the locksmith guy and I snuck Rollo out and took him home."

"What did Carrie Anne say about all that?"

"She said that if I ever interfered with things like that again, I could just pack up my things. I don't want to do that. They might fire me then."

"You're right about that, Gail. So, where's Rollo?"

"He's staying with me. Only 'til you get out. You can have him back, then."

"What if I don't get out? They want to send me to jail for at least twenty-five years."

"I guess Rollo will be pretty old by then."

I nodded. "Pretty old. You're right about that. So, how's he behaving?"

"Real good. He sleeps on my bed and he licks my face to wake me up."

"I thought that was Dan's job."

"Oh, it is. But Rollo has a bigger tongue."

I thought I'd just leave it at that before I learned far too much.

* * *

The day before my preliminary inquiry, my old pal, Neil Furey, was back on the supper hour news. Without the baying of my former neighbour, I almost missed it. The six o'clock national news reader was a dapper, dark-skinned fellow who had nothing, if not style, about him. His voice was summoned, as if by incredible will, from some deep-delved orifice and moaned with all the satisfaction of a well-tuned stereo. I figured he had maybe two years, three tops, before he made it to the States or remained tied to a life of self-loathing on one of the national networks in Canada.

> "We go now to Paul Furey who's been following the strange story of a lawyer, his dead client and a charge of first degree murder. Paul?"

Paul had found his way, once again, to the local wheat field, now cut down to stubble. This time a tractor moved about behind him, spraying some noxious chemical or other to make sure none of us came down with root rot, leaf blight or cancerous rust. Remarkably, none of its exertions were caught on the microphones.

> "Well, thank you, Geoff. Here, in Yamnuska Centre, this small prairie city has been waiting for the next act in what must be the most extraordinary murder trial in some time."

The shot changed to a montage of police cars with their lights blinking at the site of Harry's death, followed by shots of me, coming and going from the court house.

> "Harry Popowicz, a former transportation executive and eccentric resident of the small town of Moskolsippi, was found dead in the parking lot of his rent-subsidized apartment complex in that town some four months ago. He had been a regular client of local legal aid lawyer, John Prince. In fact, Prince had represented Popowicz on at least half a dozen minor charges in the last year, charges that ranged from assaults to bootlegging. Records of those court proceedings indicate that in many of the cases, Prince was successful in his appearances on behalf of Popowicz, but quarrels had recently arisen between the two men over both the quality of Prince's representation and the tactics he chose to employ. One source close to the parties suggests that Popowicz thought Prince's representation was too conservative and that Popowicz was looking to replace Prince with another lawyer. Another stated to me, quote 'Mr. Popowicz had prepared and was in the process of filing a complaint against Mr. Prince.' Neither of these reports could be confirmed by CBC News at deadline, however."

The scene shifted to stills of Harry and me. I don't know where they got that picture of Harry but it showed him slouched in a recliner, a beer on the armrest. Mine was taken from a publicity still taken during my years of torture, marital strife and substance abuse at Whittman, Richards, Illingsworth and Tisch, LLP. It made me look, I don't know, somehow preppy. I definitely had better suits, then.

> "Last June, Harry Popowicz was found dead in the parking lot of his home, the victim of what appears to be a hit and run. Oddly enough, the day before, Prince had succeeded in engineering an acquittal on the most serious of charges faced by Popowicz to that point. Prince was apparently still in Moskolsippi, staying at a local motel, apparently not alone. Police allege that sometime during the night, Prince left his room. During that time, Harry Popowicz was run down and killed by a vehicle. Usually reliable sources have told CBC News that blood, apparently from the victim, was later found on the crumpled fender of a government-issued car Prince was driving. All this comes before a preliminary hearing in the morning before Judge Alvin Powers, who has been brought in to Yamnuska Centre for that purpose."

We were back in the wheat fields with Paul by now. He cupped his hand behind his ear to try to hear what Geoff was asking him, all the way from downtown Toronto. He obviously had a great voice. It got through pretty well.

> "Tell me, Paul, is there any indication of just what Prince's motive may have been for running down and killing his client? I should say, allegedly."

Yes, you should, Geoff.

> "Well, Geoff, there have been a number of theories about that. One of our sources has suggested that Jack Prince was upset by Harry Popowicz's antics and manner. A precise legal mind, constantly having to deal with the rather

bizarre nature of a client's carryings-on, can snap and there's no telling what will happen."

"Are we expecting some sort of mental health defence, then, Paul?"

"Legal experts I've talked to have not dismissed that out of hand. Others claim that Jack Prince was just a loose cannon on the decks of the legal aid system and it was only a matter of time before he crossed the line. And, of course, there's the further curiosity of a lawyer defending himself, after firing his legal team in what has been referred to as a bizarre twist in an already bizarre case."

"So, the preliminary hearing will occur tomorrow. Any indication of just when this matter will be decided and what the penalty will be if Prince is convicted?"

"Well, Geoff, the hearing tomorrow is set for two days. After Prince is committed for trial, it's up to the courts to decide when a trial will occur. And, of course, if convicted, John Prince faces life in prison, without the possibility of parole for at least twenty-five years."

"Thanks, Paul. We look forward to your further stories from Yamnuska Centre in the days and weeks to come. Truly a bizarre story. Turning to the continuing political scandal involving the former..."

It's always helpful to provide future members of the jury with just enough of the background to feel confident that they are doing the right thing. That way, they can start pricing rope for the hanging.

I was curious as to just who the reliable and usually reliable sources were. I expected Insp. Duceppe. The more malicious stuff had to come from Carrie Anne. I'm sure she loved the irony of my being suspended from the law society for conduct unbecoming.

CALL ATTENTION TO YOUR FAULTS FIRST...

A preliminary inquiry—never a preliminary *hearing*, at least in the minds of those of this jurisdiction—is a hearing to find out if the prosecution has enough evidence that a mythical jury made up of reasonable people could, given sufficient quantities of gullibility, imagination and liquid refreshment, conceivably convict someone. It's a pretty low standard. There's a saying that some courts could indict a ham sandwich. Here, we require condiments—slatherings of butter, a taste or two of mustard, maybe a smidgeon of cheesy spread. Any prosecutor who can't win a preliminary inquiry doesn't have the credibility to know his own name without checking his wallet for ID.

So, I wasn't too hopeful that things would work out. I knew I was innocent. That and a coffee could keep you up at night. It did. I didn't really need the coffee, either.

But, here I was, safely stowed in the dungeons below the court in Yamnuska Centre. Just me and a couple of spiders whose only prospect was any insect life that might fall from me. That wasn't too likely. The Cube had made sure I had showered and changed into the freshly laundered suit I'd had on when I was arrested. So, my vermin count was at an all-time low.

I spent the time checking out the prison writings of my predecessors. Apparently, Max had gotten six for ten B &

Es. I wasn't sure if he was proud or upset. Plot wasn't Max's forte. He was more of a headline type.

Political consciousness found voice in "White men choose, Natives lose." Not too much to argue with there. Nothing too profound, either.

Apparently, *Margie* had charms to soothe the most savage of breasts. Or she was blessed with such accoutrements. Several had commented on her charms. I made a mental note to check up on her once I found my freedom. The way things were looking, we'd both be pensioners. I might even score a cup of tea from her

I might have discovered more of the secret lives of my former clientele but a bored cop, obviously within wheezing distance of his pension, cranked open the door and led me through a warren of stairs and anterooms until we reached centre stage.

The room was packed, once again. I recognized few of the audience aside from the usual railbirds—pensioners too cheap to get cable TV who attended every trial and hearing. So, I was to be condemned from the cheap seats.

Seated at the Crown table were a young thing in glasses and a serious expression, trying her best to appear to be important, and Bobby Cherry. They say that the first year of marriage is a nesting period, where comfort and togetherness trump exercise and sociability. Newlyweds frequently pack on fifteen or twenty pounds as they lie abed and feast on bonbons or whatever. Either that or women realize they've managed to snag a sinecure—a lifetime of support in return for sex twice a week and a bit of light dusting—and they can just let it all go. In Bobby's case, it seemed to be working. He'd plumped right up. I guess he'd cast aside the nobility of being, literally, a gay blade and become more of a maul. He was settling easily into the joys of matrimony. He should have had my spouse—just about everyone else did. She kept me slim just trying to keep up with her and her menagerie of foundlings, frauds and fulsome youths, all relying on her to keep them in mai tais and massages. That, of course, meant me. They say divorce impoverishes women. They're right. They have to rely on only one income, then—their own.

Bobby sat there, fairly bursting out of his blue suit, the fleshiness of his neck bulging over the red, rep tied collar. He was getting a bit of a gut, too. Maybe, he was pregnant. Don't blame me. I almost called out to him to get on the old exercise bike and pedal his way back to health.

Packed into the front row behind him was Kathy, now resplendently pregnant and obviously proud of her accomplishments. It has long amazed me how proud people are to have accomplished what nature intended and what meal worms and grasshoppers can do without the aid of a plethora of "how to" books and on-line porn. You'd think it took an atomic physicist to knock somebody up when all it requires is a simple wedge and a bit of hydrodynamics.

Three seats down sat Her Eminence, Ms Carrie Anne Bloodworth, looking far queenlier than either Bobby or his acolyte tasked to do battle for Her Actual Majesty. She was proof, if any were necessary, that the ability to perform sexually was not attached either to talent or capacity. That there probably wasn't much of a diving board in her gene pool.

I was ruminating on this when I sensed a presence next to my left shoulder. It was Bobby. Before I had a chance to say hello or suggest a good gym to him, he uttered, "Disclosure." It was more an expletive than a greeting or description but it came with a three page document with bright azure letterhead: "Blue Genes: The DNA People." Since he didn't stay to discuss the latest Supreme Court commentary on the law of wilful blindness, I was left to learn what I could of the colourful world of genetics.

I'd made it most of the way down page one and was gratified to learn that much of what I'd seen on TV crime shows was actually science, when a figure loomed in, accompanied by the announcement of His Honour Judge Alvin Powers.

His Honour was to be of the "No Nonsense School" of judicialdom. He carried his own books which he slapped onto the bench with a sound that woke several in the back row. "All right. Let's get on with it. You Mr. Prince?" Before I could answer him, he turned to Bobby. "All right, Crown, whaddaya got for me today?" I suspected he might actually know, with all the publicity and such, but it seemed to rattle Bobby who was doing his first murder prelim and following some sort of book. He stood.

"Your Honour." Bobby looked down at his script. "This is the preliminary inquiry of Mr. John Prince, who is charged with the murder of Henry Popowicz."

"I've read the Information. You got some witnesses, Mr., uh . . . ?"

"Cherry, sir. Robert Cherry, Jr. for the Crown, along with my colleague, Allison Dempsy." The young thing in the serious glasses half rose and bowed to the judge.

"Good to meet you, Ms Dempsy, is it? Now, we've got a lot to get through here today, Mr. Cherry. I don't think your little speech is going to hoe much corn here. So, can we just get down to the evidence and see where that leads us? That okay with you, Defendant?" He looked at me, not entirely kindly, even though I said it was.

The first witness was Gail. She was appropriately nervous and wouldn't look at me. She mumbled the oath and Bobby set to work.

"Ms Deare, what do you do for a living?"

"I am an office assistant at Yamnuska Centre Legal Aid." She nodded her way through this and then thought for a second to make sure she had gotten it right.

"Who did you work for there?"

"The government."

"I beg your pardon."

"The government. We all work for the government. That's what Carrie Anne—I mean, Ms Bloodworth says."

"No, no, no. Do you work for a particular lawyer?"

"No, Mr. Prince isn't particular at all. He represents just about everybody. Even the Pooper."

All this information threw Bobby right off his game. He went through his notes, flipping pages wildly. Then, he looked up. Smiled. "Of course. But let me ask you this."

"Sure, if you'd like."

"Uh, Ms Deare, this Mr. Prince, is he here?"

"Of course, he is. You know very well he is, Bobby."

"I beg your pardon."

"He went to your wedding, didn't he?"

Bobby reddened. I hadn't thought his wedding was that much of an embarrassment. It was tasteful. I'd enjoyed it, at least. "Um, yes, I suppose he did." He looked down. "Do you, do you, uhm, see him here today?"

"Yes." He looked at her, obviously waiting for something. She looked back as if to say, 'Well, I answered your question, didn't I?'"

"Well, could you point him out?"

She turned to me, flashed a smile and pointed. "He's over there. How're things, Jack?"

I smiled and mouthed "Fine."

All this bothered the learned judge. "Defendant, I won't have you communicating with this witness under your breath. You'll have your turn." So, I looked as sternly as I could at Gail which only made her burst out laughing. "Witness, I won't have you laughing. This is a serious case and I won't have you laughing about it. A man has died and that's nothing to laugh about."

I'd had about as much as I was going to take. So, I stood.

The judge looked at me. "Have you got something to say, Defendant?"

"Actually, I do. You have assumed something that is not in evidence. I believe it is important to point that out, even at a preliminary inquiry."

"Is that an objection?"

"Yes. Your adjudication of this matter may be somewhat premature."

"And how is that? Are you accusing me of bias?"

"No."

"So what have I assumed that is not in evidence, Mr., uh, Prince, is it?" He had to fumble for the information to get that right.

"You've said that someone has died. There's been no evidence of that in this hearing."

"Surely, Mr. Prince, you wouldn't find yourself charged with first degree murder if somebody hadn't been killed."

I looked at him, considering. Then, I just let fly. Nothing was going to happen to me here other than being found in contempt. I was already in jail, in the Hole, as it were. They'd even taken away the local psycho, leaving me to entertain myself as God may well have intended—or until I went blind. "Sir, there is no evidence in this hearing about anyone dying, much less being killed. As I understand the law, without evidence there is no proof and without proof, there can be no conclusion."

He turned to me, scarlet, and jabbed a fat index finger in my direction. If it had been a gun, small parts of my anatomy would have been sprayed on the back wall. "Mr. Prince, don't try my patience. If you cannot behave, I will have you dragged out—in chains. Do I make myself clear?"

"Crystal, sir."

"I beg your pardon." It was the old teacher trick, repeating something to make it stronger. It didn't matter to me. I've sent a couple of teachers into satisfying careers in insurance and real estate.

I stared at him. "I do not grant your pardon, sir. I believe you heard me clearly. Sir." Then, I sat down.

I don't think that colour of red is possible on the face of any healthy individual. There's nothing quite like the Docket Rocket's red glare. He grunted and told Bobby, "Continue."

Bobby took Gail through the so called threats in the office.

"And once, Mr. Prince told Mr. Properwitch that he had lots of enemies and they would like to see him dead."

"Do you remember exactly what Mr. Prince said?"

"No."

"How do you know that this referred to Mr. Popowicz?"

"'Cause Jack was talking to him on the phone and I heard what Jack said."

"So, what did he say?"

"Something like 'You're the one with the enemies, Harry. I'm sure if some of them got their way, you'd be dead.' Then, he said something about his way."

"His way?"

"Yup."

"Whose way?"

"No, his way."

"Whose way is that?"

"His."

"Mr. Prince's?"

"Objection. Leading."

The judge looked at me. He knew the question was improper. He didn't like the fact that it was improper. He wanted the evidence in. "Hmph! It's part of the narrative. The witness will answer." This was going well. I wondered if this guy dug up turnips with Morceau on weekends. Probably not. Even, Morceau has his limits.

"Yes. Mr. Prince's."

"So, what did that mean?"

I stood. "Surely, the evidence speaks for itself."

He looked at me. "Is that an objection?"

"Yes."

"Overruled."

I needn't have bothered. Gail's answer was clear. "I don't know."

And so it went. Any time I'd said anything negative about Harry, someone had written it down and given it to Gail to say.

At last, it was my turn.

"Ms Deare, what sort of person was Harry Popowicz?"

Bobby was on his feet right away, complaining. His Honour couldn't think of anything else to say. "That's a pretty general question, Mr. Prince. Maybe, you should rephrase it."

"Okay. Was Mr. Popowicz a pain in the neck?"

"Oh, no, Mr. Prince, not at all."

"Really?"

"No, he was a real pain in the ass."

* * *

Carrie Anne was the next Crown witness. As a taxpayer, I might have hoped that she was actually toiling for the province in her palatial digs at Legal Aid. No such luck.

She managed to pull out every slight that I had ever made against Harry's character. She seemed to have kept an actual file on it, a file she dipped into regularly. When I objected, His Honour posited the view that she was merely "refreshing her memory." When I suggested that there was refreshing her memory and there was quoting from notes, he advised that he was the judge. And when I suggested that the difference was one set out in the law of evidence, he suggested that I might complete the inquiry from the comfort of my cell. I took his point and shut up.

The worst of it came when Carrie Anne volunteered that I had once said, "One good thing about Harry dead: the only ones who'll be disappointed will be the buzzards and worms."

But my turn came.

"Ms Bloodworth, did you have any dealings with Mr. Popowicz, yourself?"

She preened briefly, straightening the lapels of her suit and brushing away an imaginary mote. "Why, yes. We had several conversations. In fact, I found him quite charming."

"Really?"

"Yes."

"So, when he told me that he thought you were a pompous bitch, was he being charming?" So, he'd never said that. She didn't know it and the court never could.

"I don't think he would ever say such a thing."

"You don't think that?"

"Well, no."

"Really?"

She brushed the crease of her pants. "You might think that, Mr. Prince, but I am quite confident that Mr. Popowicz never did." She looked up as if to say, "Do your worst, Jack. You're the one on trial and I'm the one on the way up."

"So, you had numerous conversations with him."

"Yes, unfortunately, I had to."

"Unfortunately, because he was difficult to deal with?"

"No, as I said, he was always a perfect gentleman."

"No, you said he was charming, not a gentleman, however imperfect."

"Well, it doesn't matter. He was."

"How many conversations did you have with him, then?"

"I don't know, five, maybe six."

"Any other communications with him?"

"Is this going anywhere?"

"Yes."

She made a face and looked to the judge for some relief. "You'll just have to put up with this a bit longer, Ms Bloodworth. I'm sure you have better things to do than this."

"Of course, I am the director of Yamnuska Centre Legal Services and I really have more important things to do."

I looked at her. "Oh, really, Ms Bloodworth. What would those be?"

"Objection. What is the relevance of that question?" Obviously, something had bestirred the Crown, although this time it was Ms Dempsy who rose.

"Sustained. Why don't we concentrate on the matters at hand, Mr. Prince? I'm sure Ms Bloodworth has better things to do."

"Fine, Your Honour. Ms Bloodworth, have you ever been in a courtroom with Mr. Popowicz?"

"No."

"So, you can't say what he might get up to?"

"I'm sure, Mr. Prince, that he was provoked." She looked satisfied and, then, stuck in the needle. "You are quite, how shall I say this, quite provocative." That smile was an ugly thing but her own.

"Your conversations with him were on the telephone?"

"I had one in my office, in person."

"And he was always charming and a perfect gentleman?"

"Yes."

"So, you simply believed everything that he said, particularly about me, particularly if it was negative."

"Quite frankly, Mr. Prince, it isn't hard."

"So, when he complained that I got him off before he could testify, you believed him then."

"I don't remember any such occasion."

"And when he complained because the Crown stayed the charge and I wouldn't appeal.

You believed him then?"

"I don't believe that ever happened."

"Which? That the Crown stayed the charge or that he complained?"

"Either one."

"You actually assigned me to deal with Harry Popowicz because he was so difficult, didn't you?"

"Don't be ridiculous, Mr. Prince. I assigned him to you because he needed a lawyer and you were a lawyer."

"Would you describe his legal problems as difficult?"

"I'm not sure I can say if they were or they weren't."

"Well, you are the Legal Director of Yamnuska Centre Legal Services, right?"

"We both know that I am . . . however *you* might feel about it, Mr. Prince."

"And, as director, you are expected to be aware of the strengths and weaknesses of your staff, correct?"

"Yes, staff weaknesses were a frequent issue."

"And, being aware of your staff's strengths and weaknesses, you assigned files on that basis, am I correct?"

"Of course, Mr. Prince. I assign files on the basis of competence."

"And, as legal director, you would not keep anyone on staff who wasn't up to the task, would you?"

"Within the limits of the system. Of course."

"You came to be legal director about a year ago. Just after the election?"

"That sounds about right."

"When you came, you assessed the competencies of the existing staff?"

"With assistance from trained professionals in personnel affairs." She turned to the judge. "We felt it necessary to re-evaluate the system at the time of the turn over." She was quite bored at this.

"And you terminated at least one of the lawyers on staff at that time?"

"Yes, we were forced to re-evaluate staffing levels and competencies. They seem to have lagged over time. There was considerable dry rot in the system, as could have been predicted."

"And you did so on the basis of his competencies, right?"

"I don't know what you're getting at."

"Did you or did you not terminate Lawrence Kennedy on the basis of incompetence?"

"I'm not sure I'd call it that."

"Well, you did in the letter you gave him in our office when you were re-evaluating staffing levels and competencies. Didn't you?"

"I may have."

"And you re-assigned Mr. MacLean on that basis, as well. Correct?"

"Again, I may have."

"But, when you did all of this re-evaluating staffing levels and competencies, you didn't fire me, did you?"

"As I said, there was considerable rot in the system and there had to be some re-evaluation. Staffing levels were getting a little out of hand."

"So, the office was over-staffed?"

"You could say that."

"So, because it was over-staffed, you hired six new lawyers to replace the three who had been there."

"You have to understand the situation, Mr. Prince. We were looking for young, fresh ideas."

"But, here's the thing. You fired or moved the other three out of a concern for competence. But you didn't move me. Did you?"

"I had my reasons."

"But they weren't reasons of competence, were they?"

Bobby couldn't stand it anymore, so he objected. The judge was enjoying this so he over-ruled the objection.

The answer, when it came, was nothing if not honest. And when it came, it came with that smile. "No, we had other plans."

"And those plans were to get me to quit, weren't they?"

She nodded. "Partly."

"Is that why you gave me Harry Popowicz to deal with?"

"No."

"You knew he was a difficult man and you knew he would frustrate whoever dealt with him, maybe even make them quit."

"That's not true. Mr. Popowicz was a gentleman. I've told you that."

"You had other lawyers at your beck and call, but you always steered Harry my way, didn't you?"

"It's just the way it turned out. You can't always control these things."

"Even when you're matching competencies and needs?"

It went on a while longer. I guess Bobby was probably right. It wasn't that relevant. But it was fun.

Right up until His Honour noted in answer to yet another relevance objection, "Mr. Cherry, I believe that Mr. Prince may well be setting up a provocation defence that would reduce murder to manslaughter."

Just the sort of thing you need to hear when you're on trial.

The balance of the day was spent hearing all manner of witnesses describe the scene of Harry's demise and the causes of his death. Who knew that he was so riddled with various disease processes, high thises and low thatses? Whoever killed him may have done him a genuine service, however unintentionally.

And then, we were adjourned. And so, as Samuel Pepys might have put it, to bed.

...AND OTHER'S MISTAKES—INDIRECTLY

Trials of more than a day were something new to me. At Yamnuska Centre Legal Aid, we usually have them down the chute and doing time in an afternoon or we just don't do the work. On the other hand, longer trials give you an evening to chew over the evidence of the day and make whatever shaky plans you can for the next. Given the quality of food in The Cube, the evidence was only marginally tougher to swallow. And the plans? More shaky than I was.

The first witness on the second day was an officer who had swabbed the fender and taken what he believed was blood from the crumpled metal.

"Constable Garrity, this red substance on the fender of the car was in a crease in the fender?"

"Yes, when you brought it back, they reported it and I took the sample."

"Which you bundled all up and sent off to the lab?"

"Yes, I placed the sample in a sterile container..."

"Constable, I've already conceded what you did. I'm more interested in what the results of all that testing was."

"I've got the report right here."

"Objection." Allison Dempsy was on her feet, almost purple. "We didn't put the report in evidence. It's not supposed to be in evidence at this hearing."

His Honour was intrigued. I figure that the boredom of the morning had descended on him like an opium cloud and he needed a bit of red meat to get his heart started. If all it was a bit of dried blood, that would have to do. "Mr. Prince, are you consenting to the forensic report being entered at this time?"

"Yes, Your Honour."

"Really? There could be very serious consequences to you in its admission. You do realize that?"

"Quite, Your Honour."

"If you're absolutely sure . . . ?"

"Absolutely, Your Honour."

Ms Dempsey wasn't to be denied. "But, Your Honour, the evidence is hearsay."

He didn't want to hear her objection, only the report.

"The Crown is not prepared to submit the original of the report at this time." She was stubborn, if nothing else. I like that in a woman . . . to a point.

"Well, let's proceed on mine."

"It's only a copy. It can't be admitted."

"If it's a true copy of the original, I don't see why not. And if it isn't, I suspect that there will be serious consequences for both of you before the law society and, I would guess, the Court of Appeal." His Honour was not to be put off.

I produced my copy and handed it to the clerk. His Honour read it. He seemed to be shuffling the papers and considering things for quite some time. At last, he looked up.

"I want to be sure I am reading this correctly, Mr. Cherry. The blood found on the car was not human blood. Is that what you understand from this report?"

Bobby blushed. It was good to see he still had a sense of shame. "That is one interpretation, Your Honour."

Judge Power looked at him. "All right, what other interpretation can I put on it?"

I'll give Bobby credit; he tried. "The Crown is of the view that the blood found on the car is not dispositive of the case." His blush deepened.

"I agree. But I wasn't asking you that, Mr. Cherry. What I asked is whether your understanding of this report is that the blood found is not human blood."

"That appears to be what it says."

"It also says that the blood is animal blood, likely a sheep's."

"Uh, yes."

"Would you agree that if the blood is animal blood, it didn't come from Mr. Popowicz?"

I was so glad he hadn't asked me that question. I'm not sure how I would have answered.

Bobby was doing his valiant best to save things. "Your Honour, the results of this were quite a surprise to the Crown when we received them and we had to consider carefully what we should do. After all, Mr. Prince's freedom was at issue. We have, however, come to the conclusion that our initial theory that Mr. Prince struck him with his government vehicle was inaccurate. But we have come to an alternate theory, one that is consistent with his guilt."

"I'm sure we'll hear all about it after lunch, then. A Form 19 for the prisoner to two p.m."

* * *

When I got back from my fresh *boeuf mincée et rôtie* with ketchup and cold coffee, the lunch of the truly discerning accused, the court television system had been fired up. We were to be treated to an afternoon's movie, it seemed.

His Honour came in and we all sat. Bobby called the staff sergeant of the Moskolsippi RCMP to tell us all of the detachment security footage that had been burned to a disc. I was asked if I would consent to the playing of it. I know the rule is not to ask about anything you don't already know about. Quite frankly, I was curious.

The disc showed the back of the detachment, where vehicles were impounded. A cinematic classic it was not, even as an avatar of the *cinéma vérité* school. First, it was in black and white. It showed stop action pictures taken every three seconds of the impound lot. We sat through fifteen minutes of this before Bobby freeze-framed the player. A bolt of interference cracked across the screen

"Sergeant, could you tell us what vehicles are in this view?"

"The picture shows the impound lot at the Moskolsippi detachment. The vehicles in view are all ones that had been seized and impounded by the police at that time."

"Do you recognize any of them?"

"Yes, there is a Ford Escape, blue, that we found abandoned on the highway. That is the vehicle on the right side of the screen. The vehicle next to it is a red Dodge Caravan. It was seized as part of a drug investigation."

"I am most interested in the vehicle to the extreme left side of the screen."

"Oh, that. Yes, that's the mint green cargo van that we seized from Mr. Popowicz about a week before this was taken."

I barely recognized the right rear fender of the van. Without all its signs, it seemed naked.

"If we could just let the picture go."

It juddered along in three second chunks until the second cry of "Stop!" from Bobby. It scared me silly.

"You needn't yell, Counsel." His Honour had settled in and was likely fearing a heart attack.

Since nothing seemed to have changed, I studied the screen. The clock counter read 3:47 a.m.

"Start it up."

Again, the image jumped in three second segments. At about the fourth one along, the dome light in the van came on. Five segments later, it went off. The back lights of the van came on causing the image to flare slightly. The vehicle backed out with the back half visible. Then, it pulled out, out of the view of the camera. The ragged remnants of one of Harry's signs removed all doubt as to the identity of the vehicle.

"Would you forward the frame to 5:09 a.m., please?"

It was done as commanded. About seven segments in, the camera flared again as the van returned. The dome light came on. Eight segments later, it went out and the show was over.

The courtroom lights came up

"Just a couple of questions, sergeant. What did you find when you examined the van?"

"Well, we found that the left front fender was damaged and there was what appeared to be blood on it."

"Has it been tested?"

"We did preliminary tests to determine if it was blood. It appeared to be so we sent it off to the lab for DNA."

This was all news to me. But I was allowed to cross-examine the witness.

"Sergeant, did you lock the doors of the van when you seized it?"

"Yes, we had the keys."

"What happened to the keys?"

"They were placed in a secure locker pending disposition of the vehicle."

"Were they still there in the morning?"

"I don't know."

"Why not?"

"We didn't notice this until the police dog, Shemp, spotted it. Last week, we took him into the impound lot and he got real excited. That's when we found the damage."

"Anything else?"

"Yeah, we found a piece of cloth on the fender. It matched what the deceased, Mr. Popowicz, had been wearing."

"Did you check the van for fingerprints?"

"Oh, yeah. We found a bunch."

"Mine?"

"No, sorry, Mr. Prince. None of yours. We just found Harry's and his wife, Ada Severyn's. None we didn't expect."

"I have one more question, sergeant. Were there any complaints about any dead sheep about this time?"

"Yeah, we get lots of complaints about rustlers."

"And disappointed wives, too, no doubt."

* * *

His Honour was confused. "Mr. Cherry, you told me earlier that you had an alternate theory of Mr. Prince's guilt based on this new evidence."

"Yes, Your Honour. The Crown will be calling two more witnesses who we believe will be able to show that the accused had the opportunity to take the van in question and did so. We believe that these witnesses will show what happened here."

The courtroom glare seemed to enliven Sally Ryder, although she didn't look that much better sober. She was sworn and affected an air of sophistication. After all, she was a prime witness in a notorious murder.

Yes, she had been with me on the night before poor Mr. Popowicz had died. He was a sweet old man who apparently loved puppies and small children and young ladies like her. As she reminisced, however inaccurately, she carefully tossed her hair so it flowed about her face. I checked the back of the room. I was wondering which of the onlookers was her darling Donny, late of the affections of Ms Shirley McMurchie.

"I wonder if I could take you to the night before Mr. Popowicz's death. Where were you?"

"I was in a local drinking establishment."

"What were you doing there?"

"Drinking."

"Anything else?"

She dipped her head dramatically, then looked up. She barely whispered, "Yes. Unfortunately."

"And what was that?"

She drew in a breath, then sighed deeply. "I'm terribly ashamed about this. You don't know how many times I've wondered about it. It's a terrible memory for me and I just wish I didn't have to relive it." She wiped a tear away. "Because I wasn't true to myself that night and worse . . ." Here, she sobbed and had to retrieve a tissue from the box thoughtfully placed beside her. She rucked suddenly, then looked up. "Worse, I wasn't true to my heart. I betrayed my one true love. Donald."

I had the distinct impression that she expected an orchestra to swell in the background or, at least, some murmuring from the gallery. There was none, but she forged on. "I allowed myself to be . . . I don't know what the right term is . . . well, I was set upon by that man over there, that Jack Prince, and he convinced me to go to his hotel room with him. I was really drunk, you understand, and I wouldn't have done it otherwise but I went with him.

"I can't really remember what happened. I know he wanted to use me. He's the type that just uses girls. I know that now and I just wish I'd known it then. But he used me."

"What do you mean by that, Ms Ryder?"

"He used me as a sexual plaything and when he thought I had gone to sleep, he used me as his alibi. He pretended to sleep with me but I know he was out somewhere because I don't sleep that soundly. I know he went out and did something terrible to that wonderful old man because I saw the blood on the fender of his car. And when I think about it, it just makes me sick, seeing that blood dripping off the car and knowing I might have saved him"

It was my turn. A true cad can make a girl believe it was all her idea. I'm only an amateur. I didn't bother.

Judge Power turned to the Crown. "Any more witnesses?"

"One more, Your Honour. The Crown calls Bernard Maunder."

I barely recognized Bernie. They'd bought him a suit. They'd gotten him to comb his hair. I had the sense that they had even provided him with a pretty good story, too. He took the stand with a flair that suggested some familiarity with his surroundings.

"Mr. Maunder, what can you tell us about your dealings with the accused?" Ms Dempsey now held the reins while Bobby sat back, his pen in his mouth.

"Me and Jack, we was together in the remand, like. We was real close, if ya know what I mean. We was cellies."

"Cellies?"

"Yeah, we shared a cell . . . like, in remand."

"You are speaking of the Yamnuska Centre Correctional Centre?"

"Yeah, the Cube, like."

"And what can you tell us about what occurred between you and the accused?"

"Well, when guys're locked up like that, they don't have a lot to do. Like, you can't, you know, go down to the bar, like. So, you talk to guys about their cases and stuff."

"And did Mr. Prince talk to you about your case?"

"Naw, he was real standoffish about that stuff but when he was in the cell, he talked about his stuff, you know, like how he was in trouble for chillin' one o' his clients, like."

"Did he tell you about it?"

"Not directly, like. He told me stuff at night . . . like, when he was asleep."

It seems that in Bernie's world, at least, I had begun talking in my sleep the first night I got there. I was sort of a recumbent Lady MacBeth, murdering his sleep with my nightly ramblings, all of which he had thoughtfully recorded in a coiled notebook he said he kept for his project on dream research. If he were any sort of a faithful recorder, I had spouted such lines as "Run him down! Run him down! Die, you mother, die!"; the ever memorable, "The tires! The tires! The tires!"; and, of course, "That'll teach you, Henry. Ya don't fuck with the Princer!"

"And he said this while he was asleep?"

"Yeah, that's the way it happened."

It was my turn. I wasn't really sure if I wanted to investigate my dreams with one Bernard Maunder. But it *was* only a preliminary inquiry.

"How long have you been doing dream analysis, Mr. Maunder?"

"I don't get you, like, Jack."

"Well, let me ask you this. Where did you get the nice spiral notebook?"

"They got them in the tuck shop, like, at the Cube."

"So, when did you buy it?"

"That time."

"So, when I moved in or after I was there a while or after I went to the Hole?"

"I don't remember."

"We can look it up, if you'd like."

"Nah. It's okay."

"How much did it cost you?"

"I'm not sure."

"Did you buy it to record what I was saying in my sleep or for some other reason?"

"I can't recall."

"Sure you can. Did you buy the notebook to write down what you say I was saying in my sleep?"

"I'm not sure."

"Well, what else did you write in it?"

"Nothing I recall, like."

"In fact, nothing else. It starts with you writing down what I was saying."

"Yeah, that's a fact."

"And it's all in one colour of ink."

"What's wrong with that?"

"And it's all continuous. The writing never changes. The spelling never improves."

"Whaddaya mean by that, like?"

"You're the only guy I know who spells fuck without the 'c'".

* * *

I have to give Bobby credit. He tried hard. He argued any and every possible permutation and combination consistent with my guilt. I, for once, had nothing to say.

And so, it ended.

AND, OF COURSE, LET OTHERS SAVE FACE

I did enjoy *The National* that night, even if I wasn't quite the lead story, having been squeezed out by a sex scandal in Ottawa.

> "A surprising conclusion to a shocking case. We go first to Yamnuska Centre and our prairies correspondent, Paul Furey. Paul?"
>
> "Thank you, Jackie. Yes, in a surprising twist in a case that seems to have nothing but twists and turns, Judge Alvin Powers, today, refused to commit lawyer, John Appleby Prince, on trial on a charge of murdering his own legal aid client, local eccentric, Henry Popowicz.
>
> "The evidence showed that Prince and his client had had a long and difficult relationship, often quarreling in courthouse hallways and the local legal aid clinic. The incident in question followed Popowicz's acquittal on some of the most serious charges he had ever faced, to date. Sometime later, in the early morning hours, his body was found in the parking lot of the low cost housing project he shared with his partner, Ada Severyn. He had apparently been run

down by a vehicle and left to die. In evidence admitted by agreement at the preliminary inquiry, doctors described the cause of death to be blunt force trauma. Popowicz was found to have suffered at least twenty four fractures of various bones, at least two of which were rib fractures that punctured his lungs. Damage and bloodstains were later found on the government-issued vehicle driven by Prince at the time."

"How did his lawyer escape the charges he faced?"

"Well, Jackie, in amazing turnaround of events, it came out that the bloodstains on Prince's car came from a non-human source. Prince did not testify so it is unknown just how that blood got on his car.

"Judge Powers found (and here a graphic came on screen, reproducing the words spoken—for the literate, I suppose): 'I don't see any evidence that was presented by the Crown that shows that Mr. Prince had anything to do with the death of Henry Popowicz. It is clear that there was some animus between him and what I understand to have been a very unpleasant client. Words were said that may even be seen as a threat. And Mr. Prince was out on the night in question, at least, Ms Ryder says he was not with her in his motel room.

'This entire case hangs on the evidence that blood was found on the crumpled fender of Mr. Prince's car, or the car that had been entrusted to him by the government of this province. If it had been the late Mr. Popowicz's blood, that would be one thing. But the blood was not. It was apparently the blood of a sheep. I do not know how it got there but one thing is plain. It was not Mr. Popowicz's blood. That is the only thing that ties or should I say seemed to tie Mr. Prince to this unfortunate death.'

"Then, there was evidence from a former cellmate of the now-suspended lawyer. Bernie Maunder, a petty criminal awaiting sentence for a string of frauds, testified that Prince talked in his sleep and, during these ramblings, confessed to the killing of Popowicz. In his ruling, Judge Powers said [and here, more quotes on the screen]: 'The evidence, if it can be called that, of Mr. Maunder. He is a criminal who was awaiting sentencing. While I cannot weigh the credibility of witnesses at this hearing, it is clear to me that he may well have significant reasons to have made up his evidence. It is that evidence that is most concerning. A statement, any statement, must be the product of conscious thought. I have never heard of any court, anywhere, accepting the supposed ramblings of a sleeping accused. Even more specifically, according to Mr. Maunder, Mr. Prince repeatedly said words such as "The tires! The tires! The tires!" and "That'll teach you, Henry. Don't f__k with the Princer!" Tires were never part of this killing. Mr. Prince was never referred to by anyone as "the Princer" and no one, aside from the draftsperson of the Information ever seems to have referred to the deceased as Henry. Other than his mother, I suppose.'

"It was hardly what might be called a ringing endorsement for the admission of sleep talking as evidence. Legal experts we have consulted could only agree wholeheartedly with this finding, something that will, no doubt, be reassuring to those of us who may make admissions while sound asleep.

"All that said, Prince did not escape a scolding from the sixtyish jurist. He concluded his remarks, before discharging the young lawyer, saying there had been evidence that Prince had spent part of the night in a motel room with a young woman whom he had picked up in a bar. 'The Crown's theory, whether original or revised is that Mr. Prince left Ms R. at the motel, rode down a sheep somewhere, then travelled to the local detachment where he secured the Popowicz van. They speculate that he then drove the van to the Popowicz's residence where he knocked him down. Even if I could accept all this—and there is nothing beyond speculation here—whatever one might say about Mr. Prince's actions on that day, and his abysmal conduct in seducing the young lady, I think that there is no evidence upon which a properly instructed jury, acting reasonably, could find him guilty. And I order his discharge on this charge and his release from custody.'"

"Have the police discovered the vehicle that caused the injuries, Paul?"

"Yes, Jackie. In a surprising turn of events, it was Popowicz's own, older model, green van that killed him. Security footage revealed the van being taken from the police impound lot in the early morning hours, about the time Popowicz was killed. That video did not, however, show who the driver was. The judge found over the vehement protests of Crown Counsel that, without any indication that Jack Prince had driven the vehicle, much less that he had taken it from the impound lot, a reasonable jury, properly instructed, as he put it, could not convict the thirty-three-year-old local lawyer.

"Crown Counsel, Robert Cherry, Jr."

Here, Bobby made his national television debut, looking somewhat doughy, I thought. Maybe, they should have shot his other profile. The camera can add at least ten pounds to Myron's good home-cooking.

> "Quite frankly, I'm surprised, if I can say that. I didn't foresee this result and the Crown will be considering all its options in this case, including an appeal."
>
> "What would you say the problem was here?"
>
> "Well, I have to say that the DNA results were a bolt from the blue, an absolute shock. I mean, how could we have ever known that the blood found on the accused's car wasn't from the deceased?"
>
> "Did you have any sense that this would happen?"
>
> "Obviously not. We remain convinced—and I can't emphasize this too strongly—that what happened today was not a just result."
>
> "So, you will be appealing?"
>
> "I am taking that under advisement."

With that, Bobby wandered off with Ms Dempsey and the cameras returned to Paul Furey, standing in front of the courthouse, having abandoned his wheat field to posterity.

> "So, will we be seeing any further proceedings against Jack Prince, Paul?"
>
> "Our legal experts say no. They point to the contradictory evidence produced by the Crown and the lack of any evidence pointing to Prince."
>
> "Are there any other suspects?"
>
> "Police are very close-mouthed about that, Jackie. None of them would comment on the air and most point to the fact that, once a prime suspect is cleared, the trail has often gone cold. So, what remains is a true mystery. Paul Furey, CBC News, Yamnuska Centre."
>
> "Thanks for that, Paul. A real mystery. In other news..."

So, I would remain on Bobby Cherry's suspect list, forever. I suppose he's still trying to figure out who frenched his bed on his honeymoon, too.

My passage to freedom was not nearly as set about with press coverage and infamy as my arrival. Today's homicidal defence counsel easily gives way to tomorrow's innocent lamb slaughterer. They cared about as much about my getting off as Psycho Sammy had cared about his ewes—for the same reasons, too.

I returned home and undid all of the various things my friends had done to secure the place. Newspapers taken in from the step had been thoughtfully piled on the table. I hear that scrapbooking is a fashionable time-waster. Something tasteful in black trim with appropriate splashes of red might have done just the trick. I found several boxes and consigned my putative clippings to the tender mercies of recycling.

The bills were something else. It's a bit striking to find out exactly how much gas and electricity you use when you are safely tucked away at Her Majesty's Hostelry and Home for Wayward Boys. A quick check of my bank account revealed that the regular deposit of pay cheques more than offset this and I was quite flush for a few months before the ravages of poverty would be upon me.

I rescued a quite dispirited Rollo from Gail's clutches. He looked like he wanted to stay for good. She probably didn't send him out of the room when she had visitors. He's quite the voyeur. I was looking at a quite a bill from the psycho-veterinarian for a bit of Jungian therapy for the lad. With dogs, you never want to go the Freudian route and Adler is just so passé.

I got into the habit of sleeping until almost noon so I wasn't prepared for the telephone call I got after two weeks of my freedom.

"Mr. Prince."

"Is that you, Angus?"

"Yes, of course. Who else would it be?" In his search for identity, maybe a bit of Freudian analysis would do Angus good.

"I don't know, Angus. Are you calling with good news or bad? I can't imagine that you guys at Legal Aid Central are too thrilled with me."

"Oh, no, Mr. Prince. Can I call you Jack?"

"Sure. Why not? We're old friends, aren't we?" I was going to make my firing as painful as possible. It was just a shame that they had resorted to the desperate tactic of making Angus do it.

"I like to think so, Mr. Prince. I mean Jack. I do like to think so."

"So, you called me, Angus. What's on your mind?"

"Yes, I did, didn't I? That's right."

"So, did you have a reason or is this just LAC's idea of a little joke on their soon-to-be-former employee?"

"Oh, I don't like the sound of that, Jack. Are you leaving us? Quitting, I mean?"

"No. I just figured that with all the fuss, Carrie Anne wouldn't want me around the office and there wouldn't be any place for me anywhere else in Legal Aid. I mean, you guys at Legal Aid Central haven't been as nice as you might have been, lately."

"I'm sorry about that, Jack. You can count me out of that group. I always spoke up for you. I said, 'That Jack Prince is a fine young lawyer' when they were saying those awful things about you."

"What sort of things were those, Angus?"

"Oh, you know. They're quite the chatty group there. Like a ladies' sewing circle . . . Maybe, should rephrase that. I wouldn't want you to think that there was anything wrong about a sewing circle, much less a ladies' one . . ."

"Don't worry, Angus. Your excursion into political incorrectness is safe with me. But it does sound like the rest of them there want to get rid of me."

"There?"

"Yeah, Legal Aid Central? Where did you think I meant?"

"Oh, I guess you haven't heard. I'm not there anymore."

"What? They didn't fire you, too, did they?"

"Fire? Me? Oh, no. I'm the new director of Yamnuska Centre Legal Aid."

"What happened to Carrie Anne?"

"With all the fuss and all, it was decided that she probably should leave. You know, her testifying against you and all that. Just not a good fit."

"They canned her?" All right, so I couldn't get the excitement out of my voice.

"No, no. Ms Bloodworth has made a lateral shift. She's now a special executive assistant to the Minister of Justice, Mr. Wooster. We like to call it a win-win situation."

"For whom?"

"She obviously has talents that this government feels they can't do without."

"Yeah, she's a winner. She always seems to land on her feet by lying on her back."

"Do you think it's that, Mr. Prince?"

"No, I'm sure she has a talented mouth, an imaginative repertoire and, shall we say, integrative talents that people like Jolly Jeff really savour."

"Yes, she certainly seems to have what it takes."

"Sometimes two."

"I beg your pardon?"

"Nothing. I think you called me for a reason, Angus." He frequently has to be dragged back to the topic at hand.

"Oh, yes. I was wondering why you didn't come in to work today."

"Could be something to do with being suspended."

"Oh, that. We sent you a letter. Didn't you get it?"

"Where did you address it to, Angus?"

"Let me see . . . yes . . . the correctional centre."

"You know them, Angus. They're lousy at forwarding mail. What did the letter say?"

"That you aren't suspended anymore."

"That's Legal Aid. What about the law society?"

"They sent a letter here to tell you the same thing."

"Well, I suppose I should get up and have a shave, then. Two-thirty work for you?"

* * *

Angus was quite beside himself when I arrived. Rollo wandered off to ask Gail to adopt him again as I met Angus in his office. Actually, it was still Carrie Anne's office. Angus just didn't look right in the middle of all that pastel.

I had a sense that it was affecting him in ways he didn't even realize.

"We're in a crisis, Mr. Prince, a real crisis."

"I would have thought that Carrie Anne's leaving was more an opportunity, actually."

"It's not just that. Three of the young ladies she brought with her have requested transfers and the other two are out, sick."

"There's always Chuck Ewanchuk. Didn't Carrie Anne say he was quite accomplished?"

Angus was not a man for sarcasm. He just shook his head. "He wouldn't even last at Legal Aid Central. Jack, I need you to do the docket for the next couple of weeks and get things back in order. Can you do that for me, Jack?"

"Sure."

The rapture ended with a call from Gail that an Ada Severyn was on the line for me. I took it in Angus's office.

"I just want ya to know, Mr. Prince, I don't blame ya for what happened to Harry. It couldn't be helped."

"I know, Ada. I didn't kill him, you know. But I know you cared about him a lot."

"More'an you could ever know, Mr. Prince."

"What are you going to do now, Ada?"

"Aw, I ain't got much time, ya know, Mr. Prince. I'm in and out o' the hospital ev'ry week, mostly in, if ya gotta know."

"It's tough, not having Harry there."

"It's one thing off my mind, if ya gotta know. I don't hafta worry none about what he's up to an' where's he's gettin' inta trouble. Ya might say it's a relief."

"Still, you were with him for a long time."

"Got that right, Mr. Prince, a real long time."

"So, what's with the call?"

"Just wanted to tell ya no hard feelin's, okay?"

"No, I don't have any and I hope things work out."

"Like I say, they'll work out just fine in the Lord's good time. But, like I say, I don't blame ya none for Harry and all and like ya say, ya didn't have nothing to do with it. I know that. Pity I couldn'ta done something sooner for ya. I wouldn'ta let ya twist in the wind. You woulda got off, sooner or later. I'm just glad everything worked out for ya."

"Sure, Ada. Anytime." I hung up with a smile. No hard feelings.

"What was that all about, Mr. Prince?" I looked up at Angus, trying to look at ease in a jungle of leather and pastel.

"I guess you could call it 'The Wreck of the Old Ada Severyn.'" I turned to go.

"That's not right, Mr. Prince, not right at all."

"Oh?"

"Yes, I know it well. It's 'The Wreck of the Old Ninety-Seven.' Quite a good song, actually".

I left him humming it and didn't elaborate. I had a docket to prepare for.

* * *

I made it back the next day by 4:00 p.m. Considering everything, it was somewhat of a record, getting done in the midst of all the snide comments from His Honour and Ms Dempsey for the Crown. Gail was distraught.

"Oh, Mr. Prince, it's just terrible."

"It's not that bad, Gail, and I just had a nice walk back in the bright, late fall sunshine. We won't have snow for weeks. What's so terrible about that?"

"No, Jack. It's Carrie Anne."

"She's not back? Tell me it's all a bad dream."

"No. She won't be back, either."

"Well, what's so terrible about that?"

"Listen, listen!"

She turned up the radio. For a change it was on CBC. Maybe, she'd given up music for socialist natter.

". . . Jeff Wooster, who only months ago was named Justice Minister, dead in a car crash sixty kilometres east of Yamnuska Centre where he was elected last year in the Conservative sweep of the province."

"Paul, is there any word of who the other person killed was?"

"Yes, police reports have come in. They have named the other victim as Carrie Anne Bloodworth, his special executive assistant for Legal Aid projects. You may remember her as the former head of the Yamnuska Centre Legal Aid Clinic, who recently testified in a murder preliminary inquiry involving one of her staff lawyers. As you may recall, he was discharged at the preliminary inquiry despite her testimony. Shortly afterwards, she was named special executive assistant to the minister."

"Thank you, Paul. That was Paul Furey, the prairies regional reporter for *The National*, speaking to us from Yamnuska Centre where, today, the Minister of Justice, Jeffrey Wooster, and his special executive assistant were killed in a single vehicle accident while travelling to his constituency. We'll have further details as soon as they become available to us."

The office was up, looking at the radio as if by looking at it they could somehow conjure a better reality. Angus was hanging in his doorway looking for just the right thing to say.

"Well, Mr. Prince, what do you have to say about that?"
"I've got an alibi, Angus. Honest!"

* * *

It is a tradition of the local bar to hold a memorial service when anyone of long standing or importance in the profession dies. Usually, it's some creaky, old gaffer that no one really remembers but all have fond recollections of. Songs are sung by locals, supposedly skilled in the art: the religious get hymns; the irreligious, recycled pop melodies. Prayers are earnestly prayed and speeches given. We weren't really used to planting young ones but a hall had been rented and all were more or less required by social convention to attend.

But two things bothered me. First, as the days went by, the details of the accident had slowly leaked from the local police. I suspected Inspector Duceppe's gentle hand in this. I'm sure he still pined for his lost love. And what says "I love you" and "I'll always miss you" quite like salacious rumours?

Second, as the senior lawyer from Carrie Anne's tenure at Yamnuska Centre Legal Aid, I was given the task of eulogizing her. Angus insisted and there really wasn't anyone who knew Carrie Anne better, unless you included Ms Stockard and she was inconsolable. I've often wondered how Angus got to his position of authority and respect with no sense of decorum.

I relied on Gail to pass along such tawdry morsels as she could glean from her grapevine of informants. Apparently, her mother's brother was quite tight with a number of the more senior police officers and Gail felt free to share their many observations over lunch the day before the celebration of life.

"You know, Jack, Carrie Anne was having an affair with Inspector Duceppe."

"You shock me, Ms Deare. How could you ever conceive of our dear, departed Carrie Anne, Carrieing on, as it were?"

"But, that's not the good part."

"An affair, Gail? Good? How you have strayed from the path of righteousness and virtue! I blame it all on Dave."

"His name is Dan, Jack. You know that!"

"Yeah, yeah. That's what you tell him. So, make with the gossip. I've got a speech to write."

She leaned over the table, looking both ways before crossing the borders of good taste, especially about the late Ms Bloodworth. She whispered. "They say that there was no reason for the crash".

"I don't understand."

"It was a sunny day with a clear road. The car wasn't speeding, except near the end."

"Must you be so clever, Ms Deare? I'm sure you have something more to say."

"Let me put it this way, Jack." She gave further furtive glances to port and starboard, then hissed at me. "He was wearing his shirt and his jacket and tie and she was wearing her shoes."

"And so . . ."

"Jeez, Jack, do I have to draw a picture?"

"No, please. I might go blind."

But, here's the best part."

"You mean there's more?"

"Oh, yeah."

"I can hardly wait."

"They found part of him in her."

"What part?"

"You know. The best part."

"I think they should have gone Greyhound."

"They don't let you do stuff like that on the bus."

"Yeah, but they always say 'Leave the driving to us.' That *was* their slogan, once, you know?"

"You sure know a lot."

"Only from talking to you."

* * *

The celebration of life was well attended. The political types showed up to support their former comrade-in-arms. The older lawyers showed up to be seen by the political types.

The younger lawyers got the day off but were expected to attend. And Angus and I—we were invited guests. The two lawyerettes, who were still in town, were perched in the second row, well armed with boxes of tissue. People that I fancied might be family formed up in the front row. I thought I might see Kathy Markle there but she was, as they say, conspicuous by her absence. I couldn't disagree with her. She'll soon be a mother. It simply won't do to expose an innocent child—in this case, mine—to this sort of nonsense. It might damage the little darling for life. Heck, he might even turn into a priest. Like his paternal grandfather.

I usually attend funerals to drink afterwards and, in cases of family members, to make sure that the lid is well and tightly fastened. But we didn't have a casket—just a little box (I assumed it contained her ashes) —and we didn't really have a funeral director or minister. It was given to one of the political types to act as some sort of MC which he did by seizing the microphone and holding it far too close to his mouth. I feared, briefly, that he might break into a rendition of "Feelings" or start chewing. But his job was to keep things moving right along.

We were favoured with something from one of "Carrie's closest girlfriends," a chunky number who was probably an acolyte who suffered from the reflected glow of her friend all through high school but hung in there to make sure she could pick up some of the crumbs along the way. I think she styled it as a prayer but it was mostly self-serving slop about how Carrie was likely a sparkling angel looking down on all of us from some holy perch on high. I actually had a vision of Carrie Anne in the clouds, topped off with a knowing, if cannibalistic, smile.

The local glee club had ginned up some quasi-classical number that they butchered like a hog in a public market. After that was over, I was convinced Carrie Anne had no musical taste: no random bolts of lightning struck the choristers down.

A political aide to the premier brought us the government's and the premier's heartfelt condolences. He treated us to what I can only describe as a brief sermon arguing that death was the ultimate choice proving the true genius of the marketplace. I should have taken notes.

Other folks from within Carrie Anne's life came and went like ghosts in a bad, nineteenth century play. Things were getting fairly hot and sticky and I was looking forward to the pop and doughnuts at the end.

And then, it was my turn. "And now," intoned lubricious Les, "One of Carrie Anne's co-workers with a few words from her workplace, Yamnuska Centre Legal Services. Jack Prince." I thought about bowing and wouldn't have been surprised at an ovation right about then. Even the murmurs were subdued as I took the stage.

It is important when writing a speech for a mass public gathering either to tell a joke or quote some major writer. All the books about making speeches say so. Jokes might be out of place at a funeral or celebration of life, or whatever it was that we were doing here. And I didn't think much of the front row was looking forward to my doing ten minutes of stand up. It was even money with the rest of this crowd.

I figured Shakespeare is always a good source to crib from so I opened with, "To quote Shakespeare, one of Carrie Anne's favourite authors, 'Nothing so much became her life as the leaving of it.'" Unless you've read *MacBeth* and actually understood it, this sounds a whole lot better than it really is. Then, again, I was counting on the fact that nobody listens much at funerals and when they do, they hear what they want to.

"I got to know Carrie Anne quite well during our time together at Legal Aid. I did not know her before that. And, if you had told me who she was and what she was like, I'm sure I wouldn't have believed you. No one could be quite like Carrie Anne." I put a hand to my nose. I wanted to check for the Pinocchio effect. So far, there was none.

"Our first dealings were actually outside the office. I met her in several social settings, over drinks, walking in the park. And it was there that I discovered that Carrie Anne had a big heart, something in her that always seemed to be open for others. I can honestly say that she showed her special caring to a wide spectrum of this community and many can say they found a special friend in her. We speak about the little people and I have no doubt that many of them were probably small. But I'm sure all enjoyed that special relationship that Carrie Anne had with them. Fellow workers, prosecutors, police, ordinary people that she met on the street: they all found that special place of Carrie Anne's." And there it was, the start of a chuckle. I tried to suppress it.

"She thought constantly of the needs of our clients, looking for that special lawyer who could sit with them, counsel them and help them find a resolution for their problems, something that was individual and very personal. For Carrie Anne was a true servant of the law. Her knowledge had almost no peer in our office and she honoured its high calling with a dedication that could only be described as fierce." I tried to capture just how I felt as I sat for all those minutes, hours, days and weeks, down the range from the chain-smoking psychotic. It was like pricking your hand to find the pain.

"And what can one ever say about how fine a friend she was? In my time of trouble, when I was locked up in a jail cell, Carrie Anne visited me and assured me of just how strong her support was. Later on, when she was testifying, she kindly noted how valuable I was to her and to the legal aid system, as a whole. No one can put a price on such constancy. No one can fully express what I hold in my heart today. No one can feel what darkness has been set among us at her passing. I can only hope that in the days to come, each of us can come to realize just what sort of person Carrie Anne Bloodworth truly was.

"There is a sports saying that a true team player will take one for the team. I have no doubt that Carrie Anne was constantly taking one after another after another. It was what she did so well and so happily." Now, it came with a racking sensation. My chest heaved. I grabbed a tissue from the box on the lectern, holding it to my mouth, squeezing my eyes shut.

"I think of her, I see her face, I remember so much of what she did, and why. I see a young woman out to make her way, using all her resources and capacities to do things that each of us, in his or her heart of hearts, wishes he, or she, could do, too. I see a young professional, so special, so flexible, all too soon taken from us. I see a vibrant woman, mouth set to do what she must, all so she could accomplish her dreams and contribute to the memories of so many others.

"She died in the service of her minister. I'm sure her final words were eager and encouraging ones, ones that described all too clearly what the two of them were doing to this province and country. I know that her death was a blow. It was a blow to our government and I am confident that it is a blow felt deeply and personally by those who knew her and Minister Wooster. We can only hope that when we are in her place and we come, as she must have come, and even as we as Jeff Wooster came, to the inevitable, each of us can keep our end up, harden ourselves to the task and be spoken of and thought of as they surely are, today." The convulsions were coming faster now. I squeezed my eyes again and lifted my head, breathing deeply to stifle myself. Tears began to form. I was gripped by a paroxysm, shaking, flushing, almost sweating.

"And so, let me finish with this heartfelt prayer. Dear God, take Carrie Anne into that special place that each of us knows will suit her best. Surround her with those special angels. And may her every deed be so richly rewarded that, just as she has served us all, so shall she be served for all eternity. Amen." I was choked up at this point. I could barely cough out the final words. I was caught in a spasm of gags and shakes. Tears rolled down my cheeks. Others joined me. But mine were of laughter.

* * *

Angus came up afterwards, as I was dousing myself with ginger ale.

These people had rented the most expensive hall in town. They had taken a whole afternoon off work. They had put on their finest clothes and washed their cars. And still, they were too chintzy to buy booze. Even, cheap stuff. Goodness knows that after this, I needed something a bit stronger than warmed over Coca Cola.

"A wonderful speech, Jack. I was overcome."

"Thank you, Angus. I was pretty much overcome, too."

"You were crying weren't you, Jack?" It was Gail along with Dan, who just stood there with that lolling smile of his, nodding a lot.

"It was all the emotion." I tried looking suitably pained but could only grin.

Judge Morceau walked over to me and shook my hand. "A fine speech, Mr. Prince. Have you considered politics?"

"Frequently, but I'm afraid it might be the death of me. Look what it did to poor Carrie Anne. I think I'll stick to what I know."

He nodded and wandered off in search of other hands to shake, other claptrap to spout.

Gail pushed me off into a corner. Again, she looked furtively about. "You know all that stuff I told you about Carrie Anne?"

"Yes, it was very helpful in writing my little speech, don't you think?"

"I heard that she wasn't the only one Jeff Wooster was . . . you know . . . doing the nasty with. There were hundreds."

"Really?"

"I think he must've been one of those Chinese lover guys, you know, a Don Wong."

"I don't think that's right, Gail."

"Sure it is. He was jumping them like a kangaroo."

"No, about the Chinese guy. I think with Carrie Anne, it was more like Dong Wrong."

"Oh, yeah. Like that.

* * *

Torpor. It means listlessness. You can look it up, if you like.

Nothing much was happening. I'd been a lawyer at Yamnuska Centre Legal Aid for almost three years. I'd represented the poor and weak. I'd outlasted Carrie Anne Bloodworth and confused Judge Senuk, Judge Morceau and others elevated beyond all capacity. I'd even been charged with murder, almost fired, and become a father—almost. I must say that, right now, torpor's good.

www.ingramcontent.com/pod-product-compliance
Ingram Content Group UK Ltd.
Pitfield, Milton Keynes, MK11 3LW, UK
UKHW042002230426
12048UKWH00009B/496